# Security Governance, Policing, and Local Capacity

## Advances in Police Theory and Practice Series

### Series Editor: Dilip K. Das

Security Governance, Policing, and Local Capacity
Jan Froestad with Clifford D. Shearing

Police Performance Appraisals: A Comparative Perspective
Serdar Kenan Gul and Paul O'Connell

Police Reform in The New Democratic South Africa
Moses Montesh and Vinesh Basdeo

Los Angeles Police Department Meltdown: The Fall of the Professional-Reform
Model of Policing
James Lasley

Financial Crimes: A Global Threat
Maximillian Edelbacher, Peter Kratcoski, and Michael Theil

Police Integrity Management in Australia: Global Lessons for Combating
Police Misconduct
Louise Porter and Tim Prenzler

The Crime Numbers Game: Management by Manipulation
John A. Eterno and Eli B. Silverman

The International Trafficking of Human Organs: A Multidisciplinary Perspective
Leonard Territo and Rande Matteson

Police Reform in China
Kam C. Wong

Mission-Based Policing
John P. Crank, Dawn M. Irlbeck, Rebecca K. Murray, and Mark Sundermeier

The New Khaki: The Evolving Nature of Policing in India
Arvind Verma

Cold Cases: An Evaluation Model with Follow-up Strategies for Investigators
James M. Adcock and Sarah L. Stein

Policing Organized Crime: Intelligence Strategy Implementation
Petter Gottschalk

Security in Post-Conflict Africa: The Role of Nonstate Policing
Bruce Baker

Community Policing and Peacekeeping
Peter Grabosky

Community Policing: International Patterns and Comparative Perspectives
Dominique Wisler and Ihekwoaba D. Onwudiwe

Police Corruption: Preventing Misconduct and Maintaining Integrity
Tim Prenzler

# Security Governance, Policing, and Local Capacity

**Jan Froestad**

**With Clifford D. Shearing**

CRC Press
Taylor & Francis Group
Boca Raton London New York

CRC Press is an imprint of the
Taylor & Francis Group, an **informa** business

The cover photographs were taken by Caroline Gibello of Galleria Gibello. Her website address is www.galleriagibello.com.

CRC Press
Taylor & Francis Group
6000 Broken Sound Parkway NW, Suite 300
Boca Raton, FL 33487-2742

First issued in paperback 2019

© 2012 by Taylor & Francis Group, LLC
CRC Press is an imprint of Taylor & Francis Group, an Informa business

No claim to original U.S. Government works

ISBN-13: 978-1-4200-9014-7 (hbk)
ISBN-13: 978-0-367-86586-3 (pbk)

**Library of Congress Cataloging-in-Publication Data**

Froestad, Jan.
  Security governance, policing, and local capacity / Jan Froestad with Clifford D. Shearing.
      p. cm. -- (Advances in police theory and practice ; 17)
   Includes bibliographical references and index.
   ISBN 978-1-4200-9014-7
   1. Community policing. 2. Social justice. I. Shearing, Clifford D., 1942- II. Title.

HV7936.C83F76 2013
363.2'3--dc23                                                        2012038879

**Visit the Taylor & Francis Web site at**
**http://www.taylorandfrancis.com**

**and the CRC Press Web site at**
**http://www.crcpress.com**

*This book is dedicated to the courage, insight, and perseverance of people everywhere, who, like the people of Zwelethemba, simply get on with the job of creating a more peaceful tomorrow for themselves and those around them.*

# Contents

## 4   Multiple Accountabilities             87

## 5   Human Rights in Development        127

# Foreword

Where once modern nation states proclaimed exclusive jurisdiction over the authority, techniques and force employed to secure sovereign orders, now plural governance junctions legitimately include state, private and community modes of regulation. Established sociopolitical and legal debates have pointed out the significance of such governmental transformations, detailing the privatizing, neoliberal, neoconservative, or advanced liberal dimensions thereof. Yet, there is considerable disagreement on which changes should be enhanced or resisted, and what their cumulative impact might be on justice, democracy, and sovereignty politics more generally. The issues raised by these debates are brought into sharp relief in the South African context by postapartheid constitutional and political transformations. Its security governance has faced immense challenges, prompting new governmental responses, such as a notable rise in private security which highlights a consequential extension of private agents over areas previously reserved for state agents (e.g., police).

However, it is useful to recall that attempts to reconcile local security governance with emerging forms of sovereignty politics are certainly not new to the country. Examples of such political reasoning framed various indigenous political structures prior to European colonization and were integral to the governance of vast chieftain Kingdoms. As well, this logic contoured changing versions of corporate governance deployed by the VOC in the name of a Dutch sovereign. Equally, British colonial sovereignty was negotiated over local governmental orders (following two occupations of the Cape, one in 1795, the other just over a decade later), and Batavian quests for effective Cape governance (as enunciated in J.A. de Mist's famous Memorandum) emphasized the importance of tapping existing communal controls. Considered within the context of this lineage, *Governing Security, Policing and Local Capacity* emphasizes a novel dimension of security governance by focusing on a controversial matter — the precise role community members might play in governing security, outside of both private or public security arenas.

Within governance literatures, such local community involvement in security is often spurned as highly problematic and associated with destructive powers (e.g., excessive force, unfettered vigilantism, etc.). Against this assumption, and based on their immersion in a local community project at the Zwelethemba settlement, the authors take a guardedly different and reasoned approach. They see in such community involvement and local knowledge a clear potential; namely, a "significantly untapped capacity that could, if mobilized, have a major impact, for the good, within security governance." Besides enhancing local participation in democratic sovereignty politics, such involvement in security governance might also, if effective, make significantly positive contributions to the safety, liveability, and ubuntu of unsafe informal communities.

From this vantage, the book addresses a basic question: what grassroots practices might involve poor South Africans living in unsafe areas in the just, democratic, accountable and pluralistic governance of their communities' security? In responding to this question, and with explicit ministerial support, the authors aided a process by which members of the Zwelethemba informal settlement could define an autochthonous, community kindled model. The intent was to find a way to harness local knowledge and ability in the service of improving the safety and security of residents. This unique approach emerged out of Clifford Shearing's experiences in a Toronto Housing Authority project that sought to pluralize governmental "nodes" and to mobilize different security governance strengths of police, private security and community members. At Zwelethemba, an approach was developed through trial and error experimentation, resulting in model governance procedures outlining how local residents could help with the security governance of their informal settlement. Initially, selected local community leaders arranged meetings to solicit ideas about how members could usefully be involved in redressing local insecurity. From those meetings, a group was charged with developing an appropriate model of community governance that would meet the criteria of being "robust," "sustainable," and "legitimate." This group became the Community Peace Programme (CPP) which coordinated the Peace Committees. Besides developing governance models to address conflict in local areas, the group was to formulate procedures to monitor, regulate, and render such governance accountable — this became known as the Zwelethemba model.

By the end of 2009, there were 240 peace committees operating in the Western Cape Province. The CPP recorded data on each gathering, eventually logging some 50,000 cases. The Zwelethemba model was focused on intervening in disputes and conflicts early on, seeking to prevent conflicts from escalating into damaging security matters for the wider community. Disputants were thus able to bring conflicts to the peace committees, who then organized appropriate gatherings. With overtones of restorative justice's conferences and circles, but with more emphasis on forward-looking solutions, the Zwelethemba model proposed a culturally resonant way of dealing with conflicts. At its center were organized gatherings of community members who could contribute to future focused resolutions. A code of good "practice" developed by the community program for such gatherings was read to all participants at the start of meetings, allowing participants to hold those running meetings "horizontally" accountable to the enunciated ideal. In each other's absence, the disputants were by turn given an opportunity to voice their versions of the conflict. Focusing their considerations on the root causes of conflicts, these gatherings deliberated on future directed solutions and plans designed to end the conflict. All disputants signed off on these plans and agreed to any monitoring requirements.

Despite noted successes, state funding for the program was eliminated following the 2009 National general elections. This setback prompted the authors to reflect on the lessons learned from the initiative and how its governance nodes could more effectively have linked with other nodes, such as the police. Their further reflections on the Zwelethemba experiment produce a narrative on what the model can teach us about how the "local knowledge" and "capacities" of community participation could be mobilized as nodes in appropriate security governance arrangements for, especially, informal settlements.

The authors conclude that while the dangers of excess are always possible, there are ways to mitigate them by ensuring that any such model actively pursues "good governance." Good governance, however framed, is of course applicable to any governance node, whether located within or outside state formations. Yet, for them, community governance ought to involve, at least, the active pursuit of these core values: a sense of justice followed within the limits of framing constitutions; deliberative and participatory processes that add to ("deepen") the country's overall democratic sovereignty politics; inbuilt accountability processes consistent with the values articulated in the constitution; and, cosmopolitan values and human rights discourses that serve as both ideals and resources for community members who by participating in security governance help to develop South Africa's capacities.

Pursuing such values is, of course, dependent upon how one conceptualizes them, and this is precisely where the book's theoretical engagements help to extract key lessons learned from the Zwelethemba program. For example, the model suggests that justice in security governance arenas may not be achieved through abstracted principles imposed from without. Instead, the authors argue for a view of justice as an ideal that can only be appropriated pragmatically through day-to-day experiments that aspire to just outcomes. Depending largely on Dewey and Polanyi to theorize a "sense of justice," the discussion proposes that justice is always an accomplishment, gradually developed in local contexts through trial and error. A sense of justice that emerged from the Zwelethemba gatherings was formulated through proactive, future-directed plans aiming to generate better futures, and often enough these involved reconciliations of one sort or another. The model did bring to the fore the need to circumvent excesses of popular justice. As such, the pragmatic aspirations of the experiment were coupled with accountability processes and were always subordinated to the limits of constitutional provisions, including the state's monopoly over the use of legitimate force.

This sense of justice is contrasted with the abstractions of prevalent criminal justice formulations framed around backward-looking notions of "just deserts." The latter emphasizes the need to identify a culpable offender and calculate punishments that would simultaneously avenge society and deter others. At the same time, however, even though the model implies closer links with restorative approaches, its conception of justice is directed less at finding ways to heal harms, and more at closing disputes, or planning for "better futures." This forward-looking emphasis contrasts with a restorative justice inclination to delve into past events as a way to heal damaged relationships, relying on "restored" relationships as a passage to conflict resolution.

Similarly, the authors' analysis of democracy as an "essentially contested concept" works against such classical formulations as Hobbes but with those found in Tocqueville and Polanyi. They argue against a prevalent conflation of state institutions with democracy and seek to broaden understandings of democratic practice. By embracing an expanded concept of democracy and pursuing a "decentered, polycentric pattern of nested democratic forums," this book considers the local, deliberative, and active participation of citizens as a practical center for democratic politics. Democracy here emerges as a vital, dynamic, and "practical accomplishment" but which, like justice, always remains within the context of law and the constitution. In the security governance realm, the aim is to expand the spaces for democratic participation and assist local community members to creatively deliberate on problems; thus having their say, within limits, on the safety of their neighborhoods.

In efforts to "deepen" democracy, the Zwelethemba model was equally clear on the importance of holding any local initiatives accountable. The whole matter of political accountability within and outside of state structures is vexed, especially as assorted and polycentric nodes of governance fan out over regulatory arenas. A key lesson from the model speaks to the importance of establishing various, differently focused and independent, accountability measures that operate both horizontally and vertically to monitor practices. These are meant to warrant that initiatives are well regulated and that they operate according to design. In addition, the book indicates how expanded local community capacities can help to develop the country in ways that balance autonomy with broader cosmopolitan values and human rights. In this light, the Zwelethemba project may be seen as a response to developmental challenges by assisting the state to find local resolutions to human security issues in ways that foster political capacities and knowledge.

In sum, *Governing Security, Policing and Local Capacity* provides a theoretically informed analysis of an experiment in the informal settlement of Zwelethemba that actively involved members in the governance of their own safety. The text raises key questions about the adequacy of our attempts to understand and perhaps further the pluralizing, polycentric ways by which the governance of security is changing around us. It is an intrepid attempt to venture into discussions that require revamping because of new challenges posed by considerable insecurities facing poor people who live in informal settlements on the one hand, and the consequential shifts whereby security is increasingly governed through and outside of state structures on the other. The implications for emerging notions of local security governance framed around justice, democracy, accountability and cosmopolitan values will likely assume greater, rather than lesser, importance in the years ahead.

**George Pavlich**
*Professor of Law and Society*
*University of Alberta*

# Series Preface

While the literature on police and allied subjects is growing exponentially its impact upon day-to-day policing remains small. The two worlds of research and practice of policing remain disconnected even though cooperation between the two is growing. A major reason is that the two groups speak in different languages. The research work is published in hard-to-access journals and presented in a manner that is difficult to comprehend for a layperson. On the other hand, the police practitioners tend not to mix with researchers and remain secretive about their work. Consequently, there is little dialogue between the two and almost no attempt to learn from one another. Dialogue across the globe, among researchers and practitioners situated in different continents, is of course even more limited.

I attempted to address this problem by starting the IPES (www.ipes.info), where a common platform has brought the two together. IPES is now in its 15th year. The annual meetings that constitute most major annual events of the organization have been hosted in all parts of the world. Several publications have come out of these deliberations and a new collaborative community of scholars and police officers has been created whose membership runs into several hundreds.

Another attempt was to begin a new journal, aptly called *Police Practice and Research: An International Journal* (PPR), that has opened the gate to practitioners to share their work and experiences. The journal has attempted to focus upon issues that help bring the two on a single platform. PPR completed its 10th year in 2009. It is certainly an evidence of growing collaboration between police research and practice that PPR, which began with four issues a year, expanded into five issues in its fourth year, and now it is issued six times a year.

Clearly, these attempts, despite their success, remain limited. Conferences and journal publications do help create a body of knowledge and an association of police activists but cannot address substantial issues in depth. The limitations of time and space preclude larger discussions and more authoritative expositions that can provide stronger and broader linkages between the two worlds.

It is this realization of the increasing dialogue between police research and practice that has encouraged many of us—my close colleagues and I connected closely with IPES and PPR across the world—to conceive and implement a new attempt in this direction. I am now embarking on a book series, *Advances in Police Theory and Practice*, that seeks to attract writers from all parts of the world. Further, the attempt is to find practitioner-contributors. The objective is to make the series a serious contribution to our knowledge of the police as well as to improve police practices. The focus is not only in work that describes the best and successful police practices but also one that challenges current paradigms and breaks new ground to prepare a police for the twenty-first century. The series seeks for comparative analysis that highlights achievements in distant parts of the world as well as one that encourages an in-depth examination of specific problems confronting a particular police force.

This first volume of the series explores an African experiment, located in South Africa's Western Province, to establish legitimate and effective non-state security governance within poor urban settlements.

There has been, and continues to be, much reticence to endorse private forms of security governance that operate outside of state institutions within local communities. Such initiatives have often governed security in ways that violate established standards of good governance, dispelled punishment arbitrary and brutally, and used force illegally. At the same time, it has also been acknowledged that while many local, and especially informal, communities can be exceptionally unsafe, state institutions often struggle to effectively promote safety.

This book considers a model developed to enhance safety within poor communities within South Africa by mobilizing local knowledge and capacity. It explores the extent to which the practices the model enabled realized key public goods—justice, democracy, accountability, and development. It concludes that poor communities are a significant source of untapped resources that can, under certain conditions, be mobilized to significantly enhance safety.

It is hoped that through this series it will be possible to accelerate the process of building knowledge about policing and help bridge the gap between the two worlds—the world of police research and that of police practice. This is an invitation to police scholars and practitioners across the world to come and join in this venture.

**Dilip K. Das, PhD**
*Founding President*
*International Police Executive Symposium, IPES, www.ipes.info*

*Founding Editor in Chief, Police Practice and Research: An International*
*Journal (PPR), www.tandf.co.uk/journals*

# Acknowledgments

Academic books emerge from collegial interaction, and this book is no exception. We thank our academic institutions, the Centre of Criminology at the University of Cape Town and the Department of Administration and Organization Theory at the University of Bergen for providing much of the "thought food" that in so many ways nurtured this monograph, along with considerable institutional support. The institutional relations between our two academic units have contributed greatly to the production of this book.

We thank some of our closest academic colleagues with whom we have had ongoing discussions about the topics covered in this book: at the centre, Julie Berg and John Cartwright, and at the department, Thor Øivind Jensen and Thorvald Gran, as co-members of the "Politics, Innovation and Governance" research group. We are also grateful to Audun Offerdahl for his many insightful comments on several draft chapters.

We thank the many people who have shaped the development of the Zwelethemba model, modelers, those who used the model for well over a decade, and the many people who offered advice to the modelers—without them there would have been no empirical materials to examine. Especially noteworthy were the contributions of John Cartwright and Madeleine Jenneker.

This book would not have been completed had it not been for the professional assistance provided by Elaine Atkins and Ricky Rontsch, as well as the editorial work undertaken by Martin Rollo.

We are indebted to the South African Research Chairs Initiative of the Department of Science and Technology and National Research Foundation and to the Research Council of Norway, through its South Africa–Norway Program for Research Cooperation, for financial support.

While this book was jointly conceived, it was researched and written by Jan Froestad with support from Clifford Shearing.

# About the Authors

**Jan Froestad** is an Associate Professor at Department of Administration and Organization Theory, University of Bergen, Norway. He was appointed as an Honorary Research Associate, University of Cape Town in July 2011. His research interests covers studies of normality, deviance and disability, conditions for generalization of social trust, and, more recently, the governance of security and conflict management. This research interest led to a collaboration, from 2003 onwards, with Professor Clifford Shearing of the Centre of Criminology, in several research projects on the governance of security and policing, exploring, among other things, the "Zwelethemba" model of conflict management and community development. Froestad is at present involved with Environmental Security Research in collaboration with researchers at the Centre and at the University of Bergen, where a research focus is how municipalities and the insurance industry, in countries both in the South and in the North, respond to climate change.

**Clifford Shearing** is the Director of Centre of Criminology, Department of Public Law, Faculty of Law, University of Cape Town where he holds the Chair of Criminology and the South African National Research Foundation Chair in Security and Justice. He also holds a Professor II post at the University of Bergen, Norway. His research and writing has focused on the development of theoretical understandings that can be used to enhance the quality of security and justice governance. In addition to his established interests in physical security he is currently engaged in research and writing on environmental security. His most recent books are *Where's the Chicken?*, Mercury, 2012 (with Cartwright) and *The New Environmental Governance*, Routledge, 2012 (with Gunningham and Holley). Other recent books include *Innovative Possibilities: Global Policing Research and Practice*, CRC, Routledge, 2011 (ed. with Johnston); *Lengthening the Arm of the Law: Enhancing Police Resources in the 21st Century*, Cambridge, 2009 (with Ayling and Grabosky); and *Imagining Security*, Willan 2007 (with Wood).

# Introduction

1

This book is located within a literature that interrogates the producers and authorities of security governance and asks who they are and who they should be (for a review, see Bayley & Shearing, 2001; and more recently, Burris, Kempa, & Shearing, 2008; Ayling, Grabosky, & Shearing, 2006; Buur, Jensen, & Stepputat, 2007; Baker & Scheye, 2009; Baker, 2008, 2009). There are two sides to these questions. First, who authorizes and who should authorize the ordering of security—that is, who are the auspices of security governance and who should they be? Second, how is security governance provided and who should be providing it?

These are vexing questions and ones that have been at the center of political thought for centuries. Within the field of security governance these questions were regarded as more or less settled for much of the twentieth century. Contemporary security governance has for decades been understood as a governmental function that should be, and for all practical purposes is, monopolized by states through their agencies. This situation has been regarded as the outcome of a long process of state building across the globe (for an early review of this process, see Maitland, 1885/1972).

This state of affairs has been regarded as primarily a European accomplishment, albeit an accomplishment that has come to be accepted more widely in large measure as a consequence of colonization. Within this context, good governance, as a normative ideal, has been equated with effective and democratically accountable state governance. As a consequence, good security governance has been regarded, by definition, as governance undertaken through, and by, states. Good governance is thought to exist when contesting claims about who should govern have been settled by democratic states—that is, good governance is thought to exist where a strong and well-established democratic nation-state is the source of governmental authority and provision.

Around the middle of the twentieth century a variety of challenges to this conception arose. Some of these—for example, ideas that emerged under the banner of neoliberalism—have had a long philosophical history. Others, particularly within the security governance arena, were shaped by pressing pragmatic concerns. Whatever the reason, as the twentieth century drew to a close, the landscape of security governance had become more plural. This was true both in practice and at the normative level of ideals.

By the final decade of the twentieth century, while the idea that security governance should be monopolized by state governments continued to be influential, this ideal was by no means as self-evident as it had once been. This unsettled and undermined established understandings among scholars, politicians, and practitioners in ways that opened up debates, which had been regarded as settled, about the role of states in security governance. This was particularly so, both globally and locally, at the time of the South African transition to democracy in the mid-1990s. It was in the context of this debate, and particularly the local South African debate about how best to govern security in the emerging new South Africa, that the African experiment, which is the subject of this book, emerged. (We will have more to say about the history of this experiment later.)

The debate about the appropriate architecture of security governance has become even more vibrant recently, particularly within an international peacekeeping context (Bayley, 2011; Baker & Scheye, 2009; Baker, 2010; Braithwaite et al., 2010). As with earlier debates, these more recent debates have focused attention on the actual and desirable locations of both the auspices for and provision of security governance. Unsurprisingly, there are many resonances between these more recent discussions and the South African debate that took place in the context of a transition from the oppressive apartheid regime to what was hoped would be a stable and peaceful democracy—an expectation that has yet to be realized. This South African transition and the experiment reported on in this book have relevance—as will become apparent in the chapters to follow—for the contemporary peacekeeping discussions.

In the contemporary peacekeeping context there has been much discussion about how international agencies, and states intervening in the affairs of other states, can best contribute to the development of effective and democratic security governance. Until very recently there was widespread consensus that the best way for outside agencies to contribute to peaceful transitions was to strengthen states and assist them to take firm control of security governance within the boundaries of their territories. A term used to describe these initiatives is *security sector reform*—where *sector* refers to agencies concerned with security within states.

Relatively recently, within the last half decade or so, questions have been raised about the appropriateness of this state-focused reform strategy. An alternative position that has begun to be advanced, again for both pragmatic and theoretical reasons, has been one that favors a more polycentric or nodal approach to security governance. The nub of the alternative arguments has been that it is perhaps more sensible to find ways of shifting the governance focus from the state alone to what might be thought of as a "whole of society" approach to security governance.

Within this approach security reform seeks to develop nodal assemblages of auspices and providers based on hybrid arrangements that involve state, private, and civil society sector entities. The idea here has been to adopt an empirical, rather than an ideologically driven, approach to security sector reform, which argues that reform strategies should identify, and seek to build upon, historical processes and contemporary strengths—across sectors—that are useful in developing both effective and publicly accountable forms of security governance. Two of the most outspoken proponents of this line of argument, Bruce Baker and Eric Scheye, in a co-authored paper, express this position succinctly:

> It would make more sense to recognize the nature and composition of the post-conflict and fragile state without imposing upon it an idealized Western conception of what the state should be; acknowledge its inherent weaknesses and limitations; accept the ways in which state and non-state actors inter-penetrate, mingle, and merge; and then, attempt to strengthen the performance and capacities of those who actually deliver most of the security and justice in addition to building state capacities. (Baker & Scheye, 2007, p. 514)

David Bayley (2011, p. 52), in commenting on this emerging line of thinking within peacekeeping, notes that while there is much that can be said for the position of a whole of society approach to governing security in peacekeeping contexts, there is also much to be wary of. Bayley reminds us that the normative ideal of states as monopolizing security governance emerged because of the difficulties associated with more polycentric forms of governance. It is for this reason, he argues, that "government by national states is the primary way political power has become organized over the last four hundred years" (p. 61). To challenge this evolutionary trajectory as we tackle our contemporary security challenges, Bayley cautions, is a risky business indeed, as to do so "represents a profound change in global governance" (p. 62).

This caution, as Bayley recognizes, is not one that simply applies to peacekeeping situations, although it is these situations that he explicitly focuses on in his paper. Promoting and accepting polycentric forms of security governance within any context is something to approach with considerable caution because security governance affects governance more generally (p. 59).

In this book we take Bayley's cautions very seriously and use them as guides in the assessment of the development, expansion, and eventual demise of the security governance experiment we describe here. In our exploration we ask what lessons can be gleaned from the experiment with respect to the possibility of forms of legitimate and effective polycentric security governance. We locate this discussion within the context of the theoretical and political debates and contestations regarding the questions with which this experiment engaged.

In the chapters to follow we examine an African experiment, located in South Africa's Western Cape Province, to establish legitimate and effective nonstate security governance within poor urban settlements. We use this experiment to consider whether local, community-based, nonstate forms of security governance that respect liberal democratic governance ideals are possible, and if so, under what conditions. These possibilities, and attempts to realize them, are controversial because, as we have noted, it has been widely accepted that nonstate forms of security governance are, virtually by definition, both ineffective and illegitimate.

There is much irony here, as we live in a sociopolitical age in which individuals and communities are actively encouraged to engage in their own governance, including the governance of their own security. Within the governance of security this irony has been managed by a policy preference for limiting nonstate involvement in security governance to citizens acting in support of state agencies. States govern security best, it is argued, when they act with the support and cooperation of the citizens on whose behalf they are governing. While this principle has had widespread support, exactly where the boundary between appropriate and inappropriate citizen action lies, and should lie, has been the subject of considerable debate.

Within the arena of security governance, this issue has typically been addressed through asking what role citizens should play in assisting police and, through them, what role other institutions of criminal justice should play in maintaining public order. One way in which these questions have been answered has been through programs of community policing, developed by the police to encourage and enable appropriate forms of assistance by citizens. These programs have sought to establish ways in which police organizations can initiate and orchestrate activities by citizens who are willing to assist them in maintaining the public peace. What has been debated within these programs at the level of policy and implementation are the ways in which citizens, and businesses, should best assist the police to govern security effectively and legitimately.

These are not questions that we will be addressing here. Instead our concern will be with the more radical and more difficult question of whether, and if so to what extent, it is possible for citizens to engage legitimately in their own security governance independently of state agencies such as the police.

In one well-established domain of security governance—private security—the question has been clearly, and loudly, answered in the affirmative. This answer is evident by the acceptance of the role of private security entities as agents of citizens and businesses, in countries across the world, in domestic and military arenas, in the number of private security operators, and in the huge sums of money spent on them (Abrahamsen & Williams,

2011). States have almost universally endorsed, in a variety of ways, what private security operators do, and how they do it, through legislation, judicial proceedings, and policy.

At the root of this endorsement is the fact that private security, when it is operating legally (which is much of the time), acts as the agent of citizens (both individually and collectively), businesses, and governments. Much of the time (though of course not always), whatever powers private security operators exercise are the powers that have been legitimately delegated to them by citizens, businesses, and governments. These powers are varied and include the right to use physical force (see, for example, Law Commission of Canada, 2006). This authority to use force can be very significant, especially when the right to use force is devolved to security operators by property owners or by governments.

There are many questions as to whether these agents are always acting within the limits of their powers and whether the institutions designed to regulate the way in which private security operates are able to fulfill these regulatory functions adequately. What is clear, however, is that states around the world—both directly through legislation (and court proceedings) that refers specifically to private security and more generally through, for example, property law and contract law—endorse the presence and use of private security personnel in security governance.

While we will have more to say about private security, our concern in this book is with an arena of security governance that is much more controversial and where our questions have not typically been answered in the affirmative. This is the arena of community involvement in security governance outside of private security. Like private security, this security governance arena has vast resources, as the police who favor community policing initiatives realize. And yet, it is an arena in which there remains significant untapped capacity that could, if mobilized, have a major impact, for the good, within security governance. Further, this impact could be in precisely those areas where both private security and the state security governance institutions typically have had the least effect—namely, within poor communities, for example, informally housed poor communities where public policing and private security seldom engage directly on behalf of these communities. If these resources were to be effectively and legitimately mobilized they could have a significant positive impact on the security of people living within poor communities.

Globally, this, at present largely neglected, population constitutes at least a third of humanity; one in three people worldwide are said to live in slums (Davis, 2006). While it is difficult to measure the levels of security within slums, it is generally acknowledged that these are typically among the most insecure communities on the planet. Certainly within informal communities in South Africa, which is our focus in this book, all the evidence suggests that people living in these communities are particularly unsafe.

And yet there is much reticence globally to endorse local forms of security governance that operate outside of state institutions within these communities. And indeed, there are very good reasons for this concern. In example after example, home-grown initiatives violate established standards of good security governance. In particular, the evidence shows, time and time again, that such initiatives use force to govern security, and that when they do so, they fail to live up to the Weberian ideal, which requires that all force used to promote order be used in ways that are authorized by states.

Herein lies a conundrum. The conundrum is that poor communities have available to them a huge potential resource for the governance of security—namely, their local knowledge and capacity—but the use of these resources is seldom supported by states to enhance the security governance of these communities because their use has been shown, time and time again, to—in simple terms—do more harm than good. It is this conundrum that was the focus of the experiment in local security governance that we will be exploring here, and so it is this conundrum, and the possibility of finding a solution to it, that is the topic of our book.

The source of this conundrum is the possibility of, or rather what is often regarded as the impossibility of, effective regulation of local forms of community-based security governance. Such regulation is especially difficult in very poor communities, and in particular within informally housed communities, who by their very nature tend to operate outside of the reach of established regulatory mechanisms that could be used to effectively regulate their security governance.

This book is about an experiment, and the model that the experimenters developed to establish an example of local community-based security governance that would enable the routine use of local capacity and knowledge within very poor communities to govern security independently of the institutions of criminal justice and to do so within a very strictly regulated environment. The model for effective and legitimate local security governance developed in and through this (South) African experiment has come to be known as the Zwelethemba model.

Zwelethemba is the name of the township,[1] part of the municipality of Worcester, a large town about an hour's drive east of Cape Town, where the experiment was initiated. In Xhosa, the home language of most of the residents of Zwelethemba, the word means "place or country of hope"—a very fitting name for this very hopeful experiment and the model that arose out of it.

Before we turn to a consideration of the history of this experiment and the model-building process, we define some of the terms used. We will then very briefly explore some of the issues and ideas introduced above.

## Definitions

The word *security* and the closely aligned word *safety* are, as Lucia Zedner (2009) has recently shown, difficult words to pin down. To simplify things we propose to define *security* here in a way that we suggest captures the meaning, and associated way of being, that the people of Zwelethemba who worked as part of the Zwelethemba experiment had in mind when they spoke about safety within their communities. The Afrikaans (and Dutch) word *leefbaarheid*—that can roughly be translated into English as "liveability" or "liveable-ness"—more accurately captures what the people of Zwelethemba had in mind when they thought of security. A more general Xhosa/Zulu term that includes what these experimenters, and the people of Zwelethemba, had in mind is *ubuntu*—a concept that is deeply rooted in Nguni culture that references "mutual caring." Archbishop Tutu, who along with Nelson Mandela has become associated with the concept, often translates *ubuntu* into English as "a person is a person through other persons" (Tutu, 1999, pp. 34–35). Tutu has also spoken about *ubuntu* as referring to belonging in a "bundle of life"—a person with *ubuntu* "is diminished when others are humiliated or dismissed, when others are tortured or oppressed" (p. 31). This term has become so well known that it is now included in several dictionaries. The online *Oxford Dictionary of English* defines *ubuntu* as "a quality that includes the essential human virtues; compassion and humanity."

Thus, what people from Zwelethemba, and later from other similar communities, appeared to mean when they talked of safety, and of being safe, was more than ensuring that their bodies and possessions were not threatened (although this was part of it) but of the ability to be able to live with each other in peace—to have a liveability that comfortably enabled them and their children to live, work, and play in safety. This, we suggest, is very much what Thomas Hobbes (see below) had in mind when he spoke of peace and when he likened peace to good weather. For Hobbes good weather was more than a fine moment, it included more than this. It included the confident expectation that one could go about one's day without an expectation of bad weather.[2] Similarly, this applied to security for Zwelethemba and for similar communities within South Africa (and no doubt for communities generally). To be safe means to have the confident expectation that one would be able to live within one's community with a sustained, and taken for granted, sense of *leefbaarheid*.

When defining the term *experiment* we often have a scientific experiment in mind. To experiment is to test hypotheses under controlled conditions. But the term *experiment* has a much broader, expansive meaning, and it is to this broader meaning that we refer when we use the term *experiment* here.

The *Microsoft Encarta Dictionary*'s definition of *experiment* includes "doing something new" and the "use of repeated tests and trials." The *Oxford Dictionary of English* offers, as one of its definitions, "a course of action tentatively adopted without being sure of the outcome" and traces the origin of the term to the Latin *experiri*, meaning "to try."

While not an experiment in the sense of a scientific experiment, the Zwelethemba model-building process was experimental in the sense of *experiri*. This sense resonates with the way in which the American philosopher John Dewey used the term *experimentalism* to denote a way of linking practical experience to learning (Dewey, 1938b, 1962).

The Zwelethemba experiment was an attempt to try something relatively new within the realm of local security governance without being sure of the outcome. This trying took the form of a series of trials over several years beginning in 1997 to develop a set of robust and repeatable procedures for practicing legitimate and effective nonstate security governance at local levels and to develop a regulatory environment that would govern the use of these procedures.

The intention of the experiment was to explore the possibility of developing a preventative, future-focused model that drew on the knowledge and capacity of local residents to both understand the reasons for insecurity and develop forward-focused solutions that would create a better tomorrow. This, as we will see, had everything to do with the experimenters' concern to create a process that fitted within the terms of the Weberian limits that we noted earlier. Important here was the fact that the experiment was not directed at finding a way of correcting or improving upon the institutions and processes of criminal justice—institutions that have everything to do with the use of physical force and function within circumstances that comply with the Weberian ideal. Rather, the experiment sought to provide greater choice for people living in poor communities in governing their security (see Baker, 2008).

## Good Security Governance

Since Hobbes's writings and the Treaty of Westphalia in the middle 1600s, a central feature of what it meant to govern well has been a desire to shift the location of security governance from nonstate to state auspices. The historian F.W. Maitland, whom we have mentioned earlier, writing in 1885, captured this centralizing tendency nicely when he spoke of the necessity of an emerging public peace "swallowing up" what had hitherto been a multitude of contesting "private peaces" (Maitland, 1885/1972).

Central to this idea of the swallowing up of private peaces by national states have been the concepts and ideas associated with Max Weber's writing at the end of the nineteenth century, which defines states in terms of a monopoly of the legitimate distribution of physical force. Indeed, Weber defines a *human community* as constituting a state only if it has been able to successfully lay claim to a monopoly over the legitimate use of physical force within a given territory. Within this conception, others—individuals or associations—may legitimately use physical force so long as their use is authorized by state authorities (Weber, 1946, pp. 77–128).

This view of the crucial role played by states in monopolizing force is captured in the work of Thomas Hobbes, whose classic volume *Leviathan* appeared in 1648. Hobbes used the metaphor of a leviathan—a biblical sea monster that the *Oxford Dictionary of English* defines as representing "a thing that is very large and powerful"—to capture the idea that what was required for good governance was a single, legitimate, and powerful governing authority able to realize an overarching public peace by successfully resisting efforts by others to undermine it. Abraham Bosse's frontispiece to Hobbes's *Leviathan* depicts this sovereign as a giant, formed out of the bodies of citizens, standing over a landscape with a crosier (as a symbol of legitimate authority) in his left hand and a sword (as a symbol of the force the leviathan is able to use to counter resistance to his rule) in his right (Hobbes, 1651/1968).

Such a monopoly of force has come to be accepted internationally as an essential normative requirement of peace. A key mechanism for realizing this monopoly of violence has been a state police that has the will and capacity to successfully challenge those who use, or attempt to use, force outside of the bounds of state authorizations. Indeed, many histories of state police, as we have noted, view the police as a culmination of a long and difficult swallowing up process to establish a single unifying public peace based on a monopoly of the use of legitimate force. This understanding explains why scholars and laypersons alike tend to become uncomfortable, and at times alarmed, when they find evidence that suggests to them that the authority or capacity of state police organizations is being challenged or, worse still, undermined.

Given this framing, often associated with Bittner (1979), it is not surprising that evidence of nonstate security governance often triggers concern. This concern is apparent in the use of the label *vigilantism*[3] when evidence of nonstate security governance arises (Johnston, 1996). The concern here is that such a person or group may well be promoting a private peace that is in conflict with the established public peace.

This wariness was fully recognized by the Zwelethemba experimenters and was a concern that they sought to allay in developing their model on local, nonstate security governance. It is this wariness and the response of the experimenters to this as expressed in their model that will guide us as we analyze the value of the Zwelethemba model as an appropriate guide to good security governance.

With this in mind, we now turn to consider the history of the experiment—how it came about and how it developed.

## The Zwelethemba Road

If we are to explore the Zwelethemba experiment and the model it produced, in the context of the values of good governance we have briefly outlined and that we will elaborate upon in the chapters to follow, we need first to sketch the history of the process that produced the model. While the Zwelethemba process was informed by theory, it was, most importantly, a practical, trial-and-error experiment located within a longer history of practical attempts to design and develop effective forms of legitimate nonstate security governance with which Shearing has been involved for some time. This longer history spanned a couple of decades and involved work in several countries. The Zwelethemba experiment constitutes a particular point within a continuing process of "participatory action research" (Marks & Bradley, 2008).

There is a longer history to the evolution of the Zwelethemba model than we will present here. Selecting a particular time and place to locate the beginning of this history is arbitrary, as the ideas associated with it have had a long lineage that extend beyond either of our involvements. We will, for pragmatic reasons, begin this history in Toronto with a security governance project that was supported by the Metropolitan Toronto Housing Authority (see Shearing & Froestad, 2010).

A discussion over lunch in 1987 between Shearing and John Sewell, who was at the time the chairperson of the Toronto Housing Authority (hereafter "the authority") and an ex-mayor of Toronto, prompted the Toronto project. Sewell knew of the work Shearing had been undertaking with colleagues (in particular Philip Stenning) at the Center of Criminology at the University of Toronto since the mid-1970s on the pluralization of security governance.[4]

Sewell spoke about the unsafe conditions of several residential complexes in the jurisdiction of the authority and inquired whether Shearing might be interested in suggesting ways of governing security more effectively within these, and other arenas, that the housing authority managed. Shearing agreed to take on this challenge, and he and Sewell selected several pilot sites for what they thought of as experiments in urban security within a public form of "mass private property" (Shearing & Stenning, 1981; Kempa, Stenning, & Wood, 2004).

Together Sewell and Shearing agreed to several conditions for these experiments. Two are relevant to the history of the Zwelethemba model. First, Shearing and his team would be able to shortcut existing bureaucratic requirements in getting things done. Second, Sewell would make available to the project a security governance budget, what they thought of at the time as a policing budget, a term that was used (later) in the Patten Commission report (Independent Commission on Policing for Northern Ireland, 1999), of which Shearing was a member.

The Toronto team's principal *modus operandi*, as it went about this work, was to gather together people in small groups made up of the authority staff and tenants, to think about and propose solutions for security issues. The team did not use a single group of individuals, but rather brought together different sets of people depending on the issue at hand. Similarly, the mix of staff and tenants varied depending on the issue. These groups were asked to consider what could be done to improve security governance with respect to the issues they were discussing and to come up with suggestions that relied on capacities that were available locally, that could then be put to the test in a series of experiments.

The idea underlying this was to tap into local knowledge and local capacity in order to reimagine how security at the authority might be governed. The intention was to deliberately bring together sets of knowledge and capacity (staff and tenants) that were usually kept distinct and that were usually not mobilized around security issues—issues that until this point had been deemed to fall exclusively within the professional knowledge and capacity of the authority's security personnel.

While the team did not engage in any formal evaluation of what was done, the team and the groups met regularly to consider how their experiments were proceeding and how they could be improved. For those involved, this was thought of as constituting a form of evidence-based thinking. In thinking about this process they borrowed an idea from the management thinking of Tom Peters and Robert Waterman's *In Search of Excellence* (2004, p. 134): "Do it, fix it, try it." The team expressed this as a "TTI process or principle"—"try it, test it, and improve it."

In the group brainstorming sessions to elicit local knowledge, the team learned early on that there were several impediments to innovative and imaginative thinking of the sort it was trying to promote. Two are worth mentioning here.

The first was "force of habit," in particular "habits of mind" (Dewey, 1927, pp. 160–162). These had the effect of moving groups very quickly to a solution in ways that short-circuited the problem analysis phase. The team developed an antidote to such habits by treating the brainstorming as a game where players were encouraged to deliberately put established answers out of play. This required thinking to move in new directions: After all, most of the established solutions were already being used and had not proved to be particularly useful.

The second, pervasive impediment the team encountered was the "put others down" habit. What tended to happen in brainstorming was that participants acted as if a good discussion required them to find flaws with the ideas of others—this was regarded as critical thinking. The result was a spiral of criticism: People previously criticized got "their own back" by criticizing others when their turns came around in the discussion. The team developed a simple set of rules to counter this habit. Every idea presented was put up on the wall on a sheet of paper. Before the end of the brainstorming, the best idea was selected to be tested. Then all the pieces of paper were collected and put away so that none of the ideas were lost as they might prove useful later, after what was thought to be the best idea at the time had been tested.

The Toronto process nicely illustrates Dewey's (1938a, 1938b) understanding of an experimental process—as one in which the definition of a problem and the construction of its solution are created in and through practice (Kaufman-Osborn, 1985, p. 836).

What was discovered through the Toronto process were sets of knowledge and capacity that the existing, professionally focused arrangements had systematically (though not necessarily intentionally or knowingly) marginalized. This discovery sometimes led to the constitution of new governing "nodes"—understood as institutional sites of knowledge and capacity that could be routinely mobilized as a source of security governance. The idea of nodes involved in governance has since been expanded by Shearing and colleagues as nodal governance (see, for example, Johnston & Shearing, 2003).

The result of the team's gathering of people together was a series of innovative governance initiatives. Some of these died on the experimental table. Many, however, developed and extended through the TTI process. After a few months of these trial-and-error initiatives the security environment within the authority had become very different—this was evidenced both in the incident reports on safety and security and in the day-to-day experience of the staff and tenants. Areas that had been regarded as unsafe and had often been treated as no-go zones by security staff now came to be regarded as safe. Very soon what might be thought of as a tipping point (Gladwell, 2002, p. 7) occurred. A new set of practices in terms of tenant, visitor, and staff activities—that took security rather than insecurity for granted—became the status quo. Soon the downward, negative spirals that had characterized the authority were replaced by upward, positive spirals (Wood, 1996).

An intended, but nonetheless remarkable, feature of the initiatives developed within the pilot sites in Toronto was that they, for the most part, used very different sets of resources from those that are normally used to attempt to govern security. An example that illustrates this was the provision by the authority of free barbecues on summer evenings in open spaces within the public housing authority. These proved to be a useful "tipper," as spaces that had not been regarded as being safe now came to be regarded as safe. Another example involved the encouragement of older women, who regularly played bridge together in their homes to play bridge in public foyer areas of buildings that had been taken over by local gangs of youths. Yet another example was the use of beautification as a security initiative. For instance, flower gardens were used to create real and virtual boundaries. It is in examples such as these that the wisdom of having an open security budget—that is, a budget that was not preallocated to security personnel—became very clear to all those involved. Existing security budgets limited expenditures to security resources, such as security officers, and would thus not have been available for the sort of costs that these initiatives, no matter how trivial, involved.

As a consequence of these developments, security governance within the authority was deliberately pluralized, in the sense that a variety of new and different sets of resources and knowledge were mobilized and integrated as part of a diverse and integrated security program that involved police, private security, and a host of other nodes and nodal practices. Nodes were identified, created, mobilized, and integrated into a new policing assemblage. What was previously a nodally thin security governance environment was transformed into a nodally thick environment (Walzer, 1994). The normative implication here was that nodally thick environments tend to be more effective and legitimate than nodally thin ones (Shearing, 1987).

In summary, the normative conclusion reached by the authority's research team was that a critical determinant of effective, efficient, and legitimate security governance proved to be the thickening of security governance through the identification, mobilization, and integration of appropriate sets of knowledge and capacities. Some of the nodes included in this nodal mix had been "professionalized" as security resources—for example, contracted security firms—while others had not. The security governance problem within the housing authority before the project began, the team concluded, was that there were inadequate institutional arrangements for mobilizing nonprofessionalized knowledge and capacities so that they could be actively engaged in security governance. Like most models the Toronto experiment was institutionalized in spotty ways within the organization as its political environment changed (Braithwaite & Drahos, 2000, pp. 559–563).

The next phase in this history occurred during a two-year visit by Shearing to the Community Law Centre at the University of the Western Cape in Cape Town. While based at the centre, Shearing was appointed to the Goldstone Commission's Panel on the Prevention of Public Violence and Intimidation that was tasked with proposing a policy for policing demonstrations in the run-up to the 1994 elections—South Africa's first democratic elections (see Heymann, 1992, for the panel's report).

The panel asked itself, much as the housing authority research team had done, where appropriate knowledge and capacities for governing demonstrations might be found. They concluded that the organizers of demonstrations were likely to be a critically important source of knowledge about how best to govern demonstrations, and an important source of capacity for doing so. The problem in the existing arrangements, the panel reasoned, was that the knowledge and capacities were not being mobilized. Once again, the issue boiled down to the absence of institutional mechanisms that would enable this wider and more extensive knowledge and capacity to be seen and mobilized—again, what might be thought of as a nodal deficit. As in Toronto, the existing mechanisms favored the knowledge and capacity of particular security governance nodes—in this case, the police—at the expense of other nodes.

Accordingly, the panel, like the Toronto team, found itself face-to-face with a nodal governance problem: namely, how to take cognizance of the Foucaultian point that "power comes from everywhere" (Foucault, 1978, p. 93) in ways that would enhance the likelihood that the 1994 South African elections would be peaceful. In light of this analysis, the panel directed its attention to figuring out an alternative set of institutional arrangements—thicker arrangements that would depart from the police-focused ones that had dominated the governance of demonstrations in South Africa for decades. The issue was how to find, or create, nodal institutional arrangements that would enable the mobilization of the knowledge and capacity of organizers of demonstrations and coordinate these resources with police capacity and knowledge.

The essence of the panel's proposals was as follows. Everyone, the panel argued, had a right to demonstrate, but no one had a right to demonstrate in a nonpeaceful manner. This premise gave rise to the argument that a license to demonstrate should be required. To obtain such a license, demonstrators would be required, the panel recommended, to show that their proposed demonstration would be peaceful because they had developed a practical and reliable policing plan. These recommendations were implemented, first, through a regulatory agreement and later through legislation (Heymann, 1992).

Although no formal evidence was collected, there is widespread agreement that these alternative nodal arrangements were indeed a success. Demonstrations preceding the election period were remarkably peaceful. The police were involved as a backup and supervisory institution, but much of the policing of the demonstrations took place through a process of self-policing. Much of this self-policing was done by marshals who were deployed by the organizers of demonstrations (Shearing & Foster, 2007). While this model for policing public order was rigorously adhered to during the 1994 election period, and although legislation endorsing it remains in force, it seems that today it is less pertinent than it once was in regulating public demonstrations.

## Reaching Zwelethemba

The next step in this sequence of experiments on the road to the Zwelethemba model was initiated as a consequence of a conversation Shearing had with the then South African minister of justice, Dullah Omar. Minister Omar said essentially, "Why don't we adopt the same approach as was adopted during the elections in thinking about governing security within poor South African communities?" These communities had been neglected under apartheid and were then, as they still are today, particularly insecure places. Minister Omar went on to say: "Create a model that we, the government, can implement and we will take it forward." With this remark, the Zwelethemba model-building process was born. Omar and Shearing approached the Raoul Wallenberg Foundation in Lund, Sweden, for support, and selected an area (Zwelethemba) in which to explore an iterative model-building process. Shearing received funding and began the process.

Again, the focus was on developing institutional arrangements that would facilitate an ongoing process. In thinking about what these arrangements might be, the project team—a small group of researchers based at the School of Government at the University of the Western Cape—argued that these arrangements had to be (1) robust, (2) sustainable, and (3) legitimate. This thinking was in part based on the learning from the earlier initiatives outlined above and in part based on the team's theoretical explorations around the issue of polycentric security governance—some of this thinking was touched upon at the beginning of this chapter.

By robust, the team meant that the arrangements would be ones that would be easy to implement, require a minimum of professional involvement, and thus be low cost. By sustainability, the team meant that the procedures would be easy to scale up and maintain. Legitimacy was regarded as being vital, as many of the local initiatives that had developed in response to apartheid had become violent and were not accountable to either local communities or to the law—indeed, many of these initiatives were clearly illegal. In thinking of legitimacy, the team was also aware of developing processes that resonated with established cultural practices.

The process began with the identification of local community leaders within Zwelethemba who could help the team set up and advertise community meetings and then continued with a number of community meetings. All these meetings were well attended; each meeting included several hundred people. The meetings led to the emergence of a small group of people who volunteered to take the process forward. The research team and this group agreed that they would work together to develop a process that met the above criteria of being robust, sustainable, and legitimate and that could be used to assist in the governance of security within Zwelethemba.

Initially, it was thought that perhaps the best way to proceed was to adopt the approach taken in Toronto. The team soon found, however, that, while many generic issues requiring attention could be identified, and that it was indeed valuable to bring people together to discuss them, it proved difficult to get busy residents to attend these discussions and to implement ideas developed at the meetings. In Toronto there had been a housing authority with a committed staff to facilitate these sorts of discussions and engage in the implementation of the ideas proposed. Within the Zwelethemba context, without a functional equivalent of a dedicated staff, it was much more difficult to hold the discussions and to apply the solutions that were developed. Interestingly, if we jump forward to the middle of the first decade of the twenty-first century, and turn our attention to a Nexus Project that Shearing and other colleagues developed with the Victoria Police in Melbourne, Australia, we see that it is possible for a motivated police organization to fulfill a similar role within communities (Shearing & Marks, 2011; Wood, Fleming, & Marks, 2008). This was not possible within Zwelethemba, given the challenges facing the South African police as they sought to position themselves within a new democratic environment.

There was indeed a very active civil society in Zwelethemba during the mid-1990s. However, this meant that residents were faced with a constant stream of demands to attend community meetings of various sorts. Residents did not wish to engage in an additional set of meetings and demands, without an immediate and pressing reason for attending.

The team soon found, however, that as soon as there was some really pressing matter related to security—typically an argument or a dispute of some kind—people affected by this were more than willing to engage in finding a solution to it. Two of the most frequent disputes that people began to identify as issues to be addressed were arguments over moneylending and domestic quarrels. These disputes were often very energetic and at times, if not resolved, led to violence. When they did escalate, which was not infrequently, what had begun as a seemingly small and easy-to-resolve dispute might escalate into a serious and violent conflict.

Over the course of the experiment several such examples emerged. One example that soon acquired an emblematic status within the team and among residents involved with the team was the following incident—we present the story here as it unfolded as team members inquired into it (see Cartwright & Shearing, 2012). An informal dwelling was torched and burnt down. Such an event within a settlement of informal houses is extremely dangerous, as it can lead to enormous damage to persons and property. The dwellings burn easily and fires spread very easily, as dwellings are constructed close to each other. In this incident the fire was stopped in time and an inquiry by the team ensued. When the arsonist was identified he was asked why he had done such a thing. He indignantly answered that he had done so because the shack owner had on several occasions assaulted his family. When the owner was questioned about this he equally indignantly answered that the other party and his family had constantly insulted himself and his relatives—it is necessary at this point to realize that in Zwelethemba, and similar communities, slandering is a serious offense because one's identity is often one's most prized possession.

When the next round of questioning took place it was discovered that the motivation for the insults was that the one family's chickens were allowed to roam and defecate, etc., around other people's homes. So what had become a shack-burning problem was initially a "chicken shit" problem. When asked why the chicken problem had not been addressed, the answer given was that one could not seek police assistance for such minor problems; when asked why the insults were not addressed, the same response was forthcoming; when asked about the assault, the argument was that calling the police was too expensive as one would need to provide half a bottle of brandy to persuade them to attend. The police did attend the house burning! At this point a word of caution is in order. As this story became iconic within the project, its exact origins became lost, and as we write these words we are unsure of how true the details are. What is important about this story, however, is not its truth but rather the fact that it became an iconic story that was told and retold because of its emblematic significance.

At this stage in the experimental process—that is, after a period of attempting to get something similar to what had happened in Toronto going—it was decided to invite a small group of academics interested in the governance of security to visit South Africa and to assist in the model-building process by reflecting on what had been taking place. Three scholars accepted the team's invitation: David Bayley from the United States, John Braithwaite from Australia, and Enrique Font from Argentina. A little later, in a separate visit, the team hosted two Canadians: Barry Stewart, a judge from the Yukon, and Mark Ridge, a First Nations member, who had teamed up to develop "healing circles" within the context of the formal criminal justice processes (Consedine, 1999).

Soon after our formal reflection meetings had concluded, Braithwaite and Shearing visited a community of poor people who had been building their own formal houses (houses built of concrete blocks) using government subsidies. While they were there, some community members brought an alleged rapist to them, the inference being "you guys say that you know something about security, well do something about this!" This put them on the spot. Fortunately for him, Shearing had the ever-resourceful Braithwaite with him so a response emerged. Braithwaite found himself, without warning, facilitating an impromptu gathering along the lines of the family group conferencing that he had been involved in within Australia and about which he had written extensively (Braithwaite, 1989, 2002).

The model-building team's own experiences before the reflection process and Braithwaite's unexpected recruitment as a facilitator in a quickly organized gathering convinced the team of two things. First, it was not going to be possible to build a process that met the three governing criteria around general security issues of the sort that had been addressed in Toronto. Accordingly, it would be much more useful to attempt to build processes for local security governance arrangements around people's pressing problems, manifested in disputes, as they arose.

Second, the team concluded in reflecting on Braithwaite's experience, in viewing family group conferencing videos, and in reflecting on the visit of the Canadians that while the team could learn a lot from conferencing processes, it could not simply adopt them wholesale for a variety of reasons—that is, it could not simply regard them as a "good practice" to be adopted for use in this very different setting. Two issues that arose were thought to be particularly important. One was that the family group conferencing-type processes were too costly, because they were so highly professionally focused. Second, the reaction of the team was that they were focused too much on the past, when what was required in the South African context of poor communities was to move forward quickly. What was particularly attractive about these processes and other similar ones, however, was that they were gathering focused— something that had very strong cultural resonances within South Africa.

This period of critical reflection provided the impetus for rethinking the trial-and-error-based (experimental) arrangements that were beginning to emerge. This proved to be a crucial step in the emergence of the Zwelethemba model. What emerged was a model that had a strong family resemblance to family group conferencing and healing circles, but was also distinctly different. It shared similar thinking and similar design principles (Ostrom, 1990) to these other approaches; however, there were key differences. A key difference between the sets of practices that the Zwelethemba model came to endorse and promote was that it was distinctly future focused—its focus was, in the language of the Zwelethemba team members, on "creating a better tomorrow."

On the basis of this discussion it is evident that an essential feature of the Zwelethemba model is its focus on disputes. Beside the urgency and mobilizing impetus that disputes provided, another key reason for focusing on disputes was that it was precisely a failure to deal with such matters at a point when resolutions were likely to be relatively easy to discover that led to relatively small problems becoming big ones. At the core of the Zwelethemba process was the idea that disputes caught early, and indeed disputes more generally, were most likely to be resolved if a deliberately future-focused approach was adopted. The question to be asked was: What could be done to reduce the likelihood of this dispute continuing? The best way to answer this question, it was decided, was to gather local residents together who seemed likely to be able to contribute to providing an answer that could be translated into a plan of action that all present at the gathering endorsed and would contribute toward implementing. With this conception, a conception that had taken many months to finally realize and articulate, the Zwelethemba model was born.

A routine outcome of these gatherings, and the agreements they led to, was that persons who had been involved in disputes and interactions became active players in crafting and implementing peaceful resolutions. Through this process troublemakers became peacemakers. The critical condition in fostering this turnaround was the future orientation that the process encouraged. Within a future-focused context, cooperation became possible, and was elicited precisely because blaming was not a focus.

Gatherings were often concluded with gestures of reconciliation, such as handshaking or hugs, sometimes accompanied by tears. Within the model, these gestures, and the emotions they expressed, were regarded as useful to the extent that they helped create a better tomorrow. But they were not seen as necessary or central outcomes of the process. That is, while this result was not the purpose of the process, it was seen as an often useful and desirable outcome.

Incentives designed to encourage people to give up their time to facilitate the Zwelethemba process were incorporated into the model over time. Persons willing to facilitate gatherings were organized into peace committees. Peace committees were made up of a group of people, anywhere from a handful to 20 persons, who agreed to facilitate the model's processes. Monetary incentives were provided to members who facilitated gatherings, in accordance with the model's processes. These processes were routinized in two forms: steps that set out a process from the time a dispute was identified and a code of good practice that articulated the approach and sensibility that the model sought to apply (see the appendix for the code and steps). The monetary incentives were over time incorporated into the model's accountability processes. Monetary payments were awarded for following the model's procedures rather than for dispute resolutions that produced a "successful" result. Reporting processes were established to enable peace committees to show that they had indeed followed the model's steps and code. Only dispute processes or cases that followed procedures secured payments. These reporting processes also triggered remedial processes, in the form of coaching, where procedures were routinely not being followed. In the rare case where members refused to follow procedures, gatherings, using the model's procedures, were held to craft a forward-looking solution.

A crucial feature of the code was the directive that peace committees should not resort to physical coercion in organizing or facilitating a gathering or in enacting a plan of action. As we have already hinted, a resort to physical coercion had become a notorious feature of other competing informal processes, especially those known as street committees (Scharf & Nina, 2001). Theoretically, an important intention with this rule was an endorsement of the Hobbesian/Weberian position, that we canvassed earlier, that holds that states should monopolize authorizations with respect to the use of force.

While peace committee members, as citizens, did of course enjoy certain authorizations to use force (for example, citizen's arrest and self-defense), the code forbade any use of force as part of the Zwelethemba process. At a more practical level this directive was regarded as essential if peace committees, and the process they facilitated, were to be trusted and seen as legitimate within communities. In addition, the code explicitly constrained peace committee members, and those at gatherings, to act within the law and more broadly in ways that were consistent with the values endorsed by the South African Constitution. One of the intentions of this was to encourage peace committees to work collaboratively with state agencies.

An essential feature of the Zwelethemba process, and thus a central feature of the sensibility the code and the steps sought to embed, was the future/risk focus noted above. The intention here was to establish security governance nodes (peace committees) that worked explicitly to promote peaceful sets of practices that would enhance local security. The argument that emerged to support this was that blaming processes (for example, the processes of the criminal justice institutions) were useful and appropriate at times, but that they needed to be complemented by preventive future-focused technologies that conceived of prevention in terms other than deterrence. It was this niche that peace committees, and the process they facilitated, sought to fill.

The key process features of the Zwelethemba model are as follows. Disputants bring a dispute to a peace committee. The committee, after consulting with the disputants, convenes a gathering to which persons thought to be able to contribute to a forward-focused outcome are invited. At gatherings each disputant tells his or her side of the story to inform those at the gathering of the nature of the issues. No attempt is made to arrive at a single accepted account. This happens through a process whereby each disputant speaks to the gathering alone while the other waits in an anteroom of some sort.

The focus of gatherings then turns to consider the sources of the dispute (what came to be called the root causes by peace committees), and the issue of how to reduce the likelihood of the dispute, and its associated features, continuing. A plan of action to achieve this is then formulated. This plan—which typically includes a monitoring process—is then agreed to, and those present commit themselves, by signing the document on which the plan is recorded, to facilitate and support its realization.

Data were collected on each gathering (over 50,000 at the time of writing). Of these, 35,000 were analyzed in ways that will become apparent, by staff at the Community Peace Program (CPP) as part of an in-house monitoring process. The CPP arose out of the team initially established at the University of the Western Cape. In due course it was registered as a nonprofit organization to run the program that was developed to implement the model.

The accountability mechanisms embedded in the Zwelethemba model emerged through a conscious attempt to combine a range of accountability mechanisms situated along both horizontal and vertical axes (a theme we will explore in detail in Chapter 4). Within the model the code of good practice operated as an internal regulatory framework that, alongside the peacemaking steps, set out how gatherings should be run. These mechanisms structured the actions of peace committee members (and those who attended gatherings) in ways designed to embed the values and processes outlined above in these practices.

The model requires the code of good practice to be read aloud at the beginning of all gatherings. The steps to be followed are also outlined in the model. The intention in requiring this was to enable those present at the gathering to hold peace committee members accountable to the requirements of the model through a process of horizontal accountability.

In the development of the model the issue of sustainability—that is, continuing to motivate persons to give up their time to participate—proved difficult. This was particularly so for the committee members, as they did not have a stake in the particular dispute and yet had to facilitate the dispute resolution process. These persons, during the pilot phase, often raised the "free rider" problem, saying in effect, "We do all of this work from which the community benefits, but we get no compensation and the members of our households would prefer us to spend the time earning some money instead." This sentiment and the pressures associated with it prompted a relatively high turnover of committee members. The payment system outlined above was developed, in part, to reduce member turnover. It also provided, as we have noted, the basis for an embedded regulatory system, by providing incentives for compliance with the steps and the code.

In addition to the routine reviews of each case undertaken by the staff of the CPP, case report data were aggregated; audit visits of gatherings by the CPP were undertaken. Further, occasional community baseline surveys were conducted. These data were analyzed, as part of a monitoring process, in order to direct remedial engagements in the form of coaching, both through exchanges between committees and through coaching provided by CPP staff. This focus on remedial regulation involving both committee members themselves and the CPP meant that resources to support these regulatory interventions had to be supported as part of the model's activities.

By the end of 2009 the model had been rolled out to about 240 peace committees who operated in communities in the Western Cape Province in close association with schools—peace committees were established in schools with the support of teachers and in surrounding communities. The quantitative data that are cited in later chapters are drawn from the database that the CPP developed as part of recording processes we have just outlined. These data were collected by peace committee members and CPP staff and analyzed by the CPP for internal regulatory and associated payment purposes.

As will now be apparent, a crucial intention of the model's arrangements was to deepen local involvement in security governance, so as to engage a wider range of available knowledge and capacity in ways that contributed to South Africa's emerging democracy. In particular, the aim was to, in this sense, "deepen democracy" (Appadurai, 2002) by promoting regulated problem-solving deliberative forums that would encourage citizens to participate in these security governance nodal networks. One of the motivations of the experimental process reflected here was the intention to explore ways of enhancing the voice of poor and marginalized South Africans within governance processes (Wood & Shearing, 2007).

The nodal or networked policing arrangements that the Zwelethemba model sought to promote resonates with similar institutional arrangements that have been developed within many other contexts—especially in other parts of Africa (Baker, 2002, 2004b, 2008; Marenin, 2005; OECD, 2006; Dupont et al., 2003). What Zwelethemba sought to contribute to these ongoing explorations in security governance was to find ways of routinizing and extending robust and sustainable nodal forms of governance that would enhance the voice of marginalized constituencies in highly regulated and accountable ways.

## A Road Block

The funding for the experimental process we have outlined was sourced from within the international donor community—initially from the Swedish government via the Raoul Wallenberg Institute at Lund University and later by the Finnish government through its South African embassy. As the process moved increasingly out of its experimental to its rollout phase, financial support was sourced through a variety of South African government sources—initially local government sources were used to supplement Finnish support once the rollout process to other communities beyond Zwelethemba began. By 2007 the rollout process was completely funded by the South African national government.

At the end of 2009, for reasons that have yet to become fully apparent, at the time of the change from the Mbeki to the Zuma presidency, funding from the national government came, without any warning, to an abrupt end in the middle of a two-year contract term. This occurred despite the fact that the contract had anticipated a planned rollout of the program beyond the Western Cape to the whole of South Africa on a province-by-province basis according to an agreed upon timetable. We will have more to say about this in the concluding chapter.

## Roads from Zwelethemba

The Zwelethemba model was only one development to emerge from the story we have outlined. The next chapter in this story was the Independent

Commission on Policing for Northern Ireland (1999), also known as the Patten Commission, of which Shearing was a member. The proposals presented by the Commission for the policing of Northern Ireland in their final report in September 1999 bear the marks of the thinking that inspired the Zwelethemba experiment.

The Patten Commission was established to explore the renewal of policing in Northern Ireland and to develop proposals for accountable nodal policing. These proposals included recommendations for a *policing* rather than simply a *police* budget and for a *policing* rather than a *police* board, with a remit that included, but was not limited to, police (for a recent review of the developments, see Shearing, 2010).

More recently the Victoria police in Australia have been exploring how best to reimagine police, not simply as the deliverers of policing services, but as nodal coordinators, in a series of bottom-up experiments in different policing locales (Shearing & Marks, 2011; Wood et al., 2008). Also recently, the Dutch police have been actively exploring mechanisms (as part of what they call a *nodale orientatie*) that pay particular attention to flows of people and information, along with a program of "neighborhood directing" that focuses attention on identifying, mobilizing, and integrating nodal resources (Project Group Vision on Policing, 2006). This work, and the synergies between the nodal thinking of the Dutch police and Shearing's thinking on nodal governance, has led to a collaborative program being established to enhance municipal policing within South Africa between officers from Amsterdam who have been engaged in neighborhood directing and the University of Cape Town. Very recently there have been developments to extend nodal and future-focused thinking to security governance within South Africa through developments being promoted by the government of the Western Cape.

## The Road to This Book

In 2003 Froestad and Shearing initiated a long-term collaboration on the Zwelethemba experiment. Froestad, coming from a political science background, had been engaged in research in South Africa since 1999, particularly on health issues and how the health governance system, broadly defined, had evolved since 1994. A particular concern of this research, of which a central focus was on environmental health problems in poor communities, was how a lack of trust between different agencies and professional groups within the state—but also between public agencies, their officials, and members of the local communities—often prevented collective and effective problem solving (Froestad, 2005a, 2005b).

During the ensuing years this collaborative work led to new explorations on different aspects of the Zwelethemba model and its associated thinking

and practices. Over the years eight academic papers on the model were produced, first through a series of papers that explored how the model differed
from the philosophy and practice that underlies criminal justice as well as
other (more restorative) resolution models (Froestad & Shearing, 2005, 2007a,
2007b). A further paper explored how the practice of the model tended to
change when moved from urban to more rural environments (Froestad &
Shearing, 2007c), and a final paper explored how the model contributed to
human rights thinking and practice (Froestad & Shearing, 2007d). A new
series of papers published over the last couple of years focused more on how
the model relates to nodal governance thinking (Shearing & Froestad, 2010)
and to studies of justice (Froestad & Shearing, 2011; Wood, Shearing, &
Froestad, 2011).

Over the years the Zwelethemba experiment, and the publications that
were produced exploring aspects of its practice, led to an emergence of a
degree of international interest in its philosophical underpinnings and more
practical accomplishments, with several scholars commenting on the experiment in published papers. While most of these comments were positive
in their evaluations (Braithwaite, 2000b; Roche, 2002, 2003; Burris, 2004;
Gordon, 2006), some were more critical, either questioning one or more of
the founding ideas of the model or its assumed capacity to function in challenging environments (Loader & Walker, 2004; Dixon, 2004). This gradually convinced us that the Zwelethemba experiment might be in need of a
more thorough theoretical and empirical testing, in which we would explore
in greater depth the capacity of the model, on philosophical and practical
grounds, to contribute to the production of a series of public goods. The public goods upon which we decided to concentrate our exploration was justice, democracy, accountability, and (human rights-aligned) development,
as these are values considered critical by most institutions and scholars
associated with the good governance discourse (Robinson & White, 1998;
Braithwaite, 1999b; Dowdle, 2006; Pierre, 2000; World Bank, 1992, 1997).
The key question we have been and are still asking is if it is possible for a
nonstate security model such as Zwelethemba to promote such values, and
if so, on what grounds. In the chapters to follow we explore trends within
the scholarly debates, concentrating on each of these public goods. We critically examine how the Zwelethemba modelers thought about the challenges
addressed by each of the discourses, how they responded to them, and what
they were able to accomplish on a practical level.

In Chapter 2 we explore Zwelethemba's justice. Our argument is that a
form of thinking about justice and experience of justice emerges from gatherings, which eschews the idea of "just deserts," and that this is also different
from the more past-oriented blaming practice of restorative justice programs,
though there are also interesting similarities. In Chapter 3 our focus is on
how the model has sought to deepen democracy through creating forums

that allow members of poor communities a more decisive voice in their own governance of security. We explore the extent to which interactions at gatherings are sensitive both to local values and norms and to broader (cosmopolitan) values and principles. The focus in Chapter 4, on accountability, is on how the model has sought to keep local practice within the limits of the values and the principles that the experiment has endorsed. We argue, on the basis of a range of different data, that a highly regulated practice had been established. In Chapter 5 our focus is on how the model supports thinking and practice that is closely associated with human rights, human development, and human security. The model was explicitly designed to support development in a manner that balanced the need for local autonomy and self-directedness with broader cosmopolitan human rights values. In Chapter 6 we bring it all together. We discuss what we have learned as we approach the end of our journey of exploring a model designed to enable ordinary South Africans to participate actively in security governance and broader development projects. We review the lessons we have identified as we have examined the Zwelethemba experiment through our four ideals of good governance—justice, democracy, accountability, and development aligned with human rights. We end the book with some reflections on the institutional resistance that the project engendered and ask if there is any hope that the experiences of those who took up the Zwelethemba model might live on and add to the repertoire of human choice in policing and the governance of security.

## Endnotes

1. The Zwelethemba township consists of a community of about 20,000 persons, with formal housing that has been built over years with government assistance and a sizable sector of informally constructed housing—commonly called shacks in South Africa.
2. To people such as the authors, who have lived and worked in various parts of the world, most recently Cape Town, South Africa, and Bergen, Norway, what is taken to be good and bad weather is context specific. In Cape Town it is extended periods of sunshine; in Bergen it is often a day with at least a little sunshine! Much the same applies to liveability.
3. A vigilante is "a member of a self-appointed group of citizens who undertake law enforcement in their community without legal authority, typically because the legal agencies are thought to be inadequate" (*Oxford Dictionary of English*).
4. Much of what we will have to say here in setting out this history is taken from a joint paper (Shearing & Froestad, 2010).

# Justice Through Peace 2

## Introduction

Barbara Hudson, in her book *Justice in the Risk Society*, argues that "'justice' is very much under threat within the 'risk society'" (Hudson, 2003, p. x). In this chapter we consider this threat to justice through the lens of the Zwelethemba model and its processes.

The Zwelethemba modelers assumed that justice, at least in the established sense of "just deserts" (Von Hirsch, 1976) that has dominated conceptions of justice within security governance, would be a casualty of the model's processes, as these processes were concerned with anticipating and preventing future harm, a feature of risk societies, rather than with blaming and punishing those responsible for harm caused by wrongdoing. This proved to be the case. Within the Zwelethemba processes justice as just deserts, by definition, has no place.

Nonetheless, a somewhat different sense of justice—in the sense of a good and right outcome—did in fact emerge. In this chapter we seek to articulate this Zwelethemba justice.

We argue that the emergence of an alternative sense of justice provides insights into what a sense of justice, within a risk-focused set of governance processes that eschew intentionally administered "hard treatment" (Duff, 1992), might mean. What we learned from Zwelethemba is that while risk-focused processes, like those of the Zwelethemba model, do indeed threaten the justice of just deserts that is at the center of Hudson's concerns, they allow us to discern an alternative conception of justice that is worth exploring, given the high costs that are so often associated with deontological conceptions of justice. Central to these costs are the many harmful consequences that are so often endemic in punishment, and especially in imprisonment. These consequences include harm to communities (Clear, 2007), harms that go well beyond the hard treatments handed down in courts (Van Zyl Smit, 2004), and a variety of health risks that extend beyond prisons (Shearing & Johnston, 2005). In developing these arguments we draw upon, and extend, Shearing and Johnston's earlier analysis.

We begin our discussion with a review of justice as just deserts.

## Justice as Just Deserts

For the philosopher Immanuel Kant (1790/1987) the qualities of fairness and reasonableness, which are widely associated with justice, are most appropriately realized within the context of the governance of wrongdoing when a harm to a victim is balanced by an equivalent harm imposed on the offender by a legitimate authority. Justice, for Kant, is realized when an appropriate punishment, in the form of hard treatment, is imposed on an offender. Within this retributive conception, justice is realized when a wrongdoer receives his or her just deserts (Von Hirsch, 1976) in response to the harm the wrongdoer caused to a victim(s). It is not hard to find evidence for this sense of justice being done, when offenders get their just deserts, at an experiential level in daily life. The loved ones of victims of mass harms, such as massacres, for example, often express huge relief when offenders are identified and punished, even if this happens long after the events in question. Similar experiences are also reported in much more mundane circumstances, for example, when burglars are apprehended and punished. Very often victims only feel that they are "released" from the trauma of wrongdoing when the offender has been identified and received a punishment that is felt to be commensurate with the harm caused.

These experiences have been explained by scholars who argue that justice requires a return, in the form of hard treatment, to the offender of the harm that the offender caused. This conception of justice as requiring "like with like" (Kant, 1790/1987) is often associated with biblical references to "an eye for an eye" (Matthew 5:34 (English Standard Version)). In this view, punishment is justified by the act of wrongdoing itself and should not be applied in order to reduce the likelihood of future wrongdoing, although this consequence may occur. To adopt such an instrumental view, it is argued, would mean that pain would be applied not as a response to the pain caused by the offender to the victim, but in the hope that it will produce a future good.

To treat an offender in this way is to disrespect the offender, as he or she would then be treated as a means to an end rather than as an end in itself. In this view, the proper objective of punishment, and the only objective that can justify its use, is "to inflict something painful or burdensome on an offender for his offence" (Duff, 1992, p. 49). It is the offense that justifies the punishment, and nothing else. When this happens, justice as a moral order, which the wrongdoing disrupted, is reestablished. For Kantians, like Duff and Von Hirsch, punishment should never be imposed simply for instrumental reasons but only as a retributive response to wrongdoing.

To illustrate this conception of justice, Kant (1790/1987) offers a hypothetical story of an island where all the inhabitants have resolved to "separate and scatter themselves throughout the whole world." Before the inhabitants leave the island Kant insists that "the last murderer lying in the prison ought to be executed." Only then will "the desert of his deeds" be realized. And only then will they be able to leave the island with the moral order that was violated reestablished.

Kant's shadow is a long one, as the writings of Von Hirsch, Duff, and many other deontologists make clear. In their view, what punishment ensures (and what makes its correct use so crucial) is fair dealing among free and equal citizens. To blame and then to punish, it is argued, sends a necessary message to the wrongdoer: "What you did to her, she can do to you. So you are equal" (Hampton, 1992, p. 13, in Cragg, 1992).

It is this message that provides the experience of a release from the past, and it is this release that allows a different present, and hence a different future, to unfold. It is only when the "past is repaired" (Leman-Langlois & Shearing, 2004) in this way that one has justice. Justice is done when the moral damage done by a wrongful act has been made right. Within this view, punishment, when authorized by a legitimate authority, expresses moral disapproval (by the wider community in whose name the authority acts) of a wrongful act by ascribing blame to an offender and punishing him or her for his or her wrongdoing (Von Hirsch, 1976).

The argument developed by thinkers like Von Hirsch, as we have already suggested, is that courts should punish, not to deter, but to provide for justice. Von Hirsch, in particular, argues that this understanding of the relationship between punishment and justice not only justifies the use of punishment, but also places limits on its use by ensuring that it is proportionate to the harm done—something, for example, that one often does not find in instances of popular or vigilante justice.

Deontological thinkers, like Von Hirsch, have become particularly concerned about what they view as an unwarranted escalation of punishments that tends to occur when punishment is justified on the basis of instrumental arguments, such as the argument that punishment deters.

This conception of justice is certainly one that has considerable traction within South African society at all levels, and it is certainly a conception that is alive and well within communities like Zwelethemba. The Zwelethemba modelers had no quarrel with this conception. They recognized its merits as we have outlined these above. They also recognized that a retributive impulse, and corresponding sense of justice, has very deep roots within South African communities. At the same time, they recognized the harm that this retributive impulse had produced over the years as communities had sought to find ways of responding to the harms that wrongdoers were creating within their communities. Communities like Zwelethemba across South Africa were, and continue to be, places where many forms of "informal justice" are practiced through institutions such as "street committees" (Scharf & Nina, 2001, pp. 48, 100). This justice was very different from the measured and carefully calibrated justice of the deontologists. Street justice was often experienced as just deserts, but was very often brutal and cruel.

It was this way of doing justice, rather than the ideals of justice that the deontologists have celebrated, that was the concern of the Zwelethemba modelers and those who embraced the processes of the model. Put simply, these modelers and residents were as "sick and tired" of the failure of the institutions of criminal justice to live up to the promise of the deontologists as they were of the popular forms of justice that had emerged in their stead.

The modelers certainly did not seek to develop an alternative sense of what we might think of as judicial justice. They would have been very happy to see the emergence of practices within criminal justice that would realize Kantian justice. They were not abolitionists who wanted to see an end to the use of properly functioning prisons or the proper and measured application of punishment more generally. Rather, the failure of the institutions of criminal justice, and what they saw as the wrongdoing of the institutions of popular justice, concerned them and motivated them to respond to and develop the Zwelethemba model. Their concern was with the way punishment was being used to respond to wrongdoing in communities across South Africa.

In seeking to develop methods for governing security that eschewed punishment, the modelers simply accepted that what they did would not provide justice. This was one of the reasons why the model provides for disputants to take cases to the police for processing through the criminal justice system and why on occasion peace committee members themselves might, either before, during, or after a gathering, suggest that a disputant might wish to follow this route.

This meant that the motive of the Zwelethemba modelers was quite different from the motives of supporters or advocates of other forms of justice, for example, the conception of justice as healing that is so central to the notion of restorative justice, even though the model does specify steps that resemble the sorts of steps that are sometimes used with forms of restorative justice, such as family group conferencing. This difference was not accidental, as the modelers paid considerable attention to restorative justice practices during the model-building process.

Nonetheless, we turn now to a discussion of restorative justice in the same way as we have discussed the justice of just deserts—to provide a context and contrast to the conception of justice that Zwelethemba justice provides.

## Restorative Justice: Justice as Healing

The deontological view of justice as deserts, to be accomplished through blaming and punishment, began to be challenged in the early 1990s within the governance of security literature, by a variety of thinkers, who came from different contexts, and who developed an alternative conception of justice as healing, rather than as retribution, under the sign of restorative justice.

This movement has sought to rethink what justice might mean and how it might be experienced, by reimagining it as fairness that is accomplished through a restoration of the conditions that a wrongful act disrupted through a process of restitution, through healing, in which offenders play a crucial role. The movement has drawn heavily on ideas and practices from indigenous cultures. Restorative justice advocates argue that these practices provide a source of inspiration from outside a Western philosophic tradition—in particular a Kantian tradition—and provide a new way of imagining how a disruption of an order is to be restored. For restorative justice advocates, restoration can, and should, be pursued in other ways than through the idea of restoring a moral balance, which is central to retribution. In particular, two sources of indigenous practices have been extensively drawn upon by restorative justice advocates—Maori practices of family group conferencing and the North American indigenous practices of healing circles (Consedine, 1999). This movement has also drawn upon Christian thinking and practices.

Two important milestones within this movement were the publication of two books: one by the Australian criminologist John Braithwaite that drew heavily on Maori thinking and practices, and the other by Howard Zehr, an American who drew upon his Christian Mennonite background (Braithwaite, 1989; Zehr, 1990). Similar examples of restorative advocates who have drawn upon Christian traditions are Father Jim Consedine (1999) and Archbishop Desmond Tutu, who was the co-chair of the South African Truth and Reconciliation Commission (the other chair, Alex Boraine, was also a practicing Christian).

One of the features of this alternative, restorative conception of justice has been the way in which it has sought to reimagine how fairness, and the sense of closure that can be associated with this, might be conceived. These restorative thinkers retain the retributive idea of balance, but reimagine how such a balance is to be restored.

For these thinkers, the balance that provides for fairness should not be conceived of as a balancing of one harm with another (as is the case with retributive conceptions), but rather as a balancing of harm with actions taken, especially by the wrongdoer, to heal the harm that that wrongdoing has caused. This balancing is viewed as restoring the order that had been undermined by the wrongdoing. With this conception, the two orderings—instrumental and symbolic—that deontologists are so careful to keep distinct are brought together.

Crucial to this conception, is an intention to move responses to wrongdoing away from punishment as the only acceptable means of creating a fair and just outcome to responses that focus on healing the consequences of the harm that was done. This approach, like that of the deontologists, retains a focus on the past, as this is where the harm to be healed is located. Furthermore, as with the deontologists, the countervailing balance that heals the past is located in the present. Once this healing (balance) is accomplished, a new future is seen as possible, as the imbalances that made it difficult for victims to move beyond the harms of the past have now been addressed.

Again, as with deontological justice, the justice of healing opens up new futures that build upon the possibilities that the righting of a disrupted order makes possible. Restorative justice healing a past harm, through action in the present, opens up the possibility of a future that is no longer governed by the damage caused by the past harm.

When one listens to victims who have participated in restorative justice processes such as conferencing, where what Braithwaite terms a "community of care" is established, one hears utterances by participants that frequently express a sense of release from a trap of a broken past. Once this past is "repaired," a future that is no longer entrapped by a broken past becomes possible. While there are disagreements between deontologists and restorative justice thinkers as to the nature of justice, both incorporate a conception of fairness. It is this fairness that, once established, provides a release from the past.

As we have just suggested, this conception of justice builds upon established notions of restitution as the source of fairness. Restoring what was taken away is regarded as providing the basis for a platform on which to build a new future. This idea is nicely set out on the website of the South African Restitution Foundation, which states that the foundation's mission is "to be a catalyst for restitution within the South African society," and that its vision is "to model restitution that will bring justice and healing to the nation." In answering the question "What is the relationship between restitution and restorative justice?" the foundation's Web site (http://restitution.org.za) says:

> Restitution plays a critical role in restorative justice. Because restorative justice seeks not just punishment but the healing of the community, it requires more of both the perpetrator and the victim than retributive justice does. Unlike retributive justice, which frames wrongdoing as a violation of law and crime against the state, restorative justice recognizes a wrongdoing as a violation of relationship and a crime against people and community. As part of the process of healing the wounds, then, the perpetrator must acknowledge that injustices have been committed and participate, along with the victims and wider communities, in seeking solutions that will repair that frayed social fabric. Making restitution—doing what is in the power of the perpetrator to restore justice and set right what was wrong—is a critical piece of this.... By voluntarily choosing to make restitution, [perpetrators] take responsibility for the advantages they have gained and attempt to break the cyclical nature of those advantages by redistributing both material wealth and the wealth of education and skill. In doing so they begin to right the imbalance.

For the Restitution Foundation, as these words suggest, as it was with the South African Truth Commission, the location of restoration need not be at the level of the individual or small group, but can extend to a whole society. As can be seen from this statement, and many similar statements to be found within the restorative justice movement, much is retained from the deontological conception of justice—in particular that of responding to a disequilibrium, a breach of a balance, that wrongdoing is thought to create. What differs is the way in which this righting of a balance is conceived and the understanding of the actions required to right this balance.

To these core ideas of restoration and restitution, restorative justice thinkers, particularly those who draw inspiration from a Christian tradition, often add the notion of forgiveness as a form of exchange, that operates at a symbolic level, and that complements the restitution that operates on an instrumental or material level. Forgiveness, it is argued, allows the victim to let go of past wrongdoing, and the harm it is thought to have caused. This letting go is thought to provide a platform on which to build a new future.

These ideas of forgiveness leading to a new and better future were central to the processes of the South African Truth and Reconciliation Commission. The title of Archbishop Tutu's 1999 book on the Commission, *Without Forgiveness, There Is No Future*, makes clear his views on forgiveness and restorative justice. Tutu believes that forgiveness, albeit a gift that must be given voluntarily and that cannot be coerced, is crucial if a flawed past is to be left behind and a new future is to be envisioned and established. In Tutu's words,

> Forgiveness gives us the capacity to make a new start. That is the power, the rationale, of confession and forgiveness. It is to say "I have fallen but I am not going to remain there. Please forgive me." And forgiveness is the grace by which you enable the other person to get up, and get up with dignity, to begin anew. Not to forgive leads to bitterness and hatred, which gnaw away at the vitals of one's being. (Tutu & Allen, 1997, p. 61)

While this passage addresses the future that forgiveness makes possible for the perpetrator of wrongdoing, it is also seen as liberating the victim through the exchange of a sincere apology with heartfelt forgiveness.

For the Truth and Reconciliation Commission (TRC) a better future was one in which there would be "inner peace" and an "absence of revenge," as well as "peaceful communities" and "respect for democratic values" (TRC Report Vol. 1, 5, para. 13–28 (106–110)).

Forgiveness, as this suggests, is for many advocates of restorative justice a crucial ingredient of healing—healing that enables the past to be left behind and a new future to be established. It is for this reason that Jim Consedine (2005), in "Is There a Place for Forgiveness in Restorative Justice," argues that forgiveness "forms an integral component of any such restorative justice process."

A key feature of forgiveness, as we have just noted, is that it is not something that can be demanded or coerced. It is a gift that one person offers to another—or in the view of Tutu, a divine gift (preface by Archbishop Tutu, in Consedine, 1999)—that one group offers to another, often in response to an apology by an offender (Leman-Langlois & Shearing, 2008). It is this free, voluntary feature of forgiveness that is recognized by authors, such as Tutu, who point to a spiritual element in forgiveness. In recognizing this he suggests that there is something divine about forgiveness. As Consedine notes, in his comment cited by Pumla Gobodo-Madikizela in her book *A Human Being Died That Night*, there is, for Tutu, a divine element involved when forgiveness occurs:

> "We are on holy ground." There seems to be something spiritual, even sacramental, about forgiveness—a sign that moves and touches those who are witness to its enactment. (Gobodo-Madikizela, 2003, p. 95)

Underlying the possibility of forgiveness is typically a willingness on the part of offenders to admit wrongdoing and to accept responsibility for their actions and the harm they are said to have caused. This is perhaps the reason why, within restorative justice processes, there is an insistence that a distinction must be made between victims and offenders and why it is regarded as essential for the healing that restorative justice processes enable that there be an admission of guilt by offenders and why there is often so much emphasis placed on the "hailing out" or "interpellation" (Althusser, 1971, p. 174) of the gift of an apology that acknowledges the acceptance of blame for wrongdoing and the forgiveness that this apology can evoke.

This plea for an acceptance of blame and an apology as the first step required for the reciprocal giving of an apology and forgiveness was expressed in the plea Tutu, in the context of a Truth Commission hearing, made to Winnie Madikizela-Mandela, the former wife of Nelson Mandela—a woman who is viewed by many in South Africa as the mother of the nation and an icon of the South African struggle for liberation.

> I beg you, I beg you, I beg you please—I have not made any particular finding from what has happened here. I speak as someone who has lived in this community. You are a great person and you don't know how your greatness would be enhanced if you were to say sorry, things went wrong, forgive me. I beg you. (MUFC hearings, day 9, quoted in Leman-Langlois & Shearing, 2008, p. 223)

What relationship then is there between justice and forgiveness? Why would forgiveness be thought to be so essential to restorative justice? Perhaps, as we have suggested, the answer lies in the healing that forgiveness is thought to provide and the fairness and rightness that come from the reciprocal relationship of an apology and its acceptance through forgiveness. What appears to be involved is yet another notion of balance, a balance that enables an ordering at a symbolic level to take place that complements the material ordering of restitution—an ordering that enables a harm and the disruption it has caused in the past to be healed and a new future to be opened up.

What seems clear is that forgiveness requires blame and a corresponding acceptance of wrongdoing by wrongdoers.

## Restorative Justice and the Criminal Justice System

During the 1990s restorative justice emerged as a movement that challenged and sought to reform established understandings of justice. It evolved as a loosely coupled advocacy movement with a variety of threads, each with somewhat different origins and sources of conceptual inspiration.

Given the diverse nature of the restorative justice movement there have been, not surprisingly, many disagreements over just how this healing, and the justice it enables, can best be realized—for example, disagreements over whether forgiveness is essential to healing. A significant debate within the movement has been about whether it is establishing a clear defining vision that identifies the essential features of restorative justice (and that set it off from the practices of the criminal justice system), and if so, just what this vision should be (Walgrave & Bazemore, 1999, p. 371).

One feature of this debate has been a reluctance, among some advocates of restorative justice, to support attempts to specify and formalize procedures. Their concern has been that formalizing procedures would curtail the innovation that, these advocates believe, has been such a valuable feature of the restorative justice movement. As an alternative to defining restorative justice in terms of the means it deploys, many advocates have sought to define it in terms of the values it celebrates and promotes. Braithwaite, for example, states that "stakeholder deliberation determines what restoration means in a specific context" (quoted in Crawford & Newburn, 2003, p. 44) and sees this, in combination with the value of "respectful dialogue" (Braithwaite, 2002), as an alternative way of defining the restorative approach, rather than trying to outline specific procedures for realizing this value (also see Braithwaite, 1999).

One of the developments that motivated the call for clearer definitions within restorative justice has been that, in some jurisdictions, it has come to occupy a central position within criminal justice. This success has, in the eyes of some, brought with it worrying developments. The concern is that, as restorative justice processes become more and more firmly embedded within criminal justice, there is a danger that its values and processes may be corroded by the just deserts logic that is so firmly entrenched within criminal

justice. A concern has been that embedding restorative justice within criminal justice processes has resulted in a blurring of boundaries between criminal and restorative justice in ways that have undermined the transformative
potential of the restorative approach (Walgrave & Bazemore, 1999, p. 377).
This blurring has, it is argued, unduly shifted the focus away from the pathways that account for the offenses to the offenses themselves (Mika & Zehr,
2003, p. 141). A concern here has been the limited capacity that exists within
criminal justice to forge links between individual cases and their structural
sources—something that is often identified as a crucial feature of restorative
justice (Mika, 1992, p. 563; White, 1994, pp. 183–185; Levrant, Cullen, Fulton,
& Wozniak, 1999; Crawford & Clear, 2003, p. 224). Bazemore and Walgrave
(1999, p. 56), in considering this concern, have argued that remedying this
tendency that arises when the boundaries of restorative and criminal justice
are blurred requires increasing "the compatibility and resonance between
the emphasis on repairing prior harm and … more future-oriented transformative efforts."

What this, and similar critiques, argue is that a worrying cost of embedding restorative justice within criminal justice processes is that what is lost
sight of is a future peace that reestablishes order. One way in which this loss
is identified is through a comparison of the indigenous forms of restoration
with the restorative trajectory that is followed when restorative justice is
embedded within criminal justice (Morris & Maxwell, 2001). Cunneen (2002,
p. 45), for example, in comparing indigenous sentencing circles with restorative justice programs within a Canadian criminal justice context, argues
that what counts as restoration has become "very much trapped within the
confines of the Canadian justice system"—the very system that restorative
justice, he argues, was intended to challenge.

As evidence for this, Johnstone (2007), in his discussion of Ross's (1996)
study of sexual abuse and healing paths in Hollow Water, has argued that a
crucial difficulty with many restorative justice processes—especially those
embedded within criminal justice—has been its acceptance of a bifurcation
of parties into victims and offenders. Ross's study, Johnstone argues, demonstrated that attempts to divide people into offenders and victims is mistaken.
In support of this, Johnstone draws attention to the Hollow Water's insistence on a broader construction that eschews this. He argues that restorative
justice has neither acknowledged nor acted upon the full implication of this
insightful experiment, but rather has "tended to 'borrow' processes—such
as 'circle sentencing'—and utilize them in an attempt to deal with problems
that have been constructed in a much more convenient manner" (Johnstone,
2007, p. 609).

In a similar vein Blagg (2001, p. 230) has argued that restorative justice
has tended to selectively appropriate certain elements of traditional aboriginal practices without an acknowledgment of the wider cultural universe

that gave these elements their purpose and significance. He notes that while the Maori conferencing model was intended to empower aboriginal communities and reduce the degree to which the police intervened in the lives of Maori youth, the Australian "borrowing" of this model has undermined these features of aboriginal dispute resolution processes by inappropriately representing them, from an occidental perspective, as constituting shaming ceremonies. This, he argues, has resulted in an extension of already significant police powers over young aboriginal people in Australia (Blagg, 1997).

What both Johnstone and Blagg draw attention to in these examples is an appropriation of indigenous practices and innovative approaches in ways that reshape and, in doing so, undermine them. This is done in order to create a fit with the established mentalities and processes embedded within criminal justice.

Writing in a similar vein, Pavlich (2005), while acknowledging restorative justice's many contributions, argues that it has remained disciplined by the logic of the system it has sought to oppose. He argues that restorative justice, in contrast to its various self-representations, has never been able to develop a viable alternative to criminal justice's conceptualization embodied within the concept of crime. As a consequence, the idea of healing, so central to restorative justice, has been undermined. For example, when restorative justice is realized within the confines of criminal justice its processes invariably begin with an insistence of an acceptance of the claim that a crime has been committed and that there is a responsible offender and a corresponding victim. Thus, despite its claims to offer an alternative, its opposition to established forms of justice relies upon the very categories it should be seeking to transcend (Pavlich, 2005, p. 35).

What these arguments contend is that restorative justice, rather than challenging criminal justice, ends up replicating and endorsing key features of criminal justice and the logic that is expressed through them. This happens because once restorative justice becomes embedded within criminal justice it "makes up" its objects in ways that are simply too closely tied to categories of the law and criminal justice. As a result, despite its initial critical and transformative impulse and promises, restorative justice has proved to be "no match" for the "capricious old fox" of criminal justice (Pavlich, 2005, p. 105). This has led Milovanovic (2006, p. 72) to argue that if one is to find processes that realize the hopes of restorative values, it is going to be important to decouple these processes from those of criminal justice.

These concerns about the challenges of restorative justice as such programs sought to establish a relation to criminal justice were ones that the Zwelethemba experimenters were aware of (both from reading the literature and from the responses of community members to information about the restorative justice process from visits of advocates and from video materials). In developing the Zwelethemba model they sought to respond to these concerns. An important feature of this response was their decision to develop the model at arm's length from the processes of criminal justice—albeit in the shadow of these processes (what Galanter (1981) has termed the "shadow of law" and Börzel and Risse (2010) have termed the "shadow of hierarchy").

The Zwelethemba modelers, and the Zwelethemba residents who worked with them, were very aware of the core ideas of restorative justice and yet, as the Zwelethemba model makes clear, the Zwelethemba modelers did not go down a restorative justice road—not withstanding their appreciation of it.

The reasons for not choosing a restorative justice approach had to do with concerns that the restorative justice processes, at least those they had been exposed to, relied heavily on professionals and seemed to them to typically involve very time-consuming processes. Further, the response of the modelers to the videos they reviewed of several Australian examples of conferencing was that the restorative justice processes, as presented, seemed to them and others from the community to be unrealistic given their circumstances, as they required considerable time and effort to enable people who had experienced trauma to experience healing. This was similar for wrongdoers, who often were the focus of considerable effort to persuade them to recognize the harm they had done and to apologize and, ideally, seek forgiveness. The feeling expressed was that while this might be possible in some circumstances, such as the Truth Commission, what they needed was something much more expeditious, which would focus on creating conditions conducive to a more secure tomorrow quickly and routinely. Insecurity was a huge concern, and what the modelers sought to develop was primarily an instrumental process that would quickly limit the negative impacts of disputes.

What resulted was the development of the Zwelethemba processes we have outlined. These processes were ones that, as we have already noted, the modelers felt would enhance security but without the sense of justice having been done that just deserts or restorative justice bring with them. For the modelers this meant that their focus in developing the processes of the model would simply be an instrumental one that sought to create a safer tomorrow.

However, what happened when the Zwelethemba processes were put into practice was that the gatherings did seem to have a symbolic resonance that suggested that justice, in some sense, had indeed been done. What was this resonance and how, if at all, does it relate to these two established notions of justice? In short, what was this sense of justice? It is to these questions that we now turn.

## Zwelethemba's Justice

As we have noted, it was with some surprise that we, in our research, began to notice responses within the Zwelethemba processes that suggested that something certainly akin to justice, understood as a sense of fairness and rightness that provided closure to the participants, did appear to be taking place. This experience seemed to us to be associated with a sense of reconciliation and the feeling that peace between the parties had been established.

A peace gathering held in Zwelethemba in July 2006 may serve to illustrate this point. The dispute arose between two neighbors. One of the women accused the other of having insulted her by shouting loudly in public that she was a witch, a whore, and a bitch—someone who married many times and who was sleeping around. At the gathering it became clear that part of the reason for the conflict was that the insulting woman had owed the other money for a long time. The insulted woman had brought the conflict to the attention of the community—through a local street committee—who had fined the other woman and forced her to buy a bottle of brandy and some chicken for her neighbor. Obviously this had not ended the strife between them. The insulted woman had then brought the case to the peace committee, who called both of them, together with their friends and relatives, to a meeting.

Initially, as the gathering started, the peacemakers, following the steps of peacemaking, sought to reveal what had actually happened. In the beginning the insulting woman did not want to admit to her wrongdoing. She also claimed to have been drunk, so she did not remember anything. Gradually, however, with encouragement from the peacemakers and other participants, she admitted to her actions and said she was sorry. One of the peacemakers then asked the insulted woman:

> When you came here to the peace committee what did you want the committee to do for you? I want you to guide us and also tell us what do you want NN [the other woman] to do? It is clear to us that you are not after money because you did not go to the police. Instead you came to us.

The insulted woman answered:

> I want the peace committee to punish her for me. That's why I brought her here.

One of the participating community members explained to her that the peace committee "wants peace and nothing else." A peacemaker followed up on this, stating that the principles of the committee did not allow for anybody to be fined. She addressed the other disputant and asked her to express herself. The woman responded:

> I'm very sorry to you, mother, of all the things I said. Really I won't do that again. I learned a lesson that it is not right to drink and do things because you get into troubles and sometimes jail by just one mistake. I'm really sorry to you, mother.

One of the peacemakers then asked the other disputant:

What do you say, mother? Do you accept?

She answered:

I want her to promise that she won't do this again and I want the committee to monitor that something like this will never happen again.

Being asked to respond, the other woman said:

I agree with her and I also want to shake hands to show that I'm really sorry.

At the end they both shook hands and were smiling at each other.

The case is a good illustration of how, throughout the entire process, even as one explores what happened, attempting to reveal how past events and actions have nurtured a dispute, the focus is firmly tuned toward the future and the possibility of reaching an agreement that the disputants and others who offer their assistance can commit themselves to. When the process unfolds like this, people feel a sense of fairness, equality, and rightness, and having been offered a credible hope of a better tomorrow, they seem to feel that justice has been done.

At the same time, this sense was not a sense of justice as in just deserts, nor was it a sense of justice as healing, although sometimes participants did express it as a sense of healing, especially when there were expressions of forgiveness. This forgiveness sometimes took the classic form of an apology that was given and accepted. Clearly when this happened, there was a sense of healing and closure, in the restorative justice sense. As these expressions were not specifically encouraged by the model's processes, this was indeed a gift that was exchanged, in the sense that we have discussed. However, as welcome as this was when it happened, it was not considered to be essential to the working of the model. One could have a successful gathering that led to an action plan that was accepted by all, without this sense of healing. Indeed, at times the parties would leave still aggrieved, but committed to ending the dispute.

What fascinated us, as researchers, was that even when this sense of healing did not happen, participants nonetheless seemed to experience a sense of justice. This sense was not limited to the disputants but included all those involved in gatherings. This was demonstrated by the celebratory gestures that frequently followed the conclusion of a gathering in which a plan of action to end the dispute had been decided upon. These celebrations took several forms—most commonly dancing, singing, and prayer, typically accompanied by handholding or some similar touching to create a sense of a single collective that included the disputants. The question is: What was being celebrated? What was being figuratively marked as having been realized or accomplished at, and by, the gathering?

One answer might be that what was being celebrated were acts of forgiveness when they occurred. There seems to be no doubt that when they did take place, which was frequently, the acts of healing were included in what was being celebrated. What is puzzling, however, is that even when there were no acts of forgiveness these celebratory gestures were still likely to occur. So what was being celebrated? What was being symbolically marked?

At one level the answer is simple and straightforward—what was being celebrated was the successful enhancement of the possibility of a better, more peaceful future, not just for the disputants, but for those who were affected by them and their dispute. What was being celebrated was a promise of peace. Further, this promise, because there was a credible action plan to which people were committed, was, in the view of the participants, likely to be realized. It was this promise of peace that seemed to constitute a sense of justice.

How might we articulate, and then interpret, this sense of justice and its links to peace as a reduced risk of conflict? In seeking to answer this question we will, in what follows, look to two sources for insights. First, we will look back to Thomas Hobbes, who regarded achieving peace as a foundational order that made other things possible. We will then turn to the much more recent thinking of Daniel McDermott.

For the people at gatherings, as we have already suggested, achieving a promise of peace was experienced as something to celebrate. This is hardly surprising given the nature of everyday life within the communities within which these gatherings took place, where endemic insecurity, with respect to both one's body and one's property, was a routine feature of life. This insecurity, and the violence that is such an established feature of life within South African informal settlements and townships, is a constant background feature of people's lives, and for many there seems to be little, if any, hope of change.

Within such communities little is expected from the agents of criminal justice with respect to the insecure lives that, as we have just noted, are the norm for so many people. For persons from these communities life is, to borrow language from Hobbes, very often nasty, very often brutish, and frequently very short. For evidence of this one has only to look at the police statistics available, statistics that undoubtedly underestimate insecurity, as fewer and fewer poor people bother to report their victimization to the police. Murder statistics, generally regarded as the most reliable of police statistics, tell a very sad tale for South Africa as a whole and for poor South African communities in particular. While at the time of writing the most recent statistics show a reduction of incidents in several crime categories, including that of murder, this improvement (assuming that there actually is one and that the shift in statistics is not simply an artifact of the processes generating these statistics) is a small gain indeed, given the exceptionally high levels of crime that the reduced statistics record and with which most South Africans have considerable personal experience, either directly as victims of crime or through the reports of friends and acquaintances. Cities like Cape Town and Johannesburg remain, as South Africans are fond of saying, international "crime capitals" (Louw, Shaw, Camerer, & Robertshaw, 1998).

For Thomas Hobbes the critical political accomplishment that is required by any society is to ensure peace. Without peace little else is possible. With peace new horizons of possibility open up. South Africans have little difficulty agreeing with Hobbes on this. For the majority of South Africans, a decade and a half after the transition to democracy, peace remains a highly valued dream, but it nonetheless remains little more than a dream for many people. For most South Africans now, like Hobbes, peace, as we have suggested, means more than simply not being at risk of harm at any particular moment. Peace connotes a way of life in which one can be confident that one's family, property, and oneself are safe every day.

Hobbes expresses this sense of safety very clearly in *Leviathan*. A central concern of Hobbes was how to free people from an ongoing state of war, in which every person is at war with every other person, which he viewed as the central feature of a presocial state of nature. In such a state people live lives of endemic insecurity, in which they constantly expect harm from their neighbors, who are all their enemies. Hobbes uses the metaphor of weather to develop his argument. Here is what he had to say, and it is something that is worth reflecting upon:

> For WAR consisteth not in the battle only, or the act of fighting, but in the tract of time wherein the will to contend by battle is sufficiently known: and therefore the notion of **time**, is to be considered in the nature of war; as it is in the nature of weather. For the nature of foul weather, lieth not in a shower or two of rain, but in an inclination thereto of many days together: so the nature of war, consisteth not in the actual fighting, but in the known disposition thereto, during all the time there is no assurance to the contrary. All other time is PEACE. (Hobbes, 1651/1968, p. 84)

This resonates directly with the dream of peace that so many South Africans have. Many areas of South Africa are indeed, in Hobbes's sense, "war zones" in which, when there is not "actual fighting," there is a "known disposition thereto."

This concern with finding ways to move from such a state of war to a state of peace in which fighting is not expected and one can go about one's life on the assumption that peace exists and is likely to persist for some time is directly relevant to the work of peace committees. As their name suggests, peace committee gatherings offered those who came together through them the hope that not only would specific disputes be resolved, but also there would be a better, more peaceful tomorrow, not only for the disputants, but also for those around them. In short, what the action plans, agreed upon by the people at gatherings, offered was a credible promise of peace. What made this promise credible was that they had been part of crafting it and so could see for themselves how it would be realized in practice. It is this promise not only of a resolved dispute but of the possibility of a broader peace that gave cause for celebration.

Before we examine this idea of justice through peace we note that the celebratory gestures no doubt also recognized what has come to be called procedural justice. Gatherings were carefully orchestrated by a series of steps and were conducted in a manner that was consistent with a code of good practice. This meant that the procedures were deliberative and fair in the sense that those present were encouraged to voice their opinions, and these opinions were typically respectfully listened to. Typically no one was threatened and no force was used. There was thus inevitably a sense of what Thibaut and Walker (1975) term "procedural justice," and there is no doubt that this is one of the things that was celebrated at the conclusions of gatherings—procedures were perceived to be fair and so were the decision-making processes (Tyler, 1988). The exit interviews undertaken by the Community Peace Program (CPP) also draw attention to this aspect.

To explore further the sense of justice through peace that we have suggested was being celebrated at the conclusion of gatherings, we turn now to the Kantian-inspired argument developed by McDermott (2001). While McDermott's arguments are intended to justify the use of hard treatment, that is, punishment, they provide insights as to what took place at gatherings (McDermott, 2001).

McDermott, like other deontologists we have canvassed, argues that wrongdoers incur two "debts" to victims: a material debt that has to do with the material harm they have caused and a moral debt that has to do with the moral wrong that they have caused. In our terms these are debts that have been incurred at the level of instrumental or behavioral as well as moral ordering. Actions, such as restitution, that transfer material goods to the victim can, in McDermott's view, respond effectively to a material debt that a wrongdoer incurs as a consequence of the material deprivation they have suffered. This material transfer of goods, however, cannot, in his view, respond effectively to the damage to the offender that has taken place at a symbolic level. After the material debt has been set right the imbalance at the symbolic level remains. This imbalance still needs to be put right. Doing this requires a very different response, as the two debts are qualitatively different—each debt exists at a different level of reality. A response at one level, in one register, so to speak, while it may adequately respond to debts at this level, cannot, by definition, respond to debts at the other level. Each debt and each level requires a separate response.

McDermott argues, in a Kantian fashion, that punishment is an appropriate response to wrongdoing precisely because it operates at a symbolic level and not an instrumental level. It does so because it responds to the moral debt that the victim was made to suffer by the offender with a moral response that inflicts a moral debt—namely, the offender is denied the right to be treated in a way that is consistent with established notions of liberty—hence the importance of harsh treatment and the infliction of pain that punishment entails, which treats the offender in a way that our understandings of liberty normally disallow (Brodeur, 2010).

This deprivation inflicted upon the offender parallels the deprivation experienced, at a moral or symbolic level, by the victim, whose liberty rights were violated by the offender—hence the metaphoric retributive biblical adage "an eye in place of an eye," or its shortened popular statement "an eye for an eye."

A key feature of McDermott's argument is that a transfer of moral goods from the offender to the victim—in the way restitution transfers material goods—to right or correct material imbalance is not possible as there is no good that can be transferred by the offender to the victim to replace what was lost at a symbolic level. The only way to right the moral imbalance, that has been created at a symbolic level, is to impose a comparable moral loss on the wrongdoer, such as the loss that is imposed through harsh treatment. This does not mean that material goods cannot be transferred as when, for example, money is paid in response to an event that involves a moral harm, but when this is done, what is being responded to is not the moral wrong but the parallel material harm. The moral harm remains and accordingly, the imbalance at a symbolic level that this has created still requires attention.

How does this argument relate to what occurred in gatherings? In gatherings participants experienced a sense that justice had been done when a plan of action was conceived that was thought to reduce the likelihood of the people involved—that is, the victim and offender of the moment, or others present—continuing to have their liberty compromised as it was during the course of the dispute. Here, while one does not have restitution for past wrongs, steps are being outlined that hold out the promise that one's liberty will not continue to be violated. What is promised is a series of actions that are expected to simultaneously guard against violations at both a behavioral and a symbolic level. These promised actions are not intended to respond to past harms, they are not intended to repair the past, but rather act to repair a future that was expected to be harmful in the same way that the past had been.

What *balances*, in the deontologist's terms, and what *restores*, in the language of restorative justice, is a credible assurance that the liberty of those present will be respected in the future. What is promised is a better future at both a material and a symbolic level—it is this promise of a better future that is celebrated at the conclusion of gatherings. This argues against

McDermott's argument that it is not possible for a single response to operate simultaneously at both the material and symbolic levels. While this may be true when the past is the focus of attention of actions taken in the present, it is not the case when the focus of attention is the future. Whether this promise should be conceived as justice depends of course on how one defines justice. For us what makes it appropriate to think about what participants in gatherings experienced as justice is that "fixing the future" was conceived of as a right and proper response to the harm of wrongdoing. Further, this right and proper response was experienced as an outcome that was fair to all.

What we are suggesting here is that in the forward-looking ordering that is associated with risk management it may indeed be possible for a single response to operate at both an instrumental and a symbolic level in the same way the response of punishment is able to operate simultaneously at both levels. While the deontologists argue that punishment should not be justified on the basis of its material ordering effects, they nonetheless acknowledge that punishment can, and often does have, and ideally should have, effects at a material level, when it serves to deter future wrongdoing.

If these suggestions are correct, what we have is a parsimonious combination of instrumental and symbolic ordering that resonates with the parsimony offered by punishment. The plans of action that are agreed to at gatherings, and the promise of a better future they are intended to accomplish, serve to promote greater security at the same time as they respond to a breach of a symbolic order.

What is important here is that the integration of moral and instrumental responses takes place through a risk-focused, future-oriented process rather than through a past-focused process. This eschewing of the past shifts the focus away from disadvantages that are imposed through punishment to a promise of future advantages. Here fairness and right is achieved, not by a balancing of disadvantages, but rather through the creation of advantages for all involved. These advantages are constituted through a credible guarantee of future right-doing.

While the guarantee of future right-doing might involve the participation of wrongdoers, such participation is typically regarded as a useful, but often not necessary, condition, for a plan to be successful. What is necessary is that the participants have confidence that they will be better protected from wrongdoing than they were in the past, and that this protection will be fair and equitable. Their celebrations recognized that this better tomorrow would be shared by all. The 1994 democratic elections were celebrated with precisely this sense of unity by the nation, as South Africans sensed the promise of a better tomorrow.

Although, as we have noted, this sense of justice is different from established understandings, it fits within a broader conception of justice as fairness, equality, and the maintenance of right. Those at gatherings experience justice because they feel a sense of fairness, equality, and rightness.

## Mechanisms for Building Justice Through Peace

As we have argued above, the justice offered by the Zwelethemba model relies on its capacity to give a credible promise that the liberty of the disputants, as well as of attending community members affected by the dispute, will be better protected in the future and that, through the action plan, all will enjoy a safer future. Because the credibility of the model is so strongly related to the likelihood that peace agreements are honored, peacemakers are forced to take this issue very seriously. "Justice through peace" is a practical accomplishment and, for people to experience such a notion of justice, particular capacities need to be developed. As emphasized by Miller and Rose (1990), for a particular governing mentality to be effective, it needs to be transformed into technologies that support such a way of making up and acting in the world. The Zwelethemba modelers, though their concern was not explicitly focused on delivering a particular form of justice, nonetheless took great concern in developing practical mechanisms that they thought would increase the capacity of their model to deliver a credible hope for a better and more peaceful future. We end this chapter by exploring some of these techniques that have emerged within the confines of the model.

A peace gathering organized in Khayelitsha in May 2003 attended by one of us helps to illustrate this. The dispute concerned a moneylending issue. The agreement entered into by the parties was that the husband of disputant 2 would pay disputant 1 R200 a month, until the amount agreed upon had been paid. However, because, for a variety of reasons, no one else was present besides the disputants and the peace committee members, they decided to arrange a new peace gathering. The peace committee felt that it was necessary to commit additional members of the disputants' families and community to the agreement, particularly the husband of disputant 2, as he was to be the source of the money to be paid.

An equally important function contained within the Zwelethemba model is the monitoring of the implementation of plans of action. One or several of the participants at a gathering, frequently, but not always, members of the peace committee, were selected to make sure that those who had committed themselves to a peace contract fulfilled their promises. Compared to other community structures involved in solving local conflicts peace committees appeared to place more emphasis on this function. As one representative of a civic organization (SANCO) in Khayelitsha noted: "We do see that the peace committee uses much more time to follow up cases. We do not have the capacity for that."[1] The members of the peace committees recognized that the capacity to monitor agreements was a significant feature of their practice:

> Most of the disputants follow up the agreement. If some does not, we try to encourage them to keep their promises. For instance, in moneylending cases, we ask: "Could you manage to pay R50 a month?" like that. We try to encourage the disputants to keep their promises. People say to us: "We like the way you follow up." The monitoring, it is important for being trusted. Monitoring, we think of it as marketing.[2]

Conflicts involving moneylending seem to be a category of cases that sometimes lead to broken promises. This led to peace committee members assuming the role of negotiators.

> Moneylending, people are prepared to pay, but then they don't, that happens. So we call them back and when he or she comes again, they will pay. We have never experienced otherwise. If the person is unemployed he might ask if payment can wait for a while, and if so, we will ask the other disputants, if he is willing to accept that.[3]

Peace committees developed a range of measures to enhance the probability that agreements felt to be insecure (often cases involving transfer of money or other forms of value) would be honored. An example from the Mbekweni community (part of the Paarl municipality) serves to illustrate this:

> Currently, for instance, we have a domestic case. The husband does not want to be supportive of his wife. So the agreement is that each month he gives R400 of his pension to us, and we see to it that his wife really gets it.[4]

In situations like this there is, of course, a danger that there might be coercion (either implied or explicit). To avoid this, the Community Peace Program sought, through a variety of mechanisms, to monitor this, and other possibilities, through devices such as case reviews, monitors attending gatherings, exit interviews with gathering participants, and community surveys.

A follow-up study by Froestad was conducted to evaluate the extent to which the peace agreements entered into had been kept by the disputants for a period of three to six months after the peacemaking gathering. Twenty-five cases of dispute resolution organized by three peace committees were randomly selected for study, and a total of 26 disputants were interviewed. In 16 of 17 cases in which the interviewers were able to get hold of one or both of the disputants (others had moved or were inaccessible) the peace contracts were acknowledged to have been honored. No disagreement of opinions was registered in those cases where both parties to the dispute were interviewed. Only in one case was the status of the agreement ambiguous. Twenty-two of the disputants were overwhelmingly positive of the peace gathering process they had experienced, confirmed that they would use the model again if required, and gave many reasons why they preferred Zwelethemba to other forms of public or private justice. Besides being satisfied with the process and the outcome, disputants frequently reported that they preferred the peace committee due to its capacity for solving conflicts "in a rational way," "just sitting down and talk[ing]," with "no violence involved." Many also emphasized how the model made it possible to solve conflicts before "things go too far" and without people getting arrested and being put in jail. Four disputants had more mixed feelings toward the process, two of whom were quite negative because they did not get the outcome they wanted from the gathering.

What this short exploration seems to indicate is that peace committees developed a range of mechanisms that they used to increase the likelihood that the logic of justice through peace would in the vast majority of cases actually be accomplished. Through such a practice the Zwelethemba peacemakers had been able to build a reputation in local communities that they were capable of dispensing a kind of justice that does not rely on the retributive logic of criminal justice or on the healing logic of restorative justice. The justice that the model promotes is much more radically future oriented toward minimizing the risk of further harms than either of the alternatives.

## Conclusion

It is perhaps advisable now to remind ourselves of Shapiro's (1999a) argument that one might have expected too much of philosophy and too little of ordinary people's capacity and inventiveness in seeking ways of doing justice in their daily lives.

The Zwelethemba model was designed through a process of engagement between academics and members of a local community who gradually identified the core principles of never using force, and never resorting to adjudication. The model was designed with the explicit intention of giving local communities large experimental possibilities and not allowing their practice to be directed either by the philosophy of retribution or restoration.

A remarkable constant observation coming from this experiment, though, is that participants in peace gatherings felt that justice was done when a plan of action was conceived that was deemed likely to reduce the chances that the disputants and other participants would continue to have their liberty compromised. As argued by Shearing and Johnston (2005, p. 7),

> The response to the moral wrong is not a past-focused restitutive act but a future-focused preventative one. What balances ... the past encroachment of one's liberty is not a proportional encroachment of the liberty of the offender

but a credible guarantee that one's own liberty (and that of others) will be respected in the future ... rather it is entirely future-focused. This eschewing of the past is of fundamental importance as it shifts the focus from disadvantages that were imposed to a promise of future advantages.

What our discussion suggests is that it might be well to recognize that justice can be done in different ways and that establishing the conditions for a future peace provides for a sense of justice. This suggests that while conventional forms of justice may indeed, as Hudson (2003) argues, be a casualty in situations where attention is focused primarily on creating an ordered future rather than on responding to past harms, this new environment might well be giving birth to new and different conceptions of justice, and that it behooves us to be open to what these new possibilities might be. One way of doing this might be to look at expressions of the experiences of those involved in these processes for suggestions as to new symbolic ordering experiences that provide a sense of rightness and fairness that stretch the boundaries of established thinking.

What is crucial is to avoid attempts that seek only to recognize one sense of justice, but rather to recognize that justice, as symbolic ordering, can mean different things and just what it means involves choice. Who makes this choice varies. In both restorative and Zwelethemba justice the choice takes place at the level of the individuals involved. With respect to the justice of just deserts, that choice is made at a state level.

## Endnotes

1. Member of the civic organization (SANCO) in Khayelitsha, interview 14, May 2003.
2. Member of the Khayelitsha Peace Committee, interview 11, May 2003.
3. Member of the Mbekweni Peace Committee (Pola-Park), group interview, May 2003.
4. Member of the Mbekweni Peace Committee (Lonwabo), group interview, May 2003.

# Democracy in Many Places

# 3

*The generation of a commonwealth. The definition of a commonwealth.* The only way to erect such a common power, as may be able to defend them from the invasion of foreigners, and the injuries of one another, and thereby to secure them in such sort, as that by their own industry, and by the fruits of the earth, that they may nourish themselves and live contentedly; is, to confer all their power and strength upon one man, or upon one assembly of men, that may reduce all their wills, by plurality of voices, unto one will; which is much as to say, to appoint one man, or assembly of men, to bear their person; and every one to own, and acknowledge himself to be author of whatsoever he that so beareth their person, shall act, or cause to be acted, in those things which concern the common peace and safety; and therein to submit their wills, everyone to his will, and their judgments, to his judgment. (Hobbes, 1651/1968, p. 132)

## Introduction

In this chapter we explore what might be learned from the Zwelethemba processes about what Appadurai (2002) has termed "deepening democracy" (see also Fung & Wright, 2001). The Zwelethemba modelers sought to deepen South African democracy by creating processes for governing security that would provide poor constituencies with a greater voice in the governance of their own lives. This objective of strengthening what is typically thought of as grassroots or bottom-up forms of democracy was something that many South Africans expected would follow as a consequence of their liberation from the autocratic forms of governance that had been a defining feature of apartheid. It was within this context of hope and expectations that the Zwelethemba modelers set to work to develop processes that would enhance the self-direction of poor constituencies.

While, as we have noted, there was much concern among Zwelethemba residents about the forms of local decision making that had emerged during the struggle against apartheid (especially among those that had turned to violence as their principal means of governance), there was little doubt in the minds of the modelers that they should be striving to develop processes that would give residents a decisive voice in their own governance. Given the context we have just noted, however, a crucial question for the modelers was how this might be done while eschewing violence and while operating within the context of democratic values (values that they saw as embodied in, what was then, the very new South African Constitution). Indeed, every element of the model that emerged can, and should, be regarded as part of a carefully constructed and unified set of processes that would realize this ideal of locally directed solutions to local problems to support democratic values. While now, over a decade later, these aspirations have certainly been sullied for many South Africans, they were ideas that elicited considerable support and commitment. The period five years after South Africa's first democratic elections was still a time of heady idealism, and this idealism was most certainly alive and well in the minds of the modelers.

As with the previous chapter on justice, this chapter locates the ideals that informed the model builders within the context of established scholarly debates. While in the case of justice the modelers did not see the Zwelethemba model as (explicitly) seeking to promote justice, this was not the case with respect to democracy. With respect to the values associated with democracy, and especially the value of self-direction, the modelers deliberately set out to construct a set of processes that would enhance these values through the creation of deliberative forums, in the form of gatherings. The modelers sought to create a model that would deepen democracy, and through this deepening, contribute to the quality of democratic governance in South Africa by providing the residents of Zwelethemba, and communities like it, access to decision-making pathways that would enhance their self-direction.

In this chapter we argue that the Zwelethemba model deliberately, and directly, challenges the idea that democratic debate should be confined to state forums at national, regional, and municipal levels. In developing our argument we propose, in contrast to this Hobbesian framing, that ways need to be found to multiply decision-making forums and action pathways, and that doing so does not threaten democracy but rather enhances and deepens it. We conclude, on the basis of an analysis of several gatherings, that the Zwelethemba model in practice did indeed put in place mechanisms for deepening democracy in ways that managed to avoid the dangers of popular democracy that are so often used to question the possibility of shifting away from Hobbesian framings.

In this chapter we consider established conceptions of democracy, challenges to them, and the ways in which the Zwelethemba model builders sought to engage in this debate at a practical grassroots level by instituting the experimental processes that led to the development of their model. The processes that the model institutionalized, we will argue, provided pathways that deepened democracy in Dewey's sense of "democratic experimentalism" (Dewey, 1927, 1938a, 1938b). We will argue further that this was done through the creation of "local publics" that enhance local self-direction within local governance arenas in ways that challenge and move beyond the neoliberal ideal of local implementation of centrally determined decisions.

This was done through the creation of local deliberative forums that, infused by democratic ideas of providing a voice to all, mobilize local knowledge and capacity in shaping the flow of events within local contexts.

As we do this we consider the ways in which the Zwelethemba modelers were mindful of the need to locate these local dialogical forums within the context of broader democratic forums. The modelers' concern was to ensure that local decisions were always taken within what Galanter (1981), in his classic paper on "justice in many rooms," called the "shadow of the law." The modelers, in devising the Zwelethemba processes, sought to bring this shadow very directly into play within peace gatherings, at the same time as they sought to enable gathering participants to play a direct role in defining and governing the issues that were of concern to them.

Before we consider the extent to which the model's processes realized the modelers' objective of deepening democracy by providing for the possibility of local publics governing in, and through, many rooms, we turn first to ideas and discussion within the literature on governance that are relevant to our concerns.

## Shifting Conceptions

Since Hobbes, democratic theory in the West has typically viewed states as the only legitimate source of sovereign authority. In taking this stance this body of theory has viewed the "one assembly of men" that Hobbes speaks about in the passage that heads this chapter as the only appropriate institutional home of a democratic politic. An important consequence of this is that institutions and processes of the Western liberal democratic state, voting, political parties, representative institutions, and so on, have come to be equated with democracy (Kymlicka, 1989/1991).

Within this context, the notion of representative democracy has been, and is still, conceived by many as both a significant and unique Western innovation and institution. There is certainly much to be said for this view. Indeed, the institutions and practices of representative democracy may well prove to be Western culture's most significant contribution to political theory and to democratic practice. Western political culture has contributed enormously to questions such as how representation is possible and how people's wishes and interests should best be expressed without them participating directly in decision making about themselves (Pitkin, 1967). Recent scholarly debate has also raised new questions as to how political representation might adapt to the changing political realities of our time (Mansbridge, 2003; Warren & Castiglione, 2004; Dryzek & Niemeyer, 2008). This debate, exploring as it does the problems and limits of representation (Dryzek, 1996; Saward, 2008), also functions to confirm the link between representation and democracy as a core democratic assumption of Western political thought.

This issue of the proper relationship between representatives and those they represent—how can a good Hobbesian leviathan be elected to political office and held accountable?—has been a matter of much debate within Western political culture. Indeed, as a consequence of this focus, the idea of democracy has come to be equated with representative democratic institutions—to be democratic means to engage in the practices of representation and to have established effective institutions for enabling these practices. Ends and means have been concertinaed in ways that have emphasized means over ends—a "means over ends syndrome" has shaped democratic thinking (Goldstein, 1979).

This conflation of democracy and representation has been, and is being, challenged (Pateman, 1970; Barber, 1984; Dryzek, 2002). A significant theme in these challenges is that this conflation might express a Western ethnocentric view that regards the period of European/Western international dominance as being a consequence of the superiority of its political institutions (Wallerstein, 1983; Frank, 1998; Marks, 2002). Challenges to this ethnocentric view have also argued for a broader understanding of democracy that emphasizes ends over means. A common conclusion in these critiques is that democracy should be conceived expansively as intelligent problem solving through some sort of "decision making by discussion" (Lindblom, 1965; Briggs, 2008), as a "capacity for democratic self-government" (Fung, 2001, 2003, 2004; Fung & Wright, 2003; Dorf & Sabel, 1998), or as various forms of democratic deliberation (Cohen, 1989; Elster, 1998; Dryzek, 2010). If a broader conception is accepted, it immediately becomes apparent that many cultures, other than those of the West, have contributed significantly to imagining and developing institutional means and organizational technologies for establishing democratic forms of governance (Bowden, 2009).

Hindess (1997), in a critical examination of the Hobbesian political tradition, identifies two distinct problems with the idea of "one assembly of men" as the primary mechanism for representing a *demos*. First, Hindess argues that this view does not fit easily with other widely held liberal, democratic aspirations, such as the importance of fostering a range of self-regulatory systems, including the economy (the private sector), the civil society (the civil sector), and the state bureaucracy (the public sector), with capacities that democratic governments depend upon, and whose autonomy would be undermined if these spheres are unwisely interfered with by a leviathan.

Second, Hindess notes that the idea of good governance depends on the capacity to separate the political aspects of the life of a community from its nonpolitical aspects. The concern here is the fear of contaminating governance by elected politicians or public servants who promote their private interests over public ones (1997, p. 90).

Both of these concerns have proved to be very real problems in South Africa since 1994. Recently, the independence of the judiciary and the sacrosanct character of the constitution have been frequently questioned by politicians at the highest levels. Similarly, concerns about the extent and effect of corruption within the ranks of elected officials and civil servants have become an almost constant public refrain. In both cases the concern has not been that this is a departure from South Africa's past, as this is certainly not true. Rather, the concern has been about the extent to which the new South Africa has failed to walk away from significant features of its apartheid past, which was such a powerful motivator in the development of a vision for a post-1994 South Africa.

There has been much debate as to how these (and a host of other perceived) deficiencies of representative democracy, which it is argued stem in large measure from equating democracy with representation, arise and how they should be remedied. All these remedies have themselves, not surprisingly, been riddled with their own tensions and contradictions that have all been intensively researched—for example, concerns that political steering might be undermined, that plural forms of governance might enhance the influence of political factions with negative consequences for the free play of political competition in society, that accountability to a *demos* might be eroded, that reducing administrative powers might weaken professional autonomy, that neoliberal forms of plural governance might enhance social inequalities, and that the use of market models to rationalize public bureaucracy might weaken the ethos of loyalty and service in public administration (Hood, 1999, 2000; Hood & Scott, 1996; Majone, 1994, 1997, 1999; Moran, 2001, 2002; Power, 1997; Christensen & Lægreid, 1998; Jordana & Levi-Faur, 2004; Pollit & Bouckaert, 2004; Scott, 2004). All of these concerns, and similar concerns, have merit and need to be addressed where nodal forms of governance are advocated.

Hindess, in his analysis of Hobbesian aspirations as well as challenges to these aspirations, concludes that the dream of establishing democratic control over the agenda of state governments rests on a conflation between two conceptions of political power—the responsibility to direct governance and the responsibility to manage the implementation of its directions. In his view, this aspiration sets a standard for governments that no government can possibly achieve (1997, p. 91). This standard was difficult enough to achieve at a time when governments sought to engage directly in both the "steering" and the "rowing" of governance (Osborne & Gaebler, 1992), but it has become even more difficult, he argues, within a neoliberal context. In Hindess's view, Hayekian-inspired proposals (Hayek, 1944) to decouple the steering and the rowing of governance have hugely complicated the task of governing, rather than easing it. This has resulted in a considerable increase in the size of government, as governments have sought to develop institutional arrangements, within the public sector, to regulate the dispersed forms of governance that characterize our contemporary period (Levi-Faur, 2006; Braithwaite, 2008). The complications involved in regulating dispersed governance are becoming increasingly apparent as regulatory failures, especially within the financial sector. As we write, the most recent of these have been the twin financial crises of 2008 and 2011. These developments have raised profound questions about what democracy can, and should, mean and about the continuing relevance of Hobbesian-inspired conceptions, as governance becomes increasingly plural and as the nodal relationships within these plural forms become more and more complex.

Does this imply that we will be required, however reluctantly, to abandon the core democratic idea of "power with the people" and that we have little alternative but to accept more elitist forms of governance that undermine central democratic aspirations? While there is much about the actual practice of governance, both within and above states, that suggests that this may indeed be a consequence of contemporary developments within governance, our view, along with many other optimists, is that there are still grounds for retaining this ideal as an aspirational objective, while accepting that it is something that will constantly remain an elusive goal. What is clear is that as circumstances change, as they always will, we will constantly be required not only to find new and innovative ways of striving to realize this ideal, but also to fine-tune the ideal itself.

These comments recognize that democratic government will necessarily always be a failing operation. Inherent tensions in the principles of liberal rule and the constant threat of corruption (something that is a feature of governance across the globe) make clear that democratic practice is never likely to realize its ideals. This means that there will always be new problems and new challenges. The other side of this coin is that there will also always be new spaces for democratic experiments that can be exploited as people strive to keep alive, and to realize, democratic ideals.

Having said this, it is important, while retaining this ideal, to recognize democracy, not simply as a set of ever-elusive ideals, but also as an ongoing practical accomplishment of actors engaged in ongoing practical experiments as they strive to invent and reinvent ways of enhancing the quality of their day-to-day lives (Dewey, 1927, 1938a). Understood in this way, it becomes important, in tracing shifts in democracy, not simply to look to developments in theoretical thinking about democracy, as important as these may be, but also to look to these ongoing, often very local, practical accomplishments for both insight and inspiration as to the practical ways in which people can, and do, succeed in exercising greater control over the governance of their lives.

Jacobsen (1967), in reflecting on this in another context, has warned that the greatest danger to the welfare state has been the complacency that comes about when people feel that an ideal of governance, such as the vision of a welfare state, has been realized. This, of course, applies as much to the vision of democracy in its broadest sense as to particular conceptions of it, such as those of the welfare state. This danger is evident today in a tendency to associate democracy too closely with state institutions. When this happens ideas of representation that have taken root in many Western societies can reify governance in ways that limit our ability to imagine other ways of realizing democratic ideals. It has been argued that ideas of democracy—for example, as an assembly of people engaged in argument about the proper course of action with respect to any set of issues—once had a much more open horizon than is the case today. Paine (1791/1987, in Tully, 1999, p. 170), for example, in recognizing this, notes that it was only in the latter years of the eighteenth century that representation, both as an ideal and a practice of democracy, came to be tightly coupled with democracy.

The argument here is that as the state building of modern national states has gained ground, more and more practices of governance have come under the auspices of the state—as public "peaces" swallowed up private ones. As this happened, institutions of representative democracy and citizen participation, increasingly, came to be concentrated within the public sphere (Tully, 1999).

However, as Tully has observed, there are today new and different shifts taking place.

> What is now occurring, under the historical processes of "globalization," is that the multiplicity of forms of governance no longer tends to be gathered together only or predominantly under the auspices of the formal governmental institutions.... Effective political power can no longer be assumed to be located in representative governments alone. It is dispersed—shared, negotiated and contested by diverse agencies at the local, regional, national and international level. (Tully, 1999, pp. 178–79)

For Tully, the strategies citizens are deploying to gain greater freedoms and autonomy have changed. These strategies have seen citizens act to democratize service and production and participate, at specific sites of governance, to democratize global processes, which the formal democratic institutions fail to govern.

Today the quality of democratic participation depends very much on what is going on in many diverse spaces. It is no longer sufficient in assessing participation in governance to look only to what governments are doing or to the institutions of representation. These developments suggested to the Zwelethemba modelers, as they do to us, that what scholars and practitioners need to focus their attention on is ways of improving democracy as Dewey (1916) conceived of it—namely, as a way of life, as governance—and not to limit our concern for democracy to a lone focus on state government.

The transformation from government to governance requires a modification of the rules of political studies—something that these studies have been slow to recognize. As Tully noted:

> These forms of governance and strategies of freedom require political research and analysis tied closely to the specific systems in which the disputes and resolutions occur: what the contestants do and how they do it. (Tully, 1999, p. 180)

## Democratic Deficit

The idea that the disjuncture between the ideals and the practices of democracy constitutes a "democratic deficit" that varies from situation to situation is now widely recognized (see Marres (2005) for a discussion of the various ways in which this deficit has been understood and defined). This deficit is perceived, by many, to be getting worse, not better, across the globe. This trajectory is frequently associated with three recent developments: the change from welfare state policies to neoliberalism, the increasing power of corporate organizations as auspices of governance, and the fact that we live in an increasingly globalized, interrelated, and distantiated world in which decisions are taken by a few in what are, from the perspective of the many who are affected by them, distant places.

These, and related developments, have called, and are calling into question the suitability and sufficiency of representative institutions as the foundation for effective and legitimate democratic processes. In particular, state- and corporately driven transformations in governance under the sign of neoliberalism (Osborne & Gaebler, 1992; Rose & Miller, 1992) are increasingly being questioned. Participation in the rowing of governance, without much opportunity to influence the steering, constitutes, as is argued by both theorists and practical actors alike, at best a very limited form of democratic participation in governance. This contrasts with a parallel set of explorations in governance that have seen the establishment of corporations and the collectivities associated with them as governing nodes with power and resources to support their governing agendas (Braithwaite, 2004; Drahos, 2005). While this development has in many ways been facilitated by and has taken place in the shadow of the law, it has by and large not been driven, as we have already argued, through public policies.

As a consequence of these developments most observers agree that state governments should no longer be thought to monopolize the provision of governmental services. Nor should such a monopoly, it is argued, continue to be thought of as a feasible democratic ideal (Krasner, 1988, 1999, 2001, 2002). In addition to states, there are a variety of new forms of governing nodes that provide services that have traditionally been associated with states, such as health care and physical security. While these nodes continue to include state agencies, they now include business entities, nongovernmental organizations (NGOs), and community-based auspices. These polycentric (McGinnis, 1999a) or nodal forms of governance (Johnston & Shearing, 2003) operate through a wide variety of networks and partnerships within and across these sectors (Dupont, Grabosky, & Shearing, 2003).

One of the reasons put forward to account for the presence of democratic deficits that undermine self-direction in governance has been the processes of globalization. Within a Hobbesian tradition the only legitimate sites of public governance are, as we have seen, state sites (either states themselves or devolved sites). States, within this, until very recently, hegemonic view, have been seen as the only possible institutional home of democratic politics, while relations between states have been conceptualized as based on power and a "realpolitik" (Fung, 2003; Fung & Wright, 2003). With globalization it becomes increasingly difficult to imagine how democratic forms of direction and accountability can be ensured within established representative institutions (Sabel, Fung, & Karkkainen, 1999; Karkkainen, 2004). As noted by Burris, Kempa, and Shearing (2008), globalization leads to significant governance transformations. Among these, as we have already suggested, is the emergence of many new nonstate governing institutions within the global landscape. Associated with this have been shifts in the methods of governance, as governing nodes have looked to innovative strategies, such as "rule at a distance" techniques, that have enabled nodes to take advantage of the various features of dispersed governance (Rose & Miller, 1992). All of this, as we have already suggested, tends to favor powerful players. Past wins increase the likelihood of future wins, and similarly for losses. Globalization, it is argued, is making the playing field for power and services increasingly uneven (Burris et al., 2008).

One feature of this unevenness is that particular constituencies have been able to become more self-directed and have gained greater control over the provision of governmental services to them. These autonomy benefits of polycentric forms of governance have not, as we have just suggested, been evenly distributed. A growing governance disparity now parallels the wealth disparity across the globe. We have witnessed, and are witnessing, a widening democratic deficit emerge between the rich and the poor in most areas of public service provision. Today, well-to-do people tend to enjoy greater self-direction, their rights are more protected, and they enjoy more effective and efficient governmental services than poor people. Education and health care are obvious examples. For poor people, the reverse is more likely to be true (Haas, 2004). This unevenness is ironic, as polycentric or nodal governance in principle holds the promise for greater democratic direction and control for all (Held, McGrew, Goldblatt, & Perraton, 1999).

## Democracy Blackmail

We have to this point understood the democratic deficit as a deficit in governance goods. Marres (2005) argues that the term is most often used to signify a displacement of politics from its proper institutional location within a Hobbesian tradition. The democratic deficit is defined as a structural gap between the location of politics—increasingly globalized—and the established institutional sites of democratic dialogue and decision making within the nation-state. The "cosmopolitans" (Marres has in mind, in particular, Beck (1997, 2002), Habermas (2001), and Held (1999, 2000)) propose different solutions to this problem. However, they are all based on the notion of illegitimate and unaccountable powers in a globalized world, out of sync with democratic established (and appropriate) institutional structures. Habermas (2001) conceives of the problem as a question of how to create better connections through more appropriate procedural arrangements between the multiple sites and levels of contemporary politics and more global democratic institutions. Held (1999, 2000) proposes that democratic institutions at different levels of governance—from the global to the local—properly conceived and structured will be able to provide appropriate sites for democratic governance that will reduce the deficit. Beck (1997, 2002), taking a similar tack, argues for a "neorepresentative" model of democracy in which political institutions at different levels and sites will act in the name of specific constituencies (Marres, 2005, pp. 11–17). The common thread unifying the cosmopolitans is their definition of the democratic deficit in terms of a displacement of politics away from established democratic institutional sites of governance—in their view, an unfortunate gap or disconnect between the sites of politics and the sites of democracy. The various responses to this gap are designed to reconnect the sites of political engagement with democratic institutions (Marres, 2005, pp. 1–30).

While the culprit for the deficit in the above accounts is primarily seen as the emergence of global sites of governance above the level of the state, the problem of displacement and the failure of democracy that this has produced are by no means confined to the global level. Displacement of politics is also something that has been taking place both below and beside formal representative institutions.

Within this literature a recurrent theme, with respect to how the democratic deficit might be remedied, has been a focus on the ways in which the capacities of civic organizations might be mobilized to improve the quality of inputs into representative democratic institutions (Fung, 2003). These arguments have considered arenas such as political education, resistance, and the checking of governmental powers, interest aggregation and representation, and public deliberation (Fung, 2003). Recently, scholars exploring these issues have begun to focus their attention on democratic experiments that explore possibilities for direct democratic participation. Those advocating, and involved in, these experiments have challenged the appropriateness of the established focus on enhancing the performance of representative forms of government as the key to revitalizing democracy. An underlying assumption unifying this work has been that civil society constitutes an often un- or underutilized set of capacities for collective problem solving that can, and should, be identified and mobilized (Cohen & Sabel, 1997; Dorf & Sabel, 1998; Sabel et al., 1999; Fung & Wright, 2003; Fung, 2003, 2004; Briggs, 2008).

While some of this work has had a decidedly neoliberal bent to it (for example, the proposals by Drucker (1994)), other thinkers have been more concerned with deepening democracy (Appadurai, 2002; Fung & Wright, 2003) by enhancing the self-direction of local constituencies. The focus here has been on the ways in which associations and groups within civil society can participate in directing systems of governance and policies that directly affect them. Democratic experiments of this sort have been initiated in various parts of the world, both north and south, within different functional sectors—local budgeting, education, security, environment, and regulation of common pool natural resources (Ostrom, 1999; Dietz, Ostrom, & Stern, 2003; Cohen & Sabel, 1997; Sabel et al., 1999; Fung, 2004; Fung & Wright, 2003; Santos, 1998; Douglass & Friedmann, 1998; Abers, 2000; Baiocchi, 2005). Common features of these experiments are that they rely on popular engagements that recruit citizens, in particular those who will have to live within the sphere of the consequences of decision making, to engage in governance decisions. These experiments have promoted forms of participation within governance that are both direct and continuous. A critical feature of these initiatives has been their focus on the mobilization of local or "situated knowledge" (Haraway, 1988) and capacity for effective problem solving (Briggs, 2008).

Within this domain of inquiry there has been a tendency, among some scholars, to look upon these experiments with suspicion, assuming that what is going on might bring about a displacement of politics and a weakening of formal representative institutions. This tendency has been particularly strong within political science. Marres (2005) documents the link between this skepticism and well-established disciplinary worries that have arisen from research on "agenda setting" and "issue politics," especially in the 1960s and 1970s. Marres draws attention to the contributions by Schattschneider (1960), Heclo (1978), and Lukes (1974), all of whom have argued that democratic ideals and arrangements are weakened by the actions of agenda- and issue-setting actors. In exploring this Marres notes how Lukes builds much of his analysis on the Bachrach and Baratz (1970) notion of "nondecision" (Marres, 2005, p. 77). Heclo formulated his notion of issue politics as an alternative to the concept of Lowi's "iron triangles,"[1] arguing that public policy issues were increasingly defined and implemented in broader, more diffuse, and ever-changing policy networks. He conceived of these developments as threats to democracy, as they increased the influence of issue activists and issue experts in ways that served to weaken the relation of elected politicians to their electorate (Heclo, 1978).

Similar concerns that networks threaten democracy by displacing politics from its proper place can be detected in the contemporary literature on networks within political science and other disciplines. In research conducted in the United Kingdom, Marsh and Rhodes (1992) explored the ways in which networked governance had constrained the public policy agenda. Similarly, studies on networks in local governance have also tended to view policy networks with skepticism. Aars and Fimreite (2005), for example, argue that network governance is democratic only to the degree that it involves elected politicians who are in a position to monitor and sanction decisions. They maintain that networks displace political processes from the formal democratic arrangement, and thereby weaken public accountability and control.

Sørensen and Torfing (2003, 2005), though appreciating the potential democratic benefits of networked governance, conclude that local networks are neither integrative nor aggregative enough, and that they typically weaken the control exercised by elected politicians. Boltanski and Chiapello (in Marres, 2005, p. 108) explicitly argue that networks cannot serve as sites for "a politics of the common good" since "networks don't have principles." They perceive networks as ruthless mechanisms of inclusion and exclusion, while good governance requires a political process that has a principled commitment to inclusion (Boltanski & Chiapello, 1999, pp. 160–161, 167–168, 226–227).

Many of the new experiments in collaborative governance mentioned above have been criticized along similar lines. One example is the criticisms that have been leveled at the new environmental governance that has emerged in the United States. These emerging forms of governance have sought to institutionalize new governmental architecture intended to synergize local knowledge with expertise in ways that lead to a devolution of tasks and responsibilities to local stakeholders within the context of wider government-controlled regulatory arrangements (Gunningham, Holley, & Shearing, 2012; Sabel, Fung, & Karkkainen, 1999, 2000). Opponents have characterized these governance models as "wishful thinking" and "propaganda" (notably Theodor Lowi, 1999).

In responding to these criticisms the advocates of these collaborative governance models argue that their critics are operating on the basis of a Madesonian model that conceives of citizens' participation in governance as something that should be limited to "passing judgment on election day." This representative model, they argue, sees deliberation and preference formation as the exclusive province of the political and administrative elite (Sabel et al., 2000, p. 110). Even the experiment of participatory budgeting in Porto Alegre that mobilized thousands of poorer citizens as participants in a municipal political process has been criticized because it has, it is argued, displaced politics from its proper site in the legislature (Baiocchi, 2005).

Key virtues of what might be thought of as the standard democratic model, which are frequently used to critically assess new political or governmental experiments, are its formal political inclusiveness through the election of representatives, which ensures that citizens are not required to constantly participate in politics; its well-accepted procedures for decision making (majority rule); and the stability of its institutions. If this model is deployed as the basis for comparative assessment, new experiments in more direct forms of democracy will always score low and will inevitably be seen as a threat to the vitality of the accepted political arrangement.

As long as the displacement of politics from representative institutions is assessed in these terms, innovations that offer new sites of governance will always be seen as problematic. This has created what might be thought of as a regime of "democracy blackmail" that is severely constraining our ability to creatively explore the potential of new political experiences and to use them to reimagine what democracy can and should mean. Once again, means have been equated with ends and have replaced them.

Is there any way around this?

## The Displacement of Politics as a Democratic Requirement

Understanding the democratic deficit as a gap between the sites of politics and the appropriate democratic institutions is based, essentially, on an "end of history" (Fukuyama, 1992) view of democracy. Established democratic institutions are conceived of as constituting a final architecture that, at most, only needs fine-tuning (Marres, 2005, p. 136). This arises out of, and demonstrates, a severe case of what Unger (1996) has described as "institutional fetishism"—the idea that those institutions that have solved problems in the past will be best at solving problems in the future, and that institutional means become ends in themselves. This fetishism is puzzling (and certainly dysfunctional) given the wealth of empirical evidence that demonstrates that the established channels of democratic influence (voting, corporate participation, use of media, lobbyism, protesting, etc.) consistently favor the strong at the expense of the weak (Gallego, 2007; Dahl, 1989; Klingemann & Fuchts, 1995; Skocpol & Fiorina, 1999; Olsen, 1983).

John Dewey, the American political philosopher, has provided considerable inspiration to those who have sought, and are seeking, ways out of this puzzling fetishism. His prescription for a way out of the prison of this fetishism has been, as we have already noted, "institutional innovation" through "democratic experimentalism" (Dewey, 1916, 1927, 1938a, 1938b). This pragmatic approach to democracy firmly resists approaches that are premised on an acceptance of existing political architectures.

Creative invention and reinvention of democratic institutions is seen largely as a way of destabilizing systems that have over time become "gamed" by and, as a consequence, dominated by elites and insensitive to popular demands (Unger, 1996). The motive of these developments, thus, has been a search for more legitimate and effective institutional arrangements. This, it is argued, is necessary because the institutional sites where the strong pursue their politics have not proved to be hospitable for the articulation of the concerns of the weak. Braithwaite (2004), in reflecting on this, has argued that the weak, in seeking to find ways of strengthening their voice in governance, should take a leaf out of the book of the strong and engage in forum shopping, and if required, the creation of new forums, in their search for more compatible institutional arrangements.

In Dewey's view, political framings have taken on the characteristics of religious taboos, in ways that have increasingly been used to protect established institutions, especially the institutions of the nation-state. These framings, he argued, have obstructed the development of critical and transformative inquiries into social and political institutions (1927). As a consequence, Dewey came to view existing political and legal forms and arrangements as incapable of dealing with contemporary social problems and challenges. In developing this position, Dewey was especially critical of what he regarded as a scholastic tendency in political science, rendering it as no more than a supportive reflection of the established political world. As a way of countering this inclination, he argued for a more experimentally oriented discipline, a science of ideas in action (Dewey, 1927). Dewey argued that further advances in democratization in fact require a displacement of politics to new and different sites. One reason for these shifts, he argued, is institutional failures that generate, through displacement, new publics. It is, Dewey argued, the response to failures on the part of established institutions to address salient issues in a proper manner that has engendered innovative forms of public involvement in politics.

> The new public which is generated remains long inchoate, unorganised, because it cannot use inherited political agencies. The latter, if elaborate and well institutionalised, obstruct the organisation of the new public…. To form itself, the public has to break existing forms. (Dewey, 1927, pp. 30–31)

For Dewey it is a common concern that brings actors together as a public, rather than preexisting social bonds, similar preferences, interests, or a shared identity. These publics, as political entities, are assembled from many dissimilar and heterogeneous elements, across the private and public divide. Institutional failure, along with the absence of an existing political community, constitutes conditions that enable public involvement in politics to emerge. Far from seeing this as a problem of democratic displacement, Dewey appreciates it as a democratic requirement. Displacement is for him a mechanism that enables a search for democratic innovation (Dewey, 1927).

This is, however, often a difficult and laborious process because existing institutions are so robust. This robustness gives rise to what has come to be termed path dependence in political and economic development (Skocpol, 1973; Tilly, 1994; Krasner, 1988; North, 1990; Steinmo, Thelen, & Longstreth, 1992; Pierson, 2000; Pierson & Skocpol, 2002; Page, 2006).

Marres (2005) qualifies many of Dewey's arguments in order to align his thoughts with contemporary problems, opportunities, and challenges. Two particular modifications are important. The first relates to how the displacement of politics should be conceived. Dewey regarded displacement of politics from the formal institutional arrangement as a democratic requirement and acknowledged the need to constantly "reinvent the state" (Dewey, 1927). Accordingly, he still assumed actor representation as the key mechanism for channeling demands from a public. Today, Marres (2005, p. 27) argues, it is no longer sensible to assume that democratic political processes can, or should, be hosted within a single political forum.

Each time issues are displaced to different sites, the assemblage of subject definitions, procedures, and ideals is modified and the balance of power between the strong and the weak may be altered (Marres, 2005, p. 32). Marres (2005, p. 86) reminds us of Schattschneider's (1960) idea that politics is a struggle of containing or socializing conflict. As he argued, "Everything changes once a conflict gets into the political arena—who is involved, what the conflict is about, the resources available" (Schattschneider, 1960, pp. 36, 37; Marres, 2005, p. 87).

When conflicts expand, relations of sovereignty are destabilized and the balance of force between the participants changes. The outcome of the struggle becomes more open-ended as the state is recognized as only one among a range of potential locations to host an issue of concern. Latour (2007), in taking a position that supports Marres, notes that when new publics emerge around "issues of concern," different governance outcomes are possible.

One potential outcome may be an affirmation of established state forums. This may happen if the established machinery of government is invoked to define issues as belonging to a state-defined common good or as representing the "general will." Another outcome can be the emergence of other "deliberative assemblies," as citizens meet to discuss, calculate, and negotiate compromises to solve problems within suitable forums located in civil society (Latour, 2007, pp. 815–818). A concern of the Zwelethemba modelers, as we will see, was the possibility of bringing these two outcomes together—that is, creating local deliberative assemblies that confirm state sovereignty.

The way in which Dewey and Marres conceive of the displacement of politics has consequences for how the governance deficit is understood. As Marres (2005, p. 152) argues, it is disarticulation of publics from their affairs that has been the "big scandal"—the displacement of issues away from sites hospitable to their solution or, conversely, the nondisplacement of issues away from sites inhospitable to their solution.

A danger that both Dewey and Marres recognize with some displacements is privatization. This happens when the issue is moved to a closed arena, where a free exchange between partly contesting and partly cooperating groups becomes difficult and often impossible. Dewey (1927, pp. 147–148) illustrates this danger with his example of the robber band:

> The robber band cannot interact flexibly with other groups; it can act only through isolating itself. It must prevent the operation of all interests save those which circumscribe it in its separateness.

A democratic requirement of displacement politics, for both Dewey and Marres, is that the issues under concern are opened up for broader public involvement in transparent political processes. As Marres notes:

> Only when such issues are opened up for involvement by institutional outsiders, can adequate issue definitions be developed, required courses of action determined, and an addressee identified that is capable of addressing the affair (Marres, 2005, p. 149).

Issues only take on the full aspect of a public affair when a range of elements beyond the immediate concerns are drawn upon in their articulation: definitions of who the subjects are, what constitutes their democratic character, how controversies are to proceed, how solutions might be enacted, assumptions about who are affected by specific issues, ideals about rights to self-government, and so on (Marres, 2005, p. 154).

For this reason accounts of displacement politics must be concerned with these normative and procedural questions. Indeed, when democratic spaces have been modified so as to facilitate the articulation of a public affair, the identification of principles of appropriate conduct and proper procedural constraints is among the prime instruments that can be used to prevent the privatization of such spaces.

As we turn, later in the chapter, to explore the Zwelethemba experience as an instance of the displacement of politics, a key question to which we will attend is the extent to which the practice of the Zwelethemba model worked to strike a balance between democratic self-governance and the constraints of more broadly defined democratic values and principles.

A second way in which Marres qualifies Dewey concerns his conception of publics. She correctly observes that Dewey had little to say about the organization of publics as a practical accomplishment (Marres, 2005, p. 60) and tended to define them as social rather than as political communities. Dewey defined a public as all those affected by an affair, and he assumed a self-evident commonality of interest. In taking this position he assumed private interests to be external to the issues that call publics into being (Marres, 2005, p. 57).

In responding to Dewey, Marres argues that it makes more sense to assume that, typically, both private and public interests are caught up in a single tangle of issues (Marres, 2005, p. 57). As a consequence, publics emerge across the public and private divide as a heterogeneous assemblage— as a medley of previously unrelated actors are brought into close association.

In Marres's account it is precisely this assemblage of antagonistic actors, together with their sometimes irreconcilable interests, that construct political issues (issues of concern) out of problems. Drawing upon the works of Latour and others within the "science and technology studies," Marres (2005, p. 62) emphasizes the importance of recognizing knowledge formation, within publics, as a productive and contested process. Publics constitute contested landscapes within which actors strive to define their own commitments and claims and, in competition with others, struggle to influence how issues of concern are to be conceived and governed:

> Contestation over the issues at stake, and over the type of settlement they require, may equally involve contestation over the kind of (democratic) arrangements that are to host controversy over this affair. (Marres, 2005, p. 138)

How an issue is defined will significantly affect what competencies and knowledge are perceived to be relevant, and therefore who the relevant actors are, who it is assumed will be able to contribute to the settlement of the issue and to its future management. As will become apparent, this was an important concern of the modelers and is reflected in the architecture of the Zwelethemba model.

For Marres (2005, p. 139), public participation in displaced politics involves first opening up an affair for public involvement, and second, delivering an issue to a capable addressee. She argues that the condition of being affected by an issue should not be understood as a given, but rather as a learned accomplishment.

Erdèlyi (2008), in reviewing Marres's thoughts, identifies domination by elites as a significant danger in displaced politics. This raises the practical question of how this can be guarded against. If politically weak actors engage in

forums of issue contestation before they have managed to concentrate knowledge, resources, and capacities under their own control, we would expect that
they might easily be co-opted by stronger actors to realize *their* agendas.

What are the implications of this discussion for Zwelethemba as a democratic experiment? The possibility of a displacement of politics, as a democratic requirement, points to two key questions that need to be addressed.
The first is the issue of internal democracy, that is, the question of how the
new democratic spaces that the model opens up operate. Here an important
consideration is how these spaces balance self-governance with externally
defined democratic constraints—something that was a motivating concern
for the Zwelethemba modelers.

The second issue concerns capacity for influence that the model's processes generated. Here there are two subquestions. First, to what extent did
the experiment inspire new ways of conceiving of the capacity of self and
others to identify common agendas and ways to engage with them? This is a
question of motives. And second, to what extent did the experiment facilitate
a concentration of the knowledge and resources required to intervene effectively. This is a question of pathways for action. In this chapter it is the first
challenge of democracy that we explore, while we return to the question of
power and capacity in Chapter 5, where we investigate the question of development and human rights.

## Zwelethemba and the Displacement of Politics

A number of scholars, as we have already suggested, have argued that the
ascendancy of neoliberal ideology and forms of governance, and the simul-
taneous rise and popularity of private security practices, is not accidental.
Modern states are confronted with the parallel pressures of globalization,
localization, and pluralization of security governance. These pressures are
taking place within a context of recognition by states that their capacity to
deliver governmental services, including security, is limited. The vision of
states as the answer to most, if not all, of societies' problems has given way to
one of states as one governance node among many, albeit one that continues
to play a central role. Given this shift, to what has come to be thought of as a
neoliberal understanding, states have become increasingly inclined to mobilize and enroll individuals, families, groups, corporations, and other collectivities into their own governing agenda (Crawford & Clear, 2003, p. 215).

At the same time that this happened the terrain of governance increasingly came to include nonstate auspices of governance—what might be
thought of as private governments—that have emerged (Shearing, 2006).
These new auspices are engaged in authorizing governance activity that fits
with their own conceptions of good order. They too are engaged in enrolling

others to assist in delivering governmental services. This includes enrolling state agencies (Burris et al., 2008). Police officers, for example, often draw attention to instances of their enrollment by nonstate agencies (Stenning, Shearing, Addario, & Condon, 1990). An example of this would be the complaint that they have become the servants of insurance companies who use them to validate claims by clients (Ericson & Haggerty, 1997).

While this shift to plural and networked governance has the potential, as we have argued, to empower those who have historically done poorly, with respect to either the direction of governance or in terms of the service delivery they receive, this has not happened. The inequalities that have characterized state-centered governance have also been the norm with more plural forms of governance (Haas, 2004). To the extent that the less advantaged have participated in nodal governance processes, they have typically been mobilized as volunteers, as service providers, often on less than favorable terms (Garland, 1996; O'Malley, 1992, 1996a). This has often meant that poor constituencies have found themselves responsible for their own service provision, with little or no compensation for the work they are being enrolled to provide. To make matters worse, this situation has often been marketed as increased self-governance (O'Malley, 1996a).

It is precisely this sort of inequity that the Zwelethemba modelers sought to address. Their concern was to see if it was possible to develop a plural form of security governance that enhanced the self-direction of local communities as auspices of governance as well as at the level of service provision, while at the same time involving them as service providers who would be rewarded for their time and knowledge.

Put differently, the intention of the Zwelethemba modelers was to design a set of governance processes that would deepen democracy in the way Dewey had envisioned, by genuinely enhancing self-direction of poor communities. Accordingly, a central intention of the model builders was to move beyond, and indeed to challenge, a neoliberal agenda by establishing nonstate institutions that were legitimately engaged in both the steering and rowing of governance in poor communities in ways that brought benefits of self-direction and resources to these communities.

The model was built on the assumption that a focus on the governance of security, as an alternative to a focus on governing through crime, could, and hopefully would, open new democratic spaces within which local knowledge and capacity could be mobilized and the self-direction of poor communities would be enhanced.

This is what the modelers intended. We turn now to examine the extent to which these intentions were realized in practice.

In looking at how the model worked in practice, we will focus on its self-regulatory features. There has been considerable criticism in the literature over the autonomy that middle-class entities have been able to achieve through establishing themselves as private governments. Critics have argued that these private governments, through their use of private security, have done much to undermine the equitable provision of public goods, and that this has enhanced the gap between the haves and the have-nots (Bayley & Shearing, 1996). In responding to these concerns, the modelers were, of course, anxious that any new approach should not replicate—from new grounds—the same difficulties, yet again enhancing inequalities between groups. This was particularly pertinent because, as we have noted, there had been much criticism within both Zwelethemba and the country more generally about the fact that popular forms of security governance had used their procedures to promote partisan interests (Martin, 2012).

## Zwelethemba and the Challenge of Building Private Democratic Spaces

Our concern in this section is with how successful the Zwelethemba experiment was in facilitating processes and creating outcomes consistent with its democratic values and objectives. In the analysis to follow a sample of gatherings are reviewed and assessed according to two sets of criteria that are, to some extent, opposed.[2] These criteria may be thought of as constituting two horizons—on the one hand, general principles and procedures, and on the other, local values, knowledge, and capacities, as well as local possibilities. In terms of the first horizon, gatherings should be accountable to external democratic standards that are cosmopolitan rather than local. According to the second, outcomes should be attuned to local conditions and local perceptions about conditions for democratic engagement.

The analysis explores the way in which the inevitable tensions associated with these two horizons were negotiated by peacemakers. To what extent did the peacemakers facilitate dispute resolution and problem solving in ways that enhance what Evans (1995) terms "embedded autonomy." Are the model's practices, on the one hand, embedded within, and sensitive to, local values, contexts, and norms? Similarly, on the other hand, do they maintain a degree of institutional autonomy in their practices as stipulated by the external standards and principles of the model?

What the modelers hoped for was not perfection. Rather, what they hoped their model would achieve, as peacemakers negotiated these horizons, was a range of practices, with the majority being within the bounds established by the core values and procedures of the model.

Twelve of the analyzed cases were predominantly concerned with property-focused disputes, six were social disputes beyond the family unit, and three were focused on domestic issues. This distribution fits well with the overall distribution of cases handled by peace committees.

## Disputes Over Property

In the property cases gatherings proved to be effective in providing forward-looking resolutions. These cases for the most part were dealt with expeditiously. The source of the dispute was typically easily identified. An agreed upon resolution tended to follow quickly once deliberation was initiated and shared local norms were reviewed and confirmed by those attending the gathering.

### "Futures Games" Versus "Blaming Games"

Unlike other processes that take place under a restorative sign, gatherings did not require the acknowledgment of culpability. This ironically worked to encourage, rather than discourage, acceptance of responsibility—in this case responsibility for a solution rather than for culpability. Typically at gatherings disputants and others in attendance moved easily and quickly to a plan of action that involved people taking responsibility for "making a better tomorrow."

An illustrative case concerned a man who had been paid for repairing a woman's house, but had not fulfilled his obligations due to drunkenness. Initially, this person engaged in the blaming game by claiming that the fault was not his, as another had promised to finish the job for him. The gathering facilitator responded, in accordance with the model's steps, by shifting the focus to the future and what needed to be done to get the job finished. As one of the peacemakers at the gathering put it, "This is the problem [the job is unfinished], so what are you going to do if the job is still the same way you left it?" Faced with this question the gathering quickly agreed to a plan of action for making a better tomorrow. The contractor noted that he did not want the woman to remain angry with him and he agreed to finish the job over the upcoming weekend.

Most of the property cases proceeded in a similar manner. Debtors, for example, tended to accept their obligations quickly once the blaming game was replaced with a futures game. Once this happened attention was focused on the practicalities of how to commit people to a peace contract that was likely to be honored.

For example, in one of the cases a savings scheme's bank deposit slips did not have the required bank stamp on them—required by the rules of the savings scheme as proof that the monies had indeed been deposited. At the gathering the woman who did the banking, once the move to the future had taken place, agreed to sort the matter out with the bank and to pay back any monies that proved to be missing. What the futures game did was to structure deliberation so that it focused on how the problem would be solved—an issue that proved to be less contentious than the issue of what wrongdoing had taken place and who was to be blamed for it.

## Making Up and Resolving Disputes

What the case studies illustrate is that with respect to disputes over borrowed property, the discussion typically focused not on how and when the value ought to be compensated—which is taken for granted—but rather on the form that compensation should take. This is nicely illustrated in a case over borrowed earrings, in which one of the earrings was lost and not returned. To complicate matters, the earring owner had earlier borrowed clothes from the person to whom she had lent the earrings. She had also, again sometime earlier, received a loan from the earring borrower that she had used to purchase spices. These complexities serve to illustrate the point made earlier that within contexts such as these, it is seldom possible to clearly distinguish victim and offender.

In this case the deliberations recognized that any attempt to reify a victim-offender distinction would have been difficult, if not impossible, and that the search for a solution needed to take this into account. Within the gathering the women were quickly moved to forgive each other, and indeed, the loans themselves were waived. While forgiveness is not something that the model prioritizes as a value in itself, as this example illustrates, forgiveness can and does have an instrumental role if it is likely to reduce the likelihood of the dispute continuing. As is typical of most of the cases, the key, and it is a key that the model regards as essential, was the move to the future, followed by deliberation over how a better future could be secured. In the end everyone agreed that this had been an unnecessary dispute between two friends that should not be allowed to continue.

## Building Symbolic Capital

A feature of many gatherings is the reputational capital—what Bourdieu and Wacquant (1992) call "symbolic capital"—that peace committees brought to deliberations. In one repayment case plan of action, a person at the gathering, in commenting on the agreement reached, noted: "It's obvious from [discussion] that this kind of incident has occurred before. I trust that the disputant will get his money." The committee members assured him that they always followed up on cases like this to monitor the outcome of the plan of action.

As this comment indicates, the reputational capital of peace committees is of considerable value in establishing trust. An important precondition for this was that disputants entered a peace contract of their own free will, as the code of good practice stipulates that peacemakers should not take sides—a practice that was generally adhered to, as the results of exit interviews have made clear. A shack construction dispute serves to illustrate this. The dispute was concerned with when and how money should be paid and how the buyer could be assured that the work agreed to would be satisfactorily completed. In commenting on the case a peacemaker had this to say:

> We cannot ask him to give you the bungalow without paying him first because once he gives you the bungalow and you don't pay him, he is going to say, "It is you, the peace committee, who said I must give him the bungalow." So please forgive us.

This gathering ended with the buyer apologizing to the seller for not paying him the money he was owed. The seller forgave him and they shook hands as a token of peace. This case, along with similar cases, illustrates how the lack of coercion that is such a strong feature of the Zwelethemba model is also a limitation. In this instance, however, despite the "weak hand" played by the peace committee, forgiveness served to establish conditions that enabled a future-focused agreement.

In property cases such as this one, a future-focused plan of action was typically easily negotiated. These cases nicely illustrate disputes where the gathering process leads to outcomes that tightly integrate our two horizons.

## Preventing Escalation

In considering the activities of peace committees, it is not just the outcomes that were realized that are significant, but also the counterfactual possibilities that were avoided. This is a key feature of the model and a reasoning that the modelers brought to bear in developing its processes. Thus, while the disputes that peace committees dealt with were for the most part minor, and easily handled, they could, if they had not been resolved, easily have escalated into more serious conflicts. Further, had disputants taken their dispute to other, less regulated popular forums, the resolution itself might have escalated the disorder (Nina, 2001). This demand reduction feature of the peace committees was recognized and welcomed by local police who were typically attached to very busy police stations. What was also welcome, from the point of view of democratic values, and the vision of a new South Africa that was infused with these values, was the fact that these alternative demand reduction practices were carefully regulated in ways that ensured that they supported rather than challenged this vision (see Chapter 4 on accountability).

Of course, regulatory intentions are not always consistent with regulatory practice, no matter how carefully safeguards associated with them have been thought through. The Zwelethemba experiment was no exception, although these tensions were certainly contained by the model's regulatory features and safeguards. Exploring these safeguards, in Chapter 4 we consider a rare case that produced precisely the sort of problems that the carefully constructed features of the model were intended to prevent. The case also illustrates the sort of petty conflicts that were attended to by peace committees. These are exactly the sort of small disputes that, if they escalate, can and do easily lead to serious harms taking place in the form of assaults and even homicides.

## Social Disputes

With conflicts over property, the facts of the case tend, for the most part, to be relatively straightforward. In addition, in such cases there is typically agreement among the gathering participants with respect to the normative standards that should be applied—norms of private property tend to be well entrenched across most South African constituencies. This was not as often the case with respect to what we have termed social disputes, where frequently the facts are "fuzzier" and sometimes the normative standards to be applied are also unclear. In what follows we present three such fuzzy cases.

### Increasing the Level of Transparency

A husband had been drinking at his home with two friends, who were brothers. During the course of the evening the husband looked for his cell phone but could not locate it. He told his friends that he was going to inform the police of his loss. The brothers interpreted this as an accusation that they had stolen his phone. One of them was so upset by this implied accusation that he offered to buy his friend a new phone.

The mother of the two brothers, who was concerned about the false accusation, brought the matter to the peace committee. At the gathering the wife admitted that she had taken her husband's phone and hidden it, as he frequently lost his phone while drinking: an easy resolution. The gathering simply served as a place where a higher level of transparency that had not been possible previously was attained once everyone involved was brought together. Fuzzy facts became clear and the dispute disappeared.

### Drawing Upon Community Norms and Values

The function of gatherings as a source of transparency proved to be particularly apparent when dealing with disputes about rumors. In one such case a woman claimed that her neighbors had been spreading rumors that she practiced witchcraft—a matter of serious concern in many African communities.

The woman had developed a reputation for successfully treating colic in babies with traditional herbal medicines.

In the case in question a neighbor, while visiting this woman, had felt a sudden pain in her back. At that moment she looked down and saw some smoldering traditional medicines. She also reported seeing money that had been borrowed from her husband appear in the smoke. She interpreted this as evidence of witchcraft.

On returning home the woman who had seen the money in the smoke called her mother to tell her about what had happened. Her mother advised her to pray all night so that she would not be affected negatively by the experience—a story, incidentally, that reveals something about the role of religion, in this case a mixture of Christianity and African traditional beliefs, in many communities within South Africa.

According to the herbalist, her neighbor also told others about what she had experienced. As a consequence, none of them greeted the herbalist anymore. The initial step taken by the committee was to bring the two women to a gathering at which they heard the story of each and allowed each woman to comment on the story of the other woman. Both women agreed to the facts of the case except the accusation of spreading rumors. The peace committee soon concluded that the gathering had to be reconvened with the other neighbors also present so that the issue of rumor mongering could be more fully discussed.

The following week a gathering was convened but none of the other invited women attended. The gathering went ahead as planned anyway. The disputants were invited to propose a forward-focused solution. The traditional healer said she thought matters were now very difficult for her because people were "ganging up on her." She contended that people were saying that they would never come to her home again as she was a witch. One of the committee members suggested that perhaps the three nonattending neighbors were undermining the women's erstwhile friendship. Neither of the two disputants offered a solution.

The members of the committee now shifted the focus of the deliberations by asking how the herbalist could know that the other woman had really spread these rumors about her, especially as she did not understand Xhosa but spoke Setswana. The suggestion was made that she should have approached her neighbor directly. One of the committee members, who practiced traditional medicine herself, suggested to the other disputant, quite forcefully, that next time she saw something she did not understand she should not assume things, but request an explanation:

> Do you understand that you should have gone to your neighbor to ask what the money was doing next to the smoke of the traditional medicine?

The woman replied that she agreed, she regretted the assumptions she had made, but continued to insist that she had not spread rumors. At this point, both the women felt that their friendship could be renewed and the gathering was concluded on this note.

Here the committee took an assertive role, as community members themselves, by drawing upon shared community norms to help forge a solution. General values (our one horizon) structured the way in which local knowledge (the other horizon) was mobilized and used. The gathering melded these horizons to shape a solution. In doing so they drew upon local understandings—a culture understood as "the way we do things around here" (Deal & Kennedy, 1982). In this process, forgiveness emerged, not as an end in itself, but as an instrumental means to achieve a more peaceful tomorrow (Leman-Langlois & Shearing, 2004).

## Root Causes

Another rumor or gossiping case illustrates the importance of space (or lack thereof) in informal settlements. The dispute had a long history. A previous gathering had been held. The dispute originated as a land claim a woman had brought before the municipality through a petition to a local councilor. The councilor, in his capacity as a representative of the municipality, made a decision that required, and authorized, the restructuring of the yard between two houses. This case neatly points to the fact that there are often a multiplicity of peacemaking processes available within many South African collectivities (see Baker's (2008) discussion of multichoice policing). One of the disputants had been required to close and cover up a window that opened onto the neighbor's section of the yard. There had been considerable hostility between the two disputants, but as a consequence of this shift in the organization of space, peace had apparently been established. Following the reestablishment of peace the woman who had been required to close her window was permitted to reopen it.

When the case reemerged as a dispute that was brought to the attention of the peace committee it had developed into a dispute that included a third neighbor. The new disputant had a house that shared a backyard with the previous disputants. She wanted to erect a fence around her section of the previously shared yard. She first went to the woman who had made the initial land claim, but as only her daughter was home, she went to the other neighbor and discussed her proposal.

At the gathering that was convened the daughter reported that she had overheard the two other women gossiping about her mother, saying that her family was hostile to them and that "bad things" would happen to her and her mother. The two neighbors rejected this accusation and counterclaimed that the daughter had sworn at them. As can be seen from these gossiping cases (see also the slandering cases below) within communities within which peace committees worked, a person's good name, his or her identity, was and is a highly valued possession.

The gathering focused initially on exploring the circumstances of the conflict. The two women denied that they had been gossiping, claiming the daughter had never heard them herself, but had apparently been persuaded to believe this by other children who knew even less about the matter. A deliberation on the facts of the case continued for some time. The concern was not who was to blame but what precisely had taken place—an inquiry into root causes. None of the disputants was willing to shift her position and no resolution seemed possible. The gathering began to canvass suggestions for resolutions that were presented for consideration. The common thread was that what had happened had violated established community norms. This led to a discussion about fault understood as a cause. One of the members of the committee had this to say:

> The person who caused all this is [the disputant] because she went to her first neighbor's house and then to the other neighbor's house … so we find you at fault, you should have gone straight home after coming from your first neighbor's house and not gone to your other neighbor straight after, knowing their history.

This inquiry into the causes came close to blaming but managed to avoid it. Instead, the deliberations remained primarily causal. The question driving the discussion was to establish what had happened so that a peace plan could be devised. The line here between the blaming game and the futures game was a fine one, but it was maintained.

The nature of this line, and where it should be drawn, is a matter that was frequently discussed and considered in postgatherings reviews in which peace committees reflected on what had taken place. Typically these reviews were conducted by peace committees on their own; however, as we have noted, they may also, at times, have included a representative from the Community Peace Foundation. These reviews typically turned on two questions—whether the committee members could have done better in applying the model's requirements (compliance) and whether there were issues to do with these requirements that should be rethought (innovation). Review processes were an essential feature of introductory sessions. At these sessions case examples were used to introduce new peace committee members to the model and its application. A key intention of reviews is to promote an awareness of the model features and the reasons for its provisions and, very importantly, the sensibility out of which action arises that it seeks to promote (Shearing & Ericson, 1991).

To return to the witchcraft case, as the deliberations proceeded, one of the disputants had this to say in negotiating the causal blaming line:

I told my second neighbor that I caused all this because I went to my first neighbor's house and then, just after, I went to hers, not knowing things are going to turn out this way.

This disputant later reaffirmed that she had not acted in a sensible way and apologized. Her apology was accepted and the gathering ended with the disputants shaking hands as a gesture that affirmed a plan of action that committed both of them to refrain from unwarranted accusations and gossiping, and to do their best to end the strife.

The above cases all, in one way or another, attest to the capacity and experience that committee members had developed both in implementing the processes and in acting out of the sensibility that the model seeks to establish. In doing so they developed skills that enable them to facilitate the deliberative forums they organized in ways that integrated the two horizons we have identified. As they did so they enacted a process that sought to find a way of integrating cosmopolitan values with local concerns and objectives. While the design principles the model endorses cut across specifics, the particular strategies deployed as these principles were enacted were carefully attuned to the particularities of specific disputes.

Local norms were understood as complex and nuanced. Deliberations did not simply look to established norms but created and recreated them within situational contexts. Concluding discussions often took the form of normative explications that were intended to guide action in the future in ways that would promote peace. The last case discussed provides an especially clear illustration of this. At this gathering, ethical considerations were mobilized, within a causal context, to promote a consensual resolution.

Getting close to the blame edge, without straying across it, is an essential feature of the work that peace committees did and of the reputational capital that their work generated. In the last case one observes a complex process in which normative positions were presented as possible frameworks within which disputants could locate themselves in forging peace. What one sees at work here is the sophistication that is so often glossed over in terms like "local" or "situated" knowledge (Haraway, 1988). It is this, perhaps above all else, that makes the local features that the Zwelethemba model insists upon such a distinguishing feature. It is this that accounts for the very sophisticated and nuanced outcomes that it so routinely generates.

## Domestic Disputes

As we have seen, an important feature of the reasoning embedded in the model is the argument that deliberative processes, which identify and mobilize relevant local knowledge and capacities, are well suited to crafting effective responses to complex problems. We have already observed this in the cases that we have discussed. One of the arenas in which disputes are notoriously complex and nuanced is domestic disputes. It is to this subsample we now turn.

## Mobilizing Normative Standards

One of the cases in our sample concerned a conflict between a married couple, where the wife accused her husband of domestic abuse. The case had been referred to the committee by a local magistrate—yet another example of the nested location of peace committees within a nodal field of conflict management. While the other disputant waited outside—a process that is specified in the peacemaking steps—the husband was asked to give an account of what had happened. He argued that the cause of the conflict was the oldest son in the family, who had been disrespectful and had "chased him out" of his own house. In response to the treatment he had received from this son he had told him that he was, in fact, not his biological offspring. The husband explained that although he still loved his wife, he could no longer stay in his own home with her because of this son. He wanted the son to leave their home. At this point in the husband's account of what had happened, community norms were introduced into the discussion. A committee member commented that a husband should never let a child separate him from his wife or chase him out of the house. This member also argued that while the son might have to be disciplined in some way, the father should not have rejected him in the way he had:

> A child is not a child just because you slept with a woman and made a child, a child needs to be taken care of and nurtured. You raised this child and nurtured him, so he is your child. You sent him to school and to the initiation school [a Xhosa circumcision ceremony that introduces a youth into manhood]. No matter if the blood that runs through his veins is not yours, he is your child. He feels very hurt when you say to him he is not your child.

What we see the peace committee doing here is not only acting as facilitators of a deliberative discussion in which a disputant explains himself to those present at the gathering. They were not simply neutral observers. Instead, as community members, they brought to the discussion normative framings; they sometimes inject normative standards into the deliberations that take place at gatherings. This combination of roles can, and occasionally does, lead to difficulties with respect to the ability of members to act as facilitators. However, this is regarded within the model not as a tension that can or should be eliminated, but one that should be managed through review processes where the dangers of losing sight of their role as facilitators are discussed.

The character of the deliberations shifted once the wife was invited in and the husband was asked to wait outside. She was very upset because she had recently witnessed a "terrible fight" in the house between her oldest son and one of his brothers. She painted a picture of her husband as not working for his family and frequently sleeping away from home. She argued that the conflict within the family had escalated one morning when the husband returned to the house and took the food the children were eating and gave it to his dogs. When she asked him what he was doing, he kicked her in the mouth. She then left with her mother to report the incident to the police and this is how the matter came to court. The oldest son had confronted his father with his behavior and chased him out.

Those attending the gathering were convinced by the wife's account, and once the husband was invited back in and an account of the wife's statement (which had been written down by the peace committee secretary) was read to him, attention was directed toward the husband and what was regarded as his inappropriate behavior. In seeking a solution the husband continued to insist that nothing could be done to resolve the issue while the son remained at home. The gathering attempted, in various ways, to encourage him to be more conciliatory so that a consensual solution could be reached.

In light of his refusal a member drew attention to the nested set of institutions of which the gathering was a part and the possibility that the matter would be returned to court. This coercive shadow of the law (Galanter, 1981) encouraged the father to admit that there was indeed a problem in his family that involved him as a causal element and that needed to be resolved. However, he continued to insist that he could not live with the son.

They next discussed the effects of the father's statement that the boy was not his son. In the discussion a committee member invited him to empathize with his son.

> How would you have felt if you were the oldest child at home, your father arrives in the morning, takes your siblings' food and gives it to the dogs, after that comes back inside and kicks your mother with you watching? How would you feel, just put yourself in your son's shoes, your mother's mouth is swollen, beaten up by your father? ... How would you feel?

The father conceded that he would not have been happy, and acknowledged that he had acted inappropriately. The gathering concluded with the spouses shaking hands as a symbol of the peace that had been produced. A plan of action was agreed to that included the father apologizing for his actions. Committee members agreed to visit the family that afternoon to talk with the children who had been fighting. Before they arrived the father had already taken steps to restore peace. He had apologized to his oldest son for having said that he was not his child. The son, on his part, had apologized for disrespecting his father. The committee members promised to monitor the stability of the peace that had been accomplished.

This case is clearly not an instance of a neutral or value-free facilitation. On the contrary, it was a gathering in which appropriate collective norms were recognized and applied. At the gathering committee members clearly distanced themselves from the behavior of the father, as it was seen to contradict norms about appropriate domestic behavior, in particular norms about appropriate behavior toward a spouse and one's children.

Throughout the process the husband was treated with considerable respect and his right to be respected by family members was acknowledged. The gathering sought to establish an agreed understanding of the facts and their meaning. Members encouraged and facilitated a discussion that brought local cultural norms to bear, while remaining constrained by the procedures and principles of the model. Rather than simply blaming the father the members sought to restore peace within the family. A change of attitude on his part was seen as vital to accomplish this outcome. Violence by the committee or others at the gathering was neither used nor threatened. However, the state's right to use violence as part of its legal processes—the shadow of the law—was recognized.

Once more, what we observe is how a nesting of institutions brings about a melding of different value sets. In this instance a court system with colonial and Western roots is nested with emerging institutions of local security governance that have both older and contemporary roots in Africa.

## Aligning Local and Cosmopolitan Values

A second domestic dispute was between a married couple and the wife's brother and his girlfriend—here too space was an issue. The older sister of the siblings attended the gathering. The married couple had allowed the brother to live in a dwelling in their backyard with his girlfriend, but for a long time their coexistence had not been a peaceful one. The unmarried couple had to use the married couple's house for water and toilet facilities. This had become a source of much irritation that led to one conflict after another. Both couples had spread rumors about partners sleeping around. The conflict escalated into physical violence, with the brother and his girlfriend abusing his sister, who reported the incident to the police, who in turn referred the case to the committee—again an example of nodal networking.

After an initial exploration of the incidents that led to the physical abuse, a committee member drew attention to the norms of Xhosa culture.

> The things you said about affairs are things that are said about single people, people who are not married, not to a married woman. This is a married woman, what you did was wrong—running to her husband and telling him

what she did. This is your sister, no matter what. I had a sister who just passed away, she used to curse at me and say I am a priest of the devil, but I never hit her, not even once. I used to live in her backyard…. I never answered her back because, really, it was her house.

Here the member attempted to establish an agreed platform of values upon which a future-oriented resolution could be constructed. The brother accepted that he should be constrained by these values and their associated norms. Nonetheless, he remained reluctant to reconcile with his sister and argued that he was not happy with his living arrangements. Members of the peace committee assumed a clearly directive role in drawing attention to values that they hoped would provide the basis for a resolution. This was done as a way of appealing to the brother to work with his sister to establish a resolution. Another member pointed to the possibility of bringing the issue to the attention of municipal housing authorities and the associated possibility of them imposing a resolution. Again, the shadow of the law was invoked, and with it the possibility of moving the matter to a forum where a coercive response could be invoked by a different nodal authority (Galanter, 1981). In this case the committee itself was careful not to adopt an authoritative position or threaten direct coercive action—in doing so they acted in accordance with the model's dictates. In taking this position they affirmed South African law and its prescriptions concerning the legitimate use of force. This respect for the state's monopoly of coercion, it will be remembered, is central to the model.

In the shadow of this implicit coercive inducement the brother apologized to his sister. Further discussion revealed that the brother had, in fact, already taken action to move out and had erected a shack—an informally constructed dwelling typically made from largely recycled materials—in another informal settlement. The gathering agreed that this action, taken before and independently of the gathering, would very likely solve the problem. What the gathering had done was to reestablish a more cordial relationship between the siblings. The gathering ended with a mutual acknowledgment of mistakes and with a committee member inviting the wife to call on them again if the abuse continued, so that a protection order from a state authority could be obtained.

Again we see the committee skillfully treading many fine lines that enabled it to act in ways that were legal and responsive to the model's code of good practice while intertwining these with local norms. As in the previous case, members used the shadow of other, more formal processes of conflict resolution to encourage a consensual resolution.

## Reviews and Reflection on Practice

We have mentioned that the reviews of gatherings were occasions for reflection and learning. At these reviews the challenges faced by the members who had to find ways of aligning general values and principles with local knowledge and norms were identified and discussed. During this reflection counterfactual possibilities were identified and discussed. For example, at a review meeting at which the case just discussed was presented, a question arose as to whether the gathering had been too quick to introduce, and build upon, Xhosa speakers' cultural norms. Some committee members felt that perhaps, as a result, the voices of the brother and his girlfriend may not have been heard properly and contemporary understandings that were developing in urban settings might not have been considered. Was the unmarried couple unfairly treated?

A lively debate ensued in which others argued that building on this normative platform had been legitimate, as these norms had not been contested by the couple. This discussion deftly illustrates both the nuanced reflections and the complexity of the challenges faced by committees as they applied the model's principles. The references back to the model and its principles and procedures as a sounding board during the discussion attest to its usefulness in structuring practice and guiding reflection on this practice.

## Conclusion

The Zwelethemba model, as we have just argued, can be viewed as encouraging a bottom-up process of democratic experimentalism that seeks to create institutions and processes that fit comfortably under the sign democracy (as an aspirational ideal). We have in this chapter argued that the model has been consciously built to deepen democracy, particularly by providing poor constituencies with greater opportunities and capacities to govern their own lives and their own security needs. The modelers sought to do this by creating deliberative forums through which local disputes could be solved through creating habits of democratic engagement—in Dewey's sense—that do not rely on retribution or blaming, but are radically future-oriented toward increasing the likelihood for a better and safer tomorrow for all involved. A core principle of the code of good practice that the interaction builds upon is that each participant at the gathering must be given a voice and treated with equal respect as all others. Though the Zwelethemba model can be viewed as a displacement of security governance from what has conventionally been seen as its natural place within the representative institutions of the state and the public police, our argument in this chapter has been that Zwelethemba can be perceived as a democratic experiment that supports broader democratic forums and the functions of the state police, rather than the opposite. One reason for this is that the Zwelethemba modelers and practitioners have been very concerned to create these new "local security publics" in a way that, on the one hand, made them sensitive to local contexts and local cultural values and norms, but on the other hand, also located these local forums within the context of the broader democratic forums of the nation (and, as we will explore in Chapter 5, within the context of even broader cosmopolitan values, such as the various discourses on human rights). Our observations indicate that in the vast majority of cases the peacemakers managed to balance these concerns fairly well.

In our analysis we have sought to demonstrate how the model's design principles and processes worked to relate two value horizons, one global and one local, on an ongoing basis. If this way of "doing things around here" continues to produce accountable self-direction at local levels, the model might provide an important building block in the emergence of a set of democratic values that aligns our two horizons.

In the remainder of these concluding remarks we will discuss how the Zwelethemba model's processes and their outcomes align with other related experiments and scholarship. In doing so we consider the broad question of how rethinking democratic means may assist in reimagining democratic practices. This returns us to discussions that we engaged with at the beginning of this chapter—namely, the possibility of constituting impartial and unbiased decision-making governance processes that are embedded within communal life.

The conventional view, as we have seen, has been that restorative justice and other practices of informal conflict resolution lack the quality of law-based adjudicative processes. This, it has been argued, limits their ability to advance and confirm general public norms through open and principled decision-making forums. The argument has been that only legal reasoning embedded in binding precedents, through the formal declaration of general rules by courts and legislatures, is qualified to clarify the general norms and rules that create and maintain a binding social order. Further, these arguments tend to assume that such norms can only be generalized by imposing them on society through top-down legal processes.

This entrenched view has increasingly been challenged by legal and other scholars, who argue that general norms are in fact developed in many social spheres outside the formal organs of the state. For instance, legal pluralism scholars have been active in considering this challenge. Sturm and Gadlin (2007, p. 53), for example, document how scholars within conflict resolution and deliberative democracy traditions have begun to explore the many informal processes and experiments that have emerged that generate public norms through more bottom-up social practices. Similarly, scholars have increasingly challenged the idea that the adversarial system is the best method for dealing with many of the conflicts generated in complex societies (Christie, 1977; Menkel-Meadow, 2003; Menkel-Meadow, Love, Schneider, & Sternlight, 2004).

The Zwelethemba processes analyzed above suggest one way of institutionalizing these developments. The methodology embedded in the model structures deliberative processes through which implicit norms and values are made explicit and invites participants to take part in a critical democratic inquiry. During these inquiries, norms and values, within the context of the model's restrictions, are debated, justified, and rejected. The focus in these processes is not on defining norms and values as once and forever justified and declared. Rather, the processes encourage decision making that mobilizes local norms and values—again within limits—to create pragmatic future-focused plans of action that contribute to establishing a more peaceful tomorrow.

Though the Zwelethemba model, compared to many other informal dispute resolution programs, emphasizes the importance of acknowledging value pluralism, and cautions against too ambitious attempts at identifying and articulating communal identities and norms, it does incorporate a set of general values and capacities into its processes and through these into its practices. The hope is that its processes will, over time, strengthen and generalize the values of democratic inquiry and peaceful problem solving.

The cases analyzed above confirm that such second-order standards, which set up rules, principles, and processes used to address new problems, were widely adhered to by those who applied the model. This, as we have seen, enables particular public values to emerge from an informal, nonadjudicative process outside the state institutions. To the extent that such values and capacities are generalized, as the analysis above indicates can and did happen, two outcomes appear to follow.

On the one hand, practices that promote the democratic capacities and self-directedness of local communities are institutionalized, and on the other hand, norms are produced bottom-up that may have an influence on the shaping of formal policy and law in more formal arenas. One consequence of this is that a locally based normative integration of democratic values, advocated by Dewey (1916, 1927, 1938a), does indeed contribute to a revitalization of liberal democracy.

The conventional view on impartiality, as pointed out by Sturm and Gadlin (2007, p. 58), is that it is best achieved through "detached neutrality." Ideally this points to the existence of a third party facilitating the resolution of a conflict that has no direct knowledge of the conflict, or prior relationships with the participants. In Morgan's (2006) view, the model of a disinterested decision maker using objective, rationalist, and universalized forms of knowledge to justify decisions has become a predominant model in modern societies. This model is, in his view, essentially technocratic rather than actively democratic.

Sturm and Gadlin (2007, p. 59), in our view, correctly assume that a reliance on unbiased conflict resolvers, or facilitators, ought to be an essential feature of informal conflict resolution processes. They argue, however, that detached neutrality is not the only or necessarily the best way of achieving that end. In the Zwelethemba model detached neutrality has no particular salience. As the analysis above has demonstrated, the peacemakers at the peacemaking gatherings did not function as detached decision makers, nor did they take a neutral stance toward the different values and norms explored as the conflicts were dealt with. Indeed, they often expressed their opinions, as community members, on normative matters and frequently mobilized community norms and values when facilitating the process.

What the model does require, however, is that the peacemakers do not act as adjudicators who impose outcomes. Within this context what the model does allow, and indeed encourages, is the framing of the way the conflicts are addressed so that the process is fair, open, and unbiased in ways that enable all present to meaningfully participate in and influence how issues are framed and how solutions develop.

Sturm and Gadlin (2007, p. 58) suggest that facilitators of such processes might be seen adopting a role of "embedded intermediaries" rather than as taking a detached and neutral stance. Zwelethemba's peacemakers actively used the knowledge they had acquired of the predominant opinions, norms, and values within their localities, while simultaneously seeking to ensure that all present at gatherings were heard and could contribute to the development of a plan of action that would contribute to a better tomorrow.

## Endnotes

1. Theodor Lowi, a major interlocutor of Heclo, shared many of Heclo's thoughts about a displacement of politics. In his book *The End of Liberalism* (1969) Lowi painted a picture of American politics as increasingly captured by powerful "iron triangles," consisting of state and nonstate actors, displacing politics from formal representative institutions and, in the process, effectively shielding themselves from popular influence and democratic controls.
2. Twenty-one peacemaking gatherings organized by four different peace committees were taped by a Xhosa-speaking research assistant, translated into English, and transcribed.

# Multiple Accountabilities

# 4

Accountability is an element of governance the Zwelethemba modelers recognized from the beginning as crucial to the success or failure of their project. As Martin (2012) and many others have pointed out, nonstate forms of security often end up as "club goods" that offer preferential treatment to some, while excluding and sometimes victimizing others. Martin (p. 16) concludes that the overall lack of state presence within such forms of security governance implies that they will always be insufficiently regulated. On the other hand, there is a sizable literature on African and South African public police that clearly shows that police forces have their own challenges in delivering accountable and efficient services to the public, particularly to poor members of the community (see, for example, Berg, 2005a, 2005b, 2005c). Making the state more responsible for the governance of private security may compound the problems faced by the state police.

As we stated in the introductory chapter, a key concern of the Zwelethemba modelers was how to build a security model that would be robust, sustainable, and legitimate. We focus on the legitimacy problem in this chapter. The concern of the modelers in this regard was how one could develop institutional arrangements that would constrain local practices so that they would resonate with established cultural practices and at the same time be accountable both to the local community and to the law and the South African Constitution. A key concern for the modelers was how to build a model that would, on the one hand, allow for local autonomy and creativity in how to respond to and solve disputes in particular local contexts, but on the other hand, would also be highly regulated in the sense of keeping the practice within the limits of the core values and principles of the model. To explicate how the modelers responded to this challenge, we examine the scholarly literature on accountability to illustrate how the modelers sought to draw ideas and inspiration from this academic discourse.

## Accountability—Where We Have Been

Hobbes's leviathan is a figure who is either explicitly referred to or is implicitly lurking in the background, in many scholarly contributions to the issue of accountability and the centuries-old debate that surrounds it. Hobbes's basic idea, as we have seen, is that by trading some of our liberties for more security, we accept that horizontal hazards between individuals or groups of citizens (that arise from different interests or values, such as competitive greed, spite, and strife) are translated into vertically provided protections. The danger, which is all too often so evident, is the possibility that governments will not act to improve our welfare and security, but rather will follow partisan agendas that result from the capture of the machinery of government by sectional interests that inject their wills and purposes into the content of public choices (Dunn, 1999).

As a consequence, an overarching issue in debates about accountability has been the question of how to hold states to account for the way in which they exercise their power. In such debates elections have been identified as a key mechanism for constraining their power. An important idea here has been that people should be willing to invest governments with the power to rule, provided that they can remove them if their performance is found lacking. In this traditional model, the approach to accountability is envisioned in terms of nested principal-agent relationships: The general public and their elected representatives are the principals, while governments and employees are their agents (Freeman, 2006).

During the early decades of the twentieth century, however, the effectiveness of such attributes of democratic government as sources of accountability—for instance, universal suffrage and multiparty elections—came, increasingly, to be questioned (Schacter, 2000). In the United States, for example, the ability of "machine-style" and "patronage-based" politics to thrive in electoral competitions caused many to question the electorate's capacity to hold political powers to public account through elections (Dowdle, 2006, p. 4).

Similarly, in Italy an effective conspiracy of career politicians, who promoted their own interests, were able to routinely counter the supposedly accountability-enhancing features of competitive electoral politics (Dunn, 1999). These, and similar developments elsewhere, prompted reformers to seek out new mechanisms intended to control political behavior. A significant consequence of these efforts was the move toward the development of the idea of a public or civil service that was relatively autonomous of partisan governments. This led to the development of rationalized, professionalized bureaucratic institutions of governance as a means of pursuing the public good to counterbalance the difficulties associated with electoral politics. As a consequence, hierarchical, organized bureaucratic accountability came, for much of the twentieth century, to enjoy relative conceptual dominance as a crucial mechanism for shaping and constraining public choice (Dowdle, 2006).

Another major tradition in political theory concerned with the issue of accountable politics is associated with Montesquieu, Locke, Madison, and others who advocated separating and dividing state powers to mitigate the problems associated with electoral competition. These ideas of "horizontal accountability" (O'Donnell, 1999) provided the basis for the development of mechanisms through which states were encouraged to constrain themselves by checking on their own operations, abuses, and inefficiencies. Montesquieu, for example, in *De l'Esprit des Loix* (1766), emphasized the importance of a separation of powers between the three major arms of government—the executive, the legislature, and the judiciary. Today, as we have already suggested, a fourth arm is sometimes included, namely, the public bureaucracy (Olsen, 1983, 2006), along with a range of other related public entities (for example, auditors general, anticorruption bodies, ombudsmen, electoral and human rights commissions, and police boards). Whatever the specifics, the central idea is that such separation will ensure that government is curtailed and contained by organizational checks and balances within states.

Recent neoliberal reforms—that have promoted private provision of governmental services with states retaining control of the steering of government—have revitalized the idea of horizontal accountability as a mechanism to combat abuses of political powers. The internationalization of the American regulatory mechanism of relatively autonomous agencies, the introduction of quasi-markets in public administration, the splitting up of the different administrative functions (such as the shaping, monitoring, and implementation of policy), and the outsourcing of service provision to private agencies can all be seen as reforms that have created new checks and balances within political systems that previously relied much more heavily on vertical structures as key mechanisms for constraining political power (Hindess, 1997).

Vertical lines of accountability—an electoral bottom-up mechanism, creating a space for citizens making claims and achievements from below, and a bureaucratic top-down process for enhancing oversight and order by the rule by law and regulations—in combination with a horizontal accountability mechanism, perceived as a system of checks and balances, have been and still are the principal mechanisms for achieving political accountability today.

This architecture has been complicated by communal or "convivial" accountability (Morgan, 2006). With this form of accountability behavior is constrained through the application of meanings and assumptions that are shared by a collectivity, by a community. Cultural or convivial accountability that is grounded in social identities and tacit knowledge regulates behavior through common identities, and accordingly thrives in small, local areas.

The national movements emerging in the latter part of the seventeenth century challenged medieval conceptions of societies as consisting of divided estates. This medieval concept gradually gave way to the new idea of a unity between people, histories, and territories. What emerged was the notion of "fatherlands," which eventually developed into the idea of nation-states (Gellner, 1983; Anderson, 1991).

The democratization of political regimes in the century that followed reinforced ideas of people belonging to distinct national communities with shared rights and obligations. Since then national states have, until quite recently, been regarded as relatively effective mechanisms for integrating communal accountability with other forms of accountability, in ways that have constrained the behavior of both citizens and governments within large-scale "imagined communities" (Morgan, 2006; Anderson, 1991). These ideas have been explored by, among others, Robert Dahl (1961), via his conception that political processes are constrained by shared ideas and norms about the "rules of the game."

The weight attributed to each of the mechanisms of accountability—electoral, bureaucratic, horizontal, and communal—has varied over time and from commentator to commentator. Many scholars and commentators have, not surprisingly, favored a combination of these mechanisms as the best way of holding governments and their agents accountable to a wider public.

## A New Crisis of Accountability?

The nexus of privatization and globalization has led many scholars to be concerned about the possibility that traditional accountability measures are being undermined, as political authority and power is shifted into the hands of private or transnational actors who often are able to operate outside the boundaries of accountability systems that have been designed with state-centered forms of governance in mind. Indeed, there is a growing perception that a crisis in political accountability may be developing, as each of the principal mechanisms for holding governmental powers accountable is conceived to be less and less reliable (Dowdle, 2006).

Today many commentators question the value of regular elections in holding governments to account. Frequently this challenge is seen as related to the growth of industrialization and the resultant economic power blocks, as well as the development of mass society. Other concerns relate to the increasing centralization of political powers in many parts of the world and the associated transformation of electoral mechanisms at local levels from ones that emphasize local governments and town meetings to ones that seek to be rationalized through the development of supra-local entities (Dowdle, 2006). These are all moves from polycentric forms of governance to ones that are more monocentric (Aligica & Tarko, 2012).

The concern is that elections become more symbolic and less functional with each step away from electorates (Freeman, 2006). Many scholars fear that globalization has led to an unresponsiveness on the part of governments to the general public—to the will of the people—as the requirement for national competitiveness in the international economy becomes a dominant concern of political regimes independent of the party or parties in power (Dryzek & Dunleavy, 2009; Dryzek, 1996). Evidence of the frustration of electorates with this distance from their governments was a signature feature of global political landscapes in 2011, where public demonstrations that expressed concerns about the accountability of governments were common—for instance, the demonstrations of the Arab Spring across North Africa, the Occupy Wall Street movement across the United States and elsewhere, the Euro crisis demonstrations in several parts of Europe, and in South Africa, numerous service delivery protests. Even more broadly, the global spread of a neoliberal mentality and its governmental consequences, even though its regulatory and market-sensitive solutions have been implemented with variable speed and attuned to a variety of national institutional realities (Christensen & Lægreid, 2001, 2009), has been interpreted as evidence of the decreased ability of established forms of competitive party politics to hold contemporary state governments to account (Dryzek, 1996, 2002).

The issue of the virtues of bureaucracy as a mechanism of accountability, and the debate surrounding it, has had a long history. Weber (1947), although he was impressed with the governance and regulatory capacities of bureaucracy, nonetheless had reservations about its inclination—especially the public bureaucracy of the German state—to become an autonomous and dominant power within society that could, and did, seriously affect the dynamics of other spheres of governance, including competitive party politics. These concerns have led Weberian scholars, like Talcott Parsons, to draw attention to both the virtues and damaging traits of bureaucratic forms of governance (Parsons & Smelser, 1956; Parsons, 1960). Most scholars working within this tradition have been careful to draw attention to the various dysfunctions of bureaucracy, such as its status quo or elitist orientation, its rigidity and "rule as a value in itself" inclination, and its unjust distributional effects (Blau, 1956; Albrow, 1970; Wilson, 1989; see also Wilson, 1887).

Many empirical studies of public bureaucracies at work have documented the discretionary powers of public officials and the limited capacity of bureaucratic rules and norms to constrain organizational decision making. Jacobsen (1960), for example, depicted public officials as occupying an ambitious landscape characterized by several, often contradictory, role demands—for example, loyalty to the political leadership, independence based on professional autonomy, and identification with clients. While creating dilemmas, with respect to role performance, such contradictory demands also serve as a source of autonomy and influence, as criticism from one perspective can be met by pointing to other obligations. Bureaucratic accountability is further restricted by the "problem of many hands," making it difficult to hold particular individuals accountable for collective organizational outcomes or abuses (Thompson, 1980).

Accordingly, while a bureaucratic office administration most certainly has advantages in comparison, for instance, to collegial forms of organization in enhancing public accountability, there are a number of disadvantages as well. As a consequence, today many scholars conceive of bureaucratic accountability as less and less capable of producing good governance outcomes in a contemporary world that requires governance to be agile, adaptable, and flexible (Dowdle, 2006). This has led many scholars to seek to identify other mechanisms of political accountability with greater capacity to accommodate the new requirements for continuous learning, innovation, and change in an increasingly globalized world (Courville, 2006; Williams, 2006; Guijt, 2010; Hammer & Lloyd, 2011).

These concerns have led to a revival of thinking about how to hold governors within the political realm accountable. As part of this there has been renewed interest in the idea of building in horizontal checks and balances into polycentric as well as monocentric political processes to respond to the sort of accountability concerns we have just reviewed within the context of globalized, neoliberal forms of governance. While more state-centric scholars have tended to limit their attention to established political domains, other scholars have questioned this limitation, as it does not, in their view, take into account the increasingly polycentric, or nodal, features of the contemporary governance landscape. State-driven transformations in governance under the sign of neoliberalism have most certainly encouraged state-centered forms of polycentric governance—that enroll nonstate resources in the rowing of governance while retaining state control of the auspices of governance—to become pervasive (Osborne & Gaebler, 1993; Rose & Miller, 1992).

However, other, more bottom-up shifts in governance have also taken hold and have become just as pervasive. These developments have, for example, seen the establishment of corporations, and collectivities associated with them, as governing nodes with power and resources to support their governing agendas (Braithwaite, 2004; Drahos & Braithwaite, 2002), necessitating new explorations as to how more efficient accountability systems may be conceived (Freeman, 2006; Scherer & Palazzo, 2011). Indeed, as we have already suggested, there is now a well-established consensus that governance is no longer the sole province of the state; it has become polycentric—involving public and private sector, civil society, and international institutions. The transition from state-centric analysis to approaches more inclined to acknowledge governance as a heterogeneous and multidimensional field has a range of disciplinary sources, eroding earlier state-centric approaches in such fields as international relations (Hobson, 2000), criminology (Wood & Dupont, 2005; Bayley & Shearing, 2001; Braithwaite, 2000a), the so-called new security studies (Buzan, Wæver, & De Wilde, 1997; Buzan & Hansen, 2009), law (there is a well-established *Journal of Legal Pluralism*), development economics (Aligica & Tarko, 2012), and poverty research and peace studies (Marenin, 2005; Bayley, 2005; Taylor & Jennings, 2005). The emergence of polycentric governance has encouraged scholars to explore how the new policy conundrums may mobilize dispersed knowledge, capacities, and resources in ways that promote not only legitimate collective or private interests, but wider public goods (Shearing & Wood, 2003a). Changed governance realities have necessitated a reconceptualization of horizontal accountability as a way of bridging the public and private realms.

The closely associated idea of constraining political powers and civic behavior through community engagement has also been revitalized by the communitarian response to conceived policy problems, especially in the United States. The idea of a moral community (Etzioni, 1993) is based on the idea that democracy, and corresponding mechanisms of accountability, can only thrive within social collectivities that share core values and conceptions of the "good life." Only within such communities, it is argued, can members be induced to follow common norms and rules. This approach finds considerable support in the writings of many of the classical social thinkers. Scholars like Tocqueville, Weber, and Durkheim all assumed that the success of regulatory systems ultimately depended on the capacity to induce the regulated to regulate themselves through an internalization of common norms (Furger, 1997; Gunningham & Rees, 1997). These ideas also underlie the tack taken by contemporary thinkers, such as Putnam (1995a, 2000, 2002, 2007; Putnam & Feldstein, 2003), who looks to a revival of communal bonds of trust and shared norms as a way of resolving the current crises in political accountability.

The likelihood of being able to integrate contemporary societies and thereby enhance political accountability through the establishment of thick normative bonds has, however, been questioned from the vantage point of several theoretical perspectives. Some scholars have criticized the communitarian project as utterly unrealistic, given the increased heterogeneity of modern societies. One outcome of this has been that liberal political theorists and "cultural pluralists" have therefore sought to identify principles of peaceful and fair coexistence that do not presuppose thick bonds—a high degree of social integration or cohesion (Rawls, 1971, 1982, 1995; Chambers, 2003, 2008). Others, taking a slightly different tack, assume that the possibility of mobilizing distinct national identities as mechanisms of political accountability has been eroded due to the increased cultural interconnectedness across nations (and national decision-making units), with the result that cultural transformation and power processes have increasingly escaped sovereign states (Falk, 1992, 1999; Held et al., 1999; Held & Koenig-Archibugi, 2005; Held & Moore, 2008; Monbiot, 2003).

Some scholars have argued that processes of internationalization and globalization have increasingly displaced territorially based communities with functional, nongeographically defined collectivities—communities that sometimes exist within cyber rather than real space-time spaces. These collectivities are often organized at an inter- or transnational level—for example, internationally organized expert networks or "epistemic policy communities" (Haas, 1990, 1992). These "global communities" are viewed as privileging abstract reasoning and universal principles over situated knowledge (Nygren, 1999) and local space-time forms of organization (Morgan, 2006). Within this context some scholars have begun to explore how alternative ways of conceiving citizenship as "cosmopolitan" (Held, 1995; Beck, 2005; Hutchings & Dannreuter, 1999) or "insurgent" (Friedmann, 1998, 2002) are creating new bonds and alliances between a plurality of actors, some locally based, others operating in the national or global arena (Shearing & Wood, 2003b). Their work explores how new mechanisms of unruly or convivial accountability emerge through such global interactions (Morgan, 2006).

As so many of the traditional mechanisms of holding governments to account show clear signs of incapacity, an emerging tendency in contemporary scholarship, as we have suggested, has been a search for fresh ideas and new approaches. As this has happened, some scholars have argued that a fundamental problem with respect to political accountability is that the traditional distinctions between bureaucracy, market, and community have been oversimplified, as these different mechanisms are usually intermingled (Marshaw, 2006; Scott, 2006). Other scholars, like Konig (1997, 1996), in response to the perceived inadequacy of established mechanisms, have argued for the use of a range of formal and informal practices to increase political accountability (Gunningham, Grabosky, & Sinclair, 1998; Freeman & Farber, 2005). The idea here is to seek out mechanisms that comply with democratic values and produce shared value, but which do not rest—at least not primarily—on the mechanisms of electoral democracy (Konig, 1996, 1997; Porter & Kramer, 2002, 2011; Scott, 2006; Braithwaite, 2006a; Harrington & Turem, 2006; Black, 2008).

As this literature review indicates, there has been a growing interest within many scholarly milieus during the last couple of decades in the conditions for good governance and how to make public—and increasingly private and corporate—practices accountable. There is a clear tendency in this literature to argue that, due to globalization, increased corporate power, emergence of more polycentric forms of governance, changes in state modes of steering, and so forth, it is becoming increasingly difficult to hold such practices to account, and that many of the traditional mechanisms for doing so are not functioning as well as they used to function (for a review see Burris, Kempa, & Shearing, 2008). The lesson that the Zwelethemba modelers drew from this was that a fresh look at how to reimagine accountability and its modalities might be necessary. Fortunately for the modelers a recent literature has emerged concerned with that particular challenge.

# New Ideas on How to Perceive
# and Strengthen Accountability

The concerns we have just canvassed raise several related questions. How might it be possible to strengthen political accountability in our contemporary globalized and pluralized world, where there are many sovereigns, both public and private, by engaging in multilevel and multinodal forms of accountability within governance? What approach should be adopted and what mechanisms should be developed?

In considering these questions and how they have been addressed, it is possible to identify four basic approaches among contemporary scholars and commentators.

As we have noted, the most influential approach to governance over the past several decades since the mid to late twentieth century has been the neoliberal sensibility. The ideas and empirical realities of this reform movement have been intensively studied and we now have a much better understanding of neoliberal normative agendas and their effects on governance.

An important, and continuing, debate about accountability mechanisms within neoliberal forms of governance has focused on the role of markets as accountability mechanisms. At one end of the spectrum the argument advanced has been that devolution of governance responsibilities to private actors does not release them from accountability, as the markets within which they operate will hold them to account. In contrast, other scholars have been less inclined to believe in the virtuous properties of markets—and their invisible hands—and have argued for the "publicization" of firms—something that they argue can, and should, be achieved by extending public law norms and values to private economic actors (Rubin, 2006).

Examples of initiatives that arise from this publicization line of thought are corporate social responsibility initiatives (Bhattacharya, Sen, & Korschun, 2011; Sun, 2010; Bansal & Roth, 2000; Fry, Keim, & Meiners, 1982), systems of self-regulation (Furger, 1997), or nonstate market-driven forms of governance that build on consumer choice (Cashore, 2002; Cashore, Auld, Newsom, & Egan, 2009). Fair trade initiatives provide a good example of how business practices have been influenced by movements that have sought to combine a mobilization of poor farmers from the "global South" with awareness campaigns directed at Northern consumers as a way of inducing and pressuring European and American corporations to include fair prices to poor producers as a value in their business models and practices (Hutchens, 2009; Raynolds, 2009; Reed, 2009; Utting, 2009; Barrientos, Conroy, & Jones, 2007; Nicholls & Opal, 2004; Raynolds, Murray, & Taylor, 2004; Murray, Raynolds, & Taylor, 2003).

An emerging literature has, however, asked critical questions about the assumptions that underlie neoliberal discourses about opportunities that they provide to widen participation in governance—the terms that define these discourses include *partnerships* and *joined-up governance*. Several scholars have argued that these claims to extending participation through public-private partnerships in neoliberal or globalized governance systems have not resolved democratic problems with regard to equity, access, and accountability, and indeed have often exacerbated them (Strange, 1996; Rosenau, 1999, 1992).

Cooke and Kothari (2001) posed the critical question in the title of their book *Participation: The New Tyranny?* The argument they present is that neoliberal-inspired forms of participation should be understood as emerging forms of social control. Rubin (2006), writing in a similar vein, claims that to describe neoliberal forms of governance as enhancing participation, and by implication accountability, is both inaccurate and dangerous. He pictures the new steering *modus operandi* as a mechanism of manipulation, undermining of free will, and continued supervision.

As insightful as these and similar analyses are, there is a danger in rejecting neoliberal ideas, of "throwing the baby out with the bath water" and of losing sight of innovative possibilities that may be retrievable from these forms of governance. There is little doubt that the neoliberal reform movement has opened up new governmental spaces and has spurred new debates and imaginations as to the variety of ways through which public goods may be produced and through which public and private powers could be held accountable. The lesson that the Zwelethemba modelers drew from this was that what seemed to be needed was to seek to combine a recognition of the dangers that scholars have identified with a more constructive engagement with the variety of ideas, thoughts, and mechanisms contained within the neoliberal reform umbrella (Gordon, 1991; Rose & Miller, 1992; Miller & Rose, 1990, 2008; Rose, 1996, 1999; Barry, Osborne, & Rose, 1996; Dean, 1999). What was required was an examination of neoliberal practices to see what they suggest about the development of new and novel solutions to the problems of governance, and in particular accountable governance.

An opposing position to the polycentric ones that we have just discussed is one that seeks to revitalize political accountability, not through Hayekian-inspired ideas of accountability through markets, but rather through more traditional institutions and mechanisms. Scholars who hold this view tend to regard regular elections and strong parliaments within national states as the only viable—albeit flawed—solutions to check increasingly powerful private powers (Loader & Walker, 2007). The basic attitude is that there is, in principle, nothing wrong with our democratic institutions and our traditional mechanisms of accountability—merely that they have been weakened for various reasons and need to be protected and revitalized (Dahl, 1998; Gardner,

1996; Manin, Goode, & Hawthorn, 1997; Williams, 2000; Hobson, 2008). This position also warns us, when seeking new solutions, not to throw the baby out with the bath water. The Zwelethemba modelers were very conscious of this danger. This position reminded them of the chief virtues of representative democracy as a necessary mechanism to check the operations of public and private powers, and therefore of the need to honor and pay due respect to the key mechanisms of this approach, such as respect for the law, the state's monopoly on the legitimate use of force, and the South African Constitution.

The modelers were also aware of the many recent attempts to reflect on how representative democracy might be revitalized in our time (Pitkin, 2004; Frenkiel, 2011). Suggested solutions have variously argued for the need to put more emphasis on one or the other of representative democracy's integral elements, such as political deliberation (Gastil, 2000; Dryzek, 2002; Mansbridge, 1992; Fishkin, 1995; Bohman, 1996), multiculturalism and inclusion (Young, 2000; Gooding-Williams, 1998), and engaged citizenship (Barber, 1984; Cronin, 1989; Haskell, 2001; International IDEA, 2008), as well as on its more agonic aspects (Shapiro, 1999b; Mouffe, 2000). Scholars reflecting on how representative democracy may be revitalized, however, often struggle to identify how one might strengthen traditional mechanisms of accountability in an age of decreasing electoral participation, loss of membership in political parties, and dwindling trust in public institutions (Dalton, 2004; International IDEA, 2002; Wattenberg, 2002; Skocpol & Fiorina, 1999; Nye, 1997; Tan, 1997; Putnam, 1995b; see also the Global Barometer Surveys, the European Election Studies, and the Edelman Trust Barometer). A key problem here is that while representative institutions and their concomitant mechanisms of accountability may be conceived as still necessary, it is more difficult to see how they can be adapted to respond to the challenges of globalization and polycentric governance.

A third approach, and one that seeks to identify a way out of the difficulties we have just noted, is the position taken by the cosmopolitans (Held, 1999, 2000; Beck, 1997, 2005). Held, for example, argues that the emergence of a global world, with problems that transcend national boundaries, requires a redefinition of the idea of democratic polities that moves beyond the limitations of nation-states. As it becomes increasingly clear that more and more political issues can now only be addressed through processes that transcend the boundaries of nation-states—global environmental changes provide an emblematic example—political processes, and accountability mechanisms associated with them, need to be reimagined in ways that shift them upwards (Held, 2003, 2005).

What is needed, Held and other cosmopolitan scholars argue, is a conception of what might be thought of as cosmopolitan democracy—a conception of democracy that will provide a framework for establishing an institutional arrangement for realizing democratic governance at an international level.

Cosmopolitans, by and large, seek one overarching political framework—institutions of global governance—where issues are systematically dealt with at higher and higher levels of democratic government according to the size of the constituency affected (Held, 2005; see also Marres, 2005). Scholars who advocate this approach argue for the need to strengthen transnational authorities, a constitution that applies at an international level that protects citizens, groups, and global common goods (Beck, 1997, 2005; Habermas, 2001; Held, 2000). The most advanced, and well known, of these supra-state systems is the European Union (Scharpf, 1999, 2010; Marks, Scharpf, & Schmitter, 1996; Olsen, 2007, 2010). To the Zwelethemba modelers the cosmopolitan approach became an inspiration of how such ideas and values could be built into the model, and particularly so in relation to the value of development and human rights, which is the subject of Chapter 5.

Cosmopolitan scholars have been criticized on several grounds. Some critics argue that they aggregate cosmopolitan realities in a world still dominated by states and international power structures. This, it is feared, could lead to global cultural homogenization, and in effect, it takes the focus away from the need to strengthen the national state to cope with global problems (Nakano, 2006). Latour (2005), while sharing Becks's critique of "methodological nationalism," argues that cosmopolitanism implies an "already unified cosmos" (p. 262), and instead emphasizes the need to recognize divergently mediated worlds and natures (see also Wardle, 2009).

Cosmopolitan scholars have also been criticized for not being able to show how real power imbalances in global governance can be overcome so that more democratic cosmopolitan solutions can be effectively institutionalized. A constant worry is that such arrangements will be as susceptible to capture as traditional state institutions have been. If state institutions of governance have been flawed in so many crucial ways, can we expect to be able to craft supra-state institutions that will be less flawed, especially if our new imaginings of governmental institutions are tightly coupled to our old ones? Some commentators fear that the cosmopolitan approach might abrogate existing rights of (nationally) based democracy and self-government and create new dependencies rather than to empower. The danger is that the cosmopolitan approach tends to extend rights beyond the state while offering no effective mechanism for ensuring accountability (Chandler, 2003).

The fourth basic approach to the question of how political accountability might be rethought fully accepts that our world is becoming increasingly polycentric (McGinnis, 1999a) and explicitly seeks to rethink democratic institutions within this context. In doing so its proponents give attention to nodes and networks in an approach in which the focus of interest shifts explicitly from government to governance (Rhodes, 1997). The first generation of studies within this tradition sought to identify forms of interaction within networks and to associate them with variations in policy outcomes and the distribution of governance goods (Atkinson & Coleman, 1992; Jordan & Schubert, 1992; Marsh & Rhodes, 1992). The second generation of these studies has been more concerned with searching for criteria to be used in evaluating what has happened and what is now happening (Sørensen & Torfing, 2007) and to identify design principles that will promote democratic values and accountable practices under conditions of dispersed and pluralized governance (Levi-Faur, 2005; Drahos & Braithwaite, 2002; Wood & Shearing, 2007).

Compared to the cosmopolitans, network scholars take a more radical stance with respect to conventional models of democracy that typically presuppose highly centralized policy regimes. Instead, democracy is conceived as decentralized and the key challenge is seen as how to make institutions, elites, and governments accountable to a plurality of voices (Kaldor, 2003, 2007; Wood & Dupont, 2006). An important set of studies within this approach has been that of Elinor and Vincent Ostrom, which began with their studies of metropolitan forms of governance (see, for example, Ostrom & Ostrom, 1961). The Ostroms, perhaps more than anyone, have focused attention on polycentric forms of governance, although the term *polycentric* was first used in relationship to governance, as far as we are aware, by Polanyi in his term *polycentric organization* (Polanyi, 1951). Vincent Ostrom (1972, in McGinnis, 1999b, p. 53), in a paper on polycentricity, "identified a polycentric political system as having many centers of decision making that were formally independent of each other" (see also Aligica & Tarko, 2012; Ostrom, Tiebout, & Warren, 1961). The Ostroms' work has gained considerable prominence since Elinor was awarded a Nobel Prize in Economics in 2009.

As we have already noticed, a key observation that emerges from the various literatures on the emergence of polycentric forms of governance has been that its benefits have been varied and unequal (Haas, 2004). In considering this, some scholars have explored how the experiences and interests of those whose voices are usually not mobilized in dispersed forms of governance might be included in nodal forms of governance, and how overall systems of governance might be remodeled to reduce this governance disparity (Wood & Shearing, 2007; Fung, 2003; Fung & Wright, 2003). In attempting to reimagine forms of polycentric governance that are both more thoroughly democratic and accountable, attention has been directed to the idea inspired by Hayek (1944) that *local knowledge and local capacity* are crucial to good governance. Just how local knowledge and capacity should be located within networks of polycentric governance has emerged as a crucial, and possibly the key, policy nut to crack (Braithwaite, 2000a). Though this problem remains in need of much further theoretical and empirical work, several promising mechanisms of promoting more accountable practices in polycentric governance have recently been identified. We now examine each of these suggestions in turn, as each of them became a source of inspiration to the Zwelethemba modelers as they sought to build modalities of account-ability into their own model.

First, the neoliberal principle of devolution of tasks and "responsibiliza-tion" (Garland, 1996, p. 452) of actors to self-regulate their own practices does contain ideas that are worth elaborating on, as Braithwaite has done in his numerous considerations of the idea of responsive regulation that he first developed with Ayres (Ayres & Braithwaite, 1992). As Braithwaite has put it, the advantage of such thinking is not simply to impose controls, but to acti-vate and draw upon the talents and morality of those regulated (Braithwaite, 1989, 2002, 2006a). The hope is that through more sophisticated strategies of regulation it will be possible to avoid accountability mechanisms that encourage the regulated to work defensively to avoid blame or to seek to escape controls through defiance strategies of creative compliance and the like (Ayres & Braithwaite, 1992).

An obvious danger, however, is that programs of responsive regulation, and similar strategies, will lean too heavily on predefined policy agendas and fixed criteria of evaluating performance that are external to the regu-lated entities, and therefore detrimental to the development of self-rule and self-direction (Morgan, 2006). Scott (2004) criticizes the model of respon-sive regulation for not adequately conceiving the realities and complexities of contemporary polycentric governance systems. In an early elaboration of his model, however, Braithwaite does respond to this criticism, articulating some of the more horizontal aspects of his model. Within this elaboration all implicated actors relate to and negotiate with the others through multiple and varied regulatory pyramids (Braithwaite, 1993).

What is necessary, if the danger we have just identified is to be avoided, is to discover ways of building in assurances that responsibilization will enable the devolution of both steering and rowing functions. This needs to be combined, as numerous critics have pointed out, with access to necessary resources and with processes of horizontal accountability, if such devolution is to empower rather than oppress. This, of course, is particularly relevant in arenas where a policy favoring polycentricity is intended to improve the lives of poor and marginalized groups. This was a crucial insight that the Zwelethemba modelers considered carefully when experimenting with their own model of security governance.

A related set of arguments about accountability has to do with the idea that there is usually a range of means by which actors can be held accountable for their actions and that one should consider the gamut of options when establishing accountability mechanisms. Empirical studies have shown that the inclination to establish firm distinctions between the various key mechanisms of accountability—hierarchy, market, or commu-nity—is unsustainable because the various means are typically intermingled (Dowdle, 2006). In developing this argument Scott (2000) has identified two potential mechanisms of what he terms extended accountability, namely, interdependence and redundancy. Accountability through interdependency (or mutuality) is often appropriate within polycentric governance systems consisting of many actors who rely on each other's resources and capacities, as in these sorts of assemblages principal actors regularly have to account for at least some of their actions to others. The second extended accountability model identified by Scott, redundancy, emerges as a possibility when overlapping accountability mechanisms reduce the centrality of any one of them. When utilized this possibility reduces the risks involved if one or more of the accountability mechanisms fails. Thus the presence of redundancy with accountability mechanisms can, if utilized, increase the robustness of accountability (Scott; see also Landau, 1969).

A number of recent empirical and theoretical studies have analyzed and debated the features of accountability mechanisms within a polycentric governance system. They identify the advantages of utilizing multiple-level mechanisms by establishing hybrid accountability arrangements (Black, 2001, 2003, 2007, 2008; Baldwin & Black, 2008; Dowdle, 2006). This suggests that plural mechanisms of accountability may offer the best option in designing robust systems of accountability, especially within plural governance assemblages. The key design principle here is that a dispersion of checks and balances that encourage and inhibit particular behavior will provide for the establishment of robust and effective accountability arrangements (Scott, 2000).

A third, and closely related, accountability strategy advocated by Braithwaite (1999a, 2006a) is what he names circular or horizontal accountability. While his model of "republican architectures" of governance has clear resemblances to other notions of hybrid or extended accountability that cross the public and the private, he more explicitly ties it to ideas of direct participatory democracy and "deliberative" (Roche, 2003) or "convivial" (Morgan, 2006) accountability. This approach does not advocate abandoning established forms of top-down accountability, but rather locating them within a larger set of possible accountability mechanisms. Nor does his argument suggest that all actors should have the same accountability responsibilities. A separation of powers and functions makes it possible for actors to concentrate on particular tasks and functions and to cope with bounded rationalities. This approach is cognizant of the difficulties associated with specialization, for example, problems associated with bounded imagination in the policy process (Braithwaite, 1993). The proposed solution is to nurture interpersonal trust in communities, where there can be open and respectful problem-solving dialogue so as to expand their powers of imagination and allow immediate face-to-face accountability. Alongside this, horizontal or circular accountability processes create spaces in which there can be a mutual checking of the activities of others. Arranging guardianship in a horizontal or circular manner potentially enables all principal actors within the space to check on the activities of others within a context of established trust (Braithwaite, 1993, 1999a). These processes resonate with the idea of "appreciative inquiry" (Cooperrider & Srivastva, 1987).

A fourth, and again associated, idea of promoting accountable practices in polycentric systems is cast as the possibility of accountability as learning. With the emergence of the idea of enterprising government within the broader neoliberal mentality, traditional standards of line accountability and adherence to predefined rules and regulations have been challenged by the ideas of entrepreneurship and output-based performance. This nexus of ideas has been mobilized to argue that questions of accountability might fruitfully be connected to organizational learning theory in ways that redefine accountability processes as activities associated with organizational creativity and innovation (Considine, 2002). This focus on learning conceives of accountability as a continual process of development. It implies that practices need to be structured in ways that combine a degree of permanence, while ensuring flexibility and space for change (Courville, 2006).

Considine (2002) suggests that innovative organizational processes can be conceived of as being accountable to the extent that change continues to reflect core values and agreed principles. One might assume that polycentric governance may strengthen learning abilities to the extent that fertile exchanges via a range of different resources, knowledge, and capacities are reinforced within such spaces of horizontal relations. Scholars working within the approach of nodal governance have argued that the issue of innovative and accountable practices in polycentric governance systems might be approached through a focus on principled rather than prescriptive formulas. Accountable practices are seen to be tuned toward a set of "design principles," while not being constrained by universal or context-insensitive rules (Wood, 2006a; Wood & Shearing, 2007).

All the proposed ideas to enhance political accountability in the modern world of plural governance confront particular problems and challenges. Responsibilization may, as already mentioned, easily lead to new and more efficient measures of social control and manipulation, so that reforms strengthen "the new regulatory state" (Braithwaite, 2000a; Harrington & Turem, 2006). Extended accountability measures may confront problems of legitimacy due to the fact that different constituencies evaluate performance by different criteria, which might limit possibilities to harmonize different relations of accountability or to substitute one mechanism of accountability for another (Black, 2008). Attempts to design robust accountability templates through a combination of two or more modalities of control (hierarchy, market, or community) might experience unforeseen interferences, the logic of one modality being disrupted by the modality of another (Scott, 2006). Polycentric governance systems might also increase problems with what Teubner (1987) styled a "regulatory trilemma," in which any attempt to reinforce any of the plural concerns that such systems are usually expected to promote—like efficiency, predictability, and responsiveness—may limit the capacity of the system to satisfy these and other valued outcomes (Marshaw, 2006). Attempts to construct republican solutions to accountability problems may see new relations of domination emerging within horizontal or circular accountability designs, eroding conditions that are necessary to foster open communication and interpersonal trust. Dispersed governance systems may pose new problems of innovation and learning, and enhance existing problems. The complexities of such systems may make it more difficult to see what happened, why it happened, and what the consequences were, and as a result may release skewed or limited learning processes.

The proposals, concerns, and challenges explored in the literature reviewed above became an essential source of critical reflection for the Zwelethemba model builders. Of the many ideas they were exposed to through this literature, the modelers came to put particular emphasis on the opportunities that were opened up by creating conditions for making local communities responsible for their own security governance, so as to draw upon the talents and morality of those regulated, as Braithwaite (1989, 2006a) has so nicely elaborated upon. The modelers felt it was essential to seek new ways of doing this in a manner consistent with the idea of transferring both steering and rowing functions to local communities, and therefore to identify mechanisms of transferring resources along with the devolution of these functions (a development issue we explore at length in Chapter 5). Another crucial source of inspiration was the idea of building a redundant practice of security governance that utilized all available accountability mechanisms, on the hierarchical and horizontal axis, to use the full range of options available to create a robust and resilient accountability model.

In the next section we analyze Zwelethemba and the innovative bottom-up governance initiatives that the Zwelethemba modelers sought to encourage within the context of the values and understandings they brought to this process. Their initiatives sought to make creative use of the possibilities for reshaping accountability within the context of multilevel and multinodal governance.

## The Zwelethemba Experience—Accountability Mechanisms and Challenges

To explore the extent to which the modelers had generated accountable local practices through the institutions of peace committees, Froestad interviewed members of the committees to see how they conceived of the model and their own role within it. He analyzed the interactions at a number of peace gatherings along with quantitative material regularly collected as part of the model to establish how community members felt they had handled their cases at the gatherings.

Many empirical studies within other arenas have shown that there is often a gap between what people say they do and what they actually do (March, 1986; Brunsson, 1989). To measure how accountable a practice is it is therefore advisable to explore both role conceptions and role practice. Gatherings were attended and a series of interviews of committee members, disputants, and participants from the local community were conducted in 2003 and 2004 to explore how the members of the peace committees thought about the principles and the values of the model and their own role in practicing it.[1] To investigate how successful the model was in creating outcomes consistent with its values and objectives, the following exploration also draws on the data obtained by the 21 peace gatherings that were attended by a Xhosa-speaking research assistant, and transcribed and translated into English. As we mentioned in Chapter 3, this investigation showed that all the gatherings, except for one, were facilitated in a manner that was clearly within the limits set by the code of good practice and the peacemaking steps. We will discuss the circumstances of the deviant case in detail in this chapter.

When asked how the principle of abstaining from adjudication is enacted in practice, most peacemakers emphasized the "how to do it" technology set out in the formal procedures of the peacemaking steps. These steps were workshopped with peace committees in preparing them to engage in peacemaking, and they were used by the Community Peace Program (CPP) in the coaching of peace committees that followed reviews of committees' practices, if problems in applying the model were detected. Together with the code of good practice these steps constituted the core of the model.

The steps provided peace committee members, who were convening gatherings, a framework within which they developed a repertoire of questions to mobilize the voices of the disputants and others attending gatherings. These procedures place responsibility for finding a solution that will promote a better tomorrow with those attending the gathering and not with the peace committee members alone, whose role it was only to facilitate the gatherings. The way in which peace committee members conceived of their role is nicely articulated in the following comments by members of the Mbekweni Peace Committee.

> Yes, I have the experience now. But I must still be able not to work as a judge. I must ask the questions that contribute to the solution, but I must remember not to be a judge. I have some questions to ask, like, "What do you think that the PC can do for you?" And the second question, digging the root cause, we can ask, "What do you think caused this to happen?"

We read the statements [of the disputants] first. We ask if they have something to add. But we also ask them, "Is there nothing you have forgotten?" And we also ask the disputants, "How do you think we [the participants at the gathering] can deal with this, how can we help you?" so that we will have their input.[2]

The basic rules and principles of the model allow for some local adaptations as to how the core technology is practiced. Members of the Nkqubela Peace Committee, a township within the Robertson municipality, mostly composed of a group of engaged community youngsters, had a tendency to emphasize and reflect upon the constructive role they themselves played in the peace process. The following statement, that emphasizes the skillful nature of the work of the committee members, serves as an illustration:

I have participated in approximately four hundred peace gatherings, chaired in half of them. None of the disputes are the same. I am much better in chairing now. As chair, you must check, in order to get the right solution. First, you must test; get an index of the dispute. You must have a plan for the gathering. I must try to see if I can start myself, or if I should let others speak first. Try to see what kind of style you can use, how you can plot the meeting, seek the right way to a solution.[3]

Nonetheless, while they might have sought to orchestrate events to increase the likelihood that participants would develop solutions, peacemakers typically demonstrated a firm commitment to the principle of never engaging in adjudication themselves. Their proper role was conceived as being limited to facilitating and controlling the peace process.

The model sets out both substantive and procedural rules that were designed to promote the mobilization and availability of local knowledge. In many ways, from the perspective of the model and its objectives, the procedural rules are most critical because the actions encouraged by these rules are likely to impact most directly on the mobilization of particular kinds of knowledge. The interviews suggested, however, that members of the peace committees were explicitly aware of the substantive rules—when asked about rules that guide their actions, members were most likely to refer to the code. This, however, as our observations made clear, did not mean that the model's procedural rules did not guide their activities. These rules were deliberately embedded in the forms members were required to complete (see the Appendix). They also became embedded within the habitual procedures that committees developed and used to guide practice within gatherings. Compliance with both these sets of rules was encouraged and audited through the Community Peace Program's review and incentive processes (see above and below).

The issue of the explicitness of rules is significant, as there was a tendency in review processes for members to want to focus on explicit rather than embedded rules. There are advantages and disadvantages to this when making decisions as to how explicit rules should be. On the one hand, being embedded allows rules to become part of the social and institutional "architecture" (Shearing & Stenning, 1981; Lessig, 1999). Embedded rules are useful in creating a "habitus" (Bourdieu & Wacquant, 1992) that structures behavior. On the other hand, if a serious slippage of conformity with embedded rules occurs, there is a danger that these "architectural rules," precisely because they are implicit, may be more difficult to clarify and mobilize in remedial processes that seek to get the process "back on track," because the track is implicit, and thus in some ways invisible. There is no simple solution to this dilemma. It rather points to a tension that has to be managed continually.

An equally important measure of accountability was the extent to which the disputants and others who attended the gatherings felt that they were treated fairly, and that their cases were managed constructively, what Tyler (2005) has called procedural justice. An analysis of 3,271 exit interviews conducted by the CPP from February 2000 to June 2008 confirmed a high degree of satisfaction by "clients." However, since these were ad hoc rather than random interviews, they may be biased in ways that we are not aware of.

When asked if the process the peace committee followed was fair, 96% answered "yes, very," 98% felt that the dispute had been resolved quickly enough, and 95% indicated that in their view the peacemaking process had improved the matter "a lot."

Clearly, while a plurality of resources can be brought together to create effective governing mechanisms, as the model seems to make clear, this approach brings with it its own regulatory requirements and difficulties (Wood & Shearing, 2007). However, the main strength of the Zwelethemba model—as measured by interviewing committee and community members and by analyzing the concrete interaction taking place at peacemaking gatherings—appears to be that it situates local security governance within a strategic and normative framework that works to keep these practices within limits and tuned toward core values. What the Zwelethemba model's processes make clear is that it was possible to hold many thousands of gatherings that, with the exception of a very small minority, remained within regulatory boundaries.

How was this possible? More specifically, what features of the model were responsible for maintaining such a high degree of regulatory compliance? In what follows we analyze each of the main modalities of regulation that the model includes.

## Communal Accountability

The Zwelethemba model includes, as already mentioned, an essential component, a regulatory tool in the form of a code of good practice. This code operates as a constitutional framework that was intended to guide and constrain what takes place at gatherings and during the course of the model's processes more generally. It was also intended to establish a common language, and a set of meanings, that would be routinely used in constituting cases and in acting on them. The code, along with the peacemaking steps, which set out how gatherings and their surrounding processes were to be enacted, was intended to structure the actions of peace committee members to encourage them to act in ways that embodied the values that guided the Zwelethemba modelers and that they had hoped that the model would promote, as it was implemented in case after case. Peace committees were typically formed after a community meeting—sometimes a general community meeting, often with scores of people in attendance, and at other times smaller meetings of interested persons—in which the objectives of the model were introduced. In the initial stages of establishing peace committees, external coaches (either from the staff of the CPP or members of neighboring peace committees) assisted new committee members to develop facilitative skills. Once a committee had been established, internal coaches were identified to ensure that learning was both localized and continuous.

To ensure transparency, peace committees made known what procedures would be used, for example, by publicizing widely the code of good practice and the steps that constitute the model and that peace committees were required to adhere to in their work. This was also done at the outset of each peace gathering, when the code was read aloud and the order of events made known. The code and steps, as key features of the Zwelethemba model, are intended to shape action in different ways. The code is designed to help establish a sensibility "out of which action flows," while the steps are intended to function more as a "recipe book" that sets out the actions to be followed (Shearing & Ericson, 1991). The purpose of publicizing these regulatory tools in both the ways just noted is to ensure that those who will be involved in the model's processes can play a role in ensuring that peace committee members are held to account for their actions in ways that will regulate them.

Because of the basic rule that solutions must never be enforced, but freely embraced by all disputants, there are clear limits as to how far the committee members can go in offering concrete advice and guidance. In commenting on these limits a respondent warned against the potential consequences of a too active or advisory role for committee members.

You know usually we don't. We don't give advice. We don't provide that service.... It is not our place and it is not our role. Even if it is advice they are
looking for.... That is not what we are here for. You can't deal with things by
taking them in your own hands. And it is one of our rules. You can't advise
because you don't know where your advice is going to go ... that person goes to
another person saying "the PC told me to do that," then the whole community
is implied in it. Because of one PC member, it can end up in one community
problem. So then, you mustn't mess directly with people's problems by giving
advice.[4]

Some experienced committee members claimed that they had developed a
capacity to anticipate the difficulty and complexity of new cases and to know how
to take the peace process forward and look for solutions. The following statement
by a member of the Nkqubela Peace Committee serves to illustrate this point:

I have chaired more than a hundred peace gatherings. I do it better than before,
I'm doing more of both, chairing and dispute facilitating. I have to know if this
is going to be a heavy dispute or not, how complicated. When people want to
speak they must raise their hands. If the chair sees that the dispute is not so
heavy, he will say, "I need only three to four hands." It is also important not to
waste time unnecessarily. I have much more ideas in my head now, usually I
can easily see the way forward.[5]

As peace committees accumulated knowledge they developed expertise in facilitating conflict resolution. This creates a potential difficulty—a
tension with the core principles of the model, as a hierarchy of the value of
local knowledge might become entrenched. The concern here is that committee members may come to think of themselves, and their capacities, as
more important than the voices and experiences of local community members whose engagements are precisely what the model seeks to accomplish.
In the coaching that takes place through review processes this potential is
frequently identified and discussed. This potential is nicely illustrated in the
following statement.

A chair, a facilitator, he or she must be someone who tries hard, someone who
tries to be clever. The chair is the head and the body of the process; it is a very
important role. He or she must be able to see the way forward, must be one
who knows what to do.[6]

It is precisely such statements that the CPP, through its monitoring processes, sought to pick up and use as a basis for discussion about the core values
of the model during review processes. To build trust and credibility it was
important that committee members knew what their role ought to be, in terms
of the model's prescriptions, and were good at practicing it. As Christie (1977)

underscores, specialization in conflict resolution entails the risk that functions required come to be seen as ones that can only be provided by experts.

A statement that fits better with the core values of the model is the following:

> I have facilitated 40 to 50 cases. The facilitator, he or she would chair the meeting. The facilitator is just there to guide, he or she is not a decision maker. The facilitator is not the most important person, it is all the participants at the gathering.[7]

In the last statement the peace committee member clearly conceived of himself as a less important figure in the resolution process than community participants, who, in terms of the principles of the model, ought to be viewed as the primary source of knowledge and experience that needed to be mobilized in the search for peace. This tension between the value of local and expert knowledge (albeit the knowledge of local experts) was a site of constant engagement within the workings of the model and one that required ongoing attention if the values of the model were to be realized.

## Directly Deliberative Accountability

Roche's (2003) study of a range of restorative justice programs revealed a number of accountability mechanisms at work in participatory forms of governance. He argued that critics of such forms of governance have overlooked the presence of the sort of informal accountability mechanisms in the deliberations of restorative meetings that we have identified. When restorative encounters are working at their best, Roche argued, the processes of negotiation and collective problem solving contain their own in-built form of immediate and mutual "deliberative accountability." In such settings people are required to give reasons for whatever they propose; they have to accept that arguments will at some point be viewed as more reasonable and carry more weight than others—including, of course, their own. In musing on this, committee members often observed that the setting of a peace gathering, if the steps were followed, tended to foster sincerity and made it difficult for participants to maintain strategic or opportunistic stances.

> At the peace gatherings, I think many people are affected. We see that they do their best to help us solve a problem. If you come with a friend, he will also be affected. He will not only support you, but correct you if it is right, tell the truth. Outside, before a meeting, we understand that people are sometimes plotting, making alliances. But the peacemaking changes things. Attitudes are changed, people come to the truth. Afterwards, when we ask them they will admit that they had plotted, but that they failed to keep it up.[8]

As we have noted, an essential principle of the model is to ensure that each peace committee engages in frequent assessments and evaluations of their own practice independently of any external review, which during the implementation period of the model was conducted by the CPP.

> We usually sit down and evaluate a case, if we got a good decision. We do an assessment, talk through the case. This is to keep the good things and to get rid of the bads. A bad approach would, for instance, be that you are not listening, that you are stopping people. Good ones may be the way we try to work together. It is important to help each other. If somebody is a slow thinker, to encourage, not to embarrass him or her in front of the disputants.[9]

Both the interviews and the transcripts of peace gatherings attested to Roche's view, developed following his research on peace committees, that there was a viable mechanism of horizontal deliberative accountability at work in the informal meetings encouraged by the CPP and other restorative justice programs. As argued by Braithwaite (2006a), the accountability of one actor present at such a meeting to the others in the circle often works better than the hierarchical accountability mechanisms relied upon by prosecutors and courts. It is to this issue of horizontal accountability that we now turn.

## Horizontal Accountability

The Zwelethemba model views peace committees as privately organized security nodes operating in a plural security landscape consisting of a variety of governing nodes, public and private, that the committees relate to, cooperate with, and to some extent, compete with (Johnston & Shearing, 2003). Peace committees, as with any other nodal player within such a governance landscape, are thus motivated to find ways of institutionalizing themselves as valued security nodes within a plural governance system.

An evaluation report on the work of the Community Peace Foundation (Whande & Nordien, 2006), commissioned by the Finnish government, indicated that local councilors and political structures like the South African National Civic Organization (SANCO) and Community Police Forum (CPF) had mixed feelings about the operations of the peace committees. To ensure the legitimacy of the peace committees in the community as a whole the CPP, over the years of the operation of peace committees, sought to avoid becoming aligned with any political structures. This proved to be difficult within the polarized landscape that so often defined and still defines South African politics. The CPP recognized that to some extent some of the local politically related organizations—structures within the local South African parlance—such as street committees and SANCO, with origins in the struggle and the campaign, especially during the 1980s, to make South African cities under apartheid ungovernable, at times regarded peace committees as nodal competitors who should be brought under the ambit of their control.

Dixon (2004) has suggested that peace committees, while prospering in townships like Zwelethemba, located on the outskirts of relatively small agricultural towns, might find it much harder to function and preserve their autonomy and accountability in places like Khayelitsha, a well-established community close to the center of Cape Town, where there is an established, diversified, and competitive market for conflict resolution and security management (see Baker's (2008) concept of multichoice policing). The peace committee in Khayelitsha, established in September 1999, provides evidence that confirm Dixon's concerns.

The committee there discovered that it was being actively opposed by the local civic organization and similar community structures because they viewed it as a competitor. While, with time, relations became more harmonious, tensions remained. These tensions—that exist between many such structures—expressed themselves in the competition for securing local funding. One of the reasons for the lessening of tensions proved to be the nature of the peacemaking processes and the impression that they created. As one member commented,

> As they participated in our peace gatherings, they saw and understood. Now we have a good mutual understanding. We get some cases referred from SANCO. They see that it eases their work. We are supported also because of the peace-building activities [activities that provide support to community initiatives].[10]

This reduction of tension was remarked on by a member of SANCO, who in this remark drew attention to the peacemaking activities of the peace committee:

> If we see that a case needs peace more, we may refer it to the PC. Those cases, it would typically be, conflicts between family members and also domestic abuse. In SANCO we have a lot to do, many cases, development projects. We need more time for such work, so the PC has relieved us of some work.[11]

There is no doubt that places like Khayelitsha are more challenging environments within which to establish and sustain peace committees than smaller townships with high rates of crime and conflict, but frequently with a lack of existing community structures that offer security. To strengthen its position within the community the peace committee in Khayelitsha, in response to the political context we have outlined, emphasized both its peacemaking and its peace-building activities. It regarded supporting local initiatives through peace building to be of the utmost importance in securing community support.

The peace making, it is very important, for marketing. The peace making, it's like a bank, but the peace building is more important for support.[12]

Now the PC is growing. In the beginning, we had no implementation of peace-building projects. But from last year, we engaged in a lot in such activities. People here got very impressed. Now we get a lot of applications for sponsoring [that is, from initiatives who are seeking sponsorship], but we do not have the means.[13]

The emphasis on peace-building projects is indicative of how this peace committee sought to adapt itself to institutional surroundings characterized by dense local structures, a competitive security market, and a strong cultural valuation of community progress. In such environments, our findings suggest, legitimacy and support depended on the ability of peace committees to demonstrate their capacity to contribute to collective development projects.

There is a danger, of course, that if the basic function of peacemaking, as the comment above makes clear, is perceived to be important for marketing, it might suffer if it becomes regarded merely as a "bank" for more essential activities. As one participant remarked at the monthly review meeting in May 2003, "If peace making is to be a bank, that will surely be done quickly."[14]

There were no signs that this peace committee was, given its political context, drifting away from the core values of the model. Members of the Khayelitsha Peace Committee demonstrated a good understanding of, and commitment to, the basic principles upon which the Zwelethemba model has been built. Interviews confirmed that the principle of abstaining from adjudication was a core value and had become a marker of a common identity that members of the committee frequently commented upon to distinguish between themselves and other local dispute resolution structures. The following comment from one of the members is illustrative in this regard:

I was in SANCO before, I was very respected. But here we are not doing things as in SANCO. They are judging, there the aim is only payment, not peace. We are seeking solutions reflecting the disputant's wills. When new members come from other community structures, from SANCO, ANC, ANC youth league, or from the political parties or the police forum, we often need to correct them. Those structures, they make judgments, not from the disputants, but by majority decisions. It is very different from what we are doing.[15]

## Hierarchical Accountability

While a fundamental idea of the Zwelethemba experiment was to avoid prioritizing established hierarchical forms of thinking, the model does, of course, along with scholars such as Braithwaite (1993, 2000a, 2002), recognize their regulatory value and does, accordingly, integrate hierarchical modalities of regulation and control into the model's processes.

## Accountability Relations Between the Peace Committees and the Community Peace Program

The Community Peace Program used the network of arrangements we have just described to regulate the activities of committees in terms of the values and procedures of the model.

The relationship between peace committees and the CPP was intended to be one of interdependence, autonomy, and accountability. On the one hand, local committees independently decided how peacemaking and peace-building processes unfolded. The model provides no specific rules or procedures that specify correct solutions in peacemaking gatherings. While there are rigid rules that set the architecture of gatherings, as we have seen, within this architecture committee members were able to articulate a personal style as well as a style that characterized particular committees. The same applied to peace-building initiatives. Within the architecture established by the code and the steps for both peacemaking and peace building, local peace committees enjoyed high degrees of autonomy and discretion.

An essential part of the Zwelethemba model involves the ongoing collection of data. In addition to reports that are prepared on every case, data collection is also an essential part of the review process, and in particular the reviews conducted by the audit teams (that were deployed by the Community Peace Program during the implementation of the model) to identify and analyze problems. As well as analyzing the reports of gatherings, the audit team may carry out interviews with persons who have attended gatherings to generate an independent source of information about the validity of the reports they receive.

In addition to the above data gathering and analysis, community surveys were conducted at irregular intervals (the intervals were dependent in part on funding) to assess the nature of community problems and in particular to whom community members typically turned (including peace committees) for assistance with their problems. The combination of data was used to assist peace committees in operating and to encourage transparency with respect to their actions.

During the implementation of the model, the role of the CPP was to facilitate, maintain, and sustain the architecture of the model. This ensured that local practices remained within the limits of the general values and principles that the model embraces.

In what follows we consider, briefly, the one peace gathering, among the 21 transcribed cases, that manifested the sort of problems that the carefully constructed regulatory features of the model were intended to prevent. The case is instructive because it illustrates precisely the sorts of problems that can and, as this case makes clear, did occur when the regulatory safeguards, intended to ensure an accountable local practice, break down. Once the Community Peace Program became aware of such problems through its audit procedures, it first took steps to remedy the problems, and if that failed, it decommissioned the peace committee. This typically involved announcing the decommissioning within a community and withdrawing the payments provided to members.

## Disrespecting the Framework

The dispute in question arose in a shebeen (drinking venues, often unlicensed, found across South Africa). A woman suggested that a group of women who had been drinking together collect money to buy a bottle of brandy for the husband of one of them who had given them two bottles. It was agreed that she should buy the brandy, deliver it, and collect contributions. The gift was delivered, but when the money was collected, one of the women did not pay her share. She refused to contribute because she said the husband had abused and assaulted her. This in turn led to a fight between her and the women to whom she owed money. At the gathering one of the women claimed that during the fight she had lost 100 rands that she had had in her pocket.

Despite extensive deliberations at the gathering held to consider this case, no collectively agreed plan emerged and the members of the committee became very frustrated because no resolution to the dispute was forthcoming. It seemed clear to them, however, that the woman who had lost her money ought to have her loss compensated by the other disputant. In response to their frustration members now sought to dictate a resolution.

> This is what will happen if you don't pay this hundred rands, we will go to your house and raid some of your clothes that amounts to a hundred rands, there's no other way.

In this case we see what might be viewed as a reversion to the culture and practices often associated with other popular justice mechanisms.

What possible remedies are there in such cases? No regulatory framework can ensure that problems such as this are eliminated entirely. In this particular case it may well be that the threats remained verbal and no violence was employed because of the culture of restraint within the peace committee that the model had engendered. The prevalence of this sort of problem, as we have already suggested, is also limited by the remedial steps that are taken when a routine review detects deviations from the model's prescriptions.

What this case highlighted, for the review process that in fact followed, was that even the presence of a researcher recording the gathering did not deter the members who clearly regarded their actions as appropriate. The typical remedial action taken in cases of this sort, as was the case here, was supportive coaching. As we have already noted, should this fail (something that rarely happened), this will result in a formal, and public, decertification of a committee or a committee member.

## Accountability Relations to the South African State and Its Constitution

On the one hand, there was no formal hierarchical relationship between the community peace committees and the South African state. Peace committees, as conceived by the model, are civil society entities, not government entities, although they could, of course, be reported to the police for acting illegally. On the other hand, the code of good practice as set out in the model explicitly requires respect for the law and the South African Constitution. In recognizing this peace committees deliberately constitute themselves as having no adjudicative or coercive powers. The Weberian argument of the modelers in support of this was that these powers are properly powers that only belong to state processes and state officials. When peace agreements in cases of conflicts are not honored, or cannot be agreed upon, a peace committee might come to the conclusion that a more coercive solution than the code of good practice permits is appropriate. In such cases the norm was to pass the case on to the police:

> If the man keeps on doing this, he keeps beating his wife ... then we have to put him to court, and then we assist. It is our role to see to it that those things do not happen again, that there is no more of this cruel beating.[16]

What the processes of the model seek to do is carve out a space for local action that is consistent with the architecture set out by South African law in ways designed to enhance democratic self-direction through which local people are enabled to develop and implement plans for creating peace in their lives. Given the contexts within which peace committees operated, this did enable the voices of the poor and the marginalized to be heard in ways that provided for greater self-direction.

An important feature of the code is its implicit argument that deliberative engagements, which draw on notions of deliberative democracy, will produce appropriate and sustainable resolutions to disputes. These deliberations are structured to promote a future orientation that sees members of a peace committee acting as deliberative facilitators rather than as judges. With respect to the South African Constitution the key right mobilized through these processes is the right of South Africans to democratic engagements.

The model's requirement of respecting the law and state sovereignty over the legitimate use of force was creatively used by peace committees, as we suggested earlier in the context of our discussion concerning Galanter's (1981) "shadow of the law" in relation to the model, as a way of encouraging disputants to come to agreement or to acknowledge their own responsibilities for the way in which a conflict had escalated. This was sometimes done by drawing attention to the nested set of institutions of which gatherings were a part—Ayres and Braithwaite's (1992) "pyramid of responsive regulation"—and the possibility that if a problem was not resolved at the peace committee level, the matter would most likely be referred to the police, and through them to the court system.

## Accountability in Learning Processes

Facilitating or chairing peace gatherings is a role that one can introduce via training workshops, but the skills required can only be learned through practice—including the practice of involvement in other community structures, although in this case habits developed elsewhere often had to be replaced with new ones. Peace committee members typically reported that learning these skills was difficult.

> In the beginning I was not confident, I was afraid of doing it. I did not have the experience from other community structures. I had to get the skills, talking skills. Now I got the confidence, I am growing.[17]

The knowledge and capacity that experienced peace committee members used when they facilitated peace gatherings seem to have been derived, on the one hand, from a combination of an accumulated knowledge of a variety of local structures and the practice of peacemaking and, on the other, from a reliance on the tacit knowledge acquired by living in communities like Zwelethemba. Together these experiences provided a jurisprudence-like store of knowledge and capacities.

> What I can do is to use earlier examples, similar cases, as tools. We try to store ideas, points, to use in later cases. It is also important to know the community, the culture, the style of life. If you don't, you might think you do the right thing, but people might think you are rude. We know our people.[18]

The capacity of peace committee members to facilitate and guide peace gatherings toward a resolution was, by and large, based on an analogical reasoning rather than on abstract, theoretical knowledge. Experiences from past cases were used as a basis for understanding and responding to new ones (see Shearing & Ericson's (1991) conception of figurative logic). Experience, however, is not only, or primarily, accumulated on an individual basis. As we have seen, an essential feature of the model is to ensure that each peace committee engages in frequent assessments and evaluations of their own practice to build a collective set of analogical tools.

An important comment made as part of the project evaluation report (Whande & Nordien, 2006) was that bottom-up learning processes in the Community Peace Program had come to a halt, and that the program's major focus had turned to monitoring and regulation of local practice. Our own data confirm these observations.

During the last five years of the program very little changed in the nature of the model other than some fine-tuning, in particular improving the efficiency of the payment processes. The reason offered for this is that nothing came up in the various review processes that would have necessitated a shift in the essential features of the model. This does not mean that there were no concerns expressed by committee members, for example, about the frustration they experienced because of the model's limitations with respect to them taking a directive role in solving a dispute or in resorting to coercion as a motivator. There most certainly were.

Besides the fine-tuning of payment processes, considerable attention was paid to audit mechanisms and shifts were occasionally made to strengthen them—for example, by insisting that more exit interviews with disputants and other participants be undertaken. This activity was directly related to concerns within peace committees, communities, and the CPP, as well as by funders, about the possibility of corrupt practices emerging. This also relates to the competition we have mentioned between different community structures and the desire by both the CPP and committees to be able to demonstrate that they were "squeaky clean."

In summary, over its life cycle, the program shifted gear from *exploring* and creating new technologies to *exploiting* and refining existing ones (March, 1991). Expressed a little differently, the emphasis in the last stages of the program was on sustaining a model that, though perhaps not perfect, had been delivering dispute resolutions that were both effective and legitimate because they had been conducted within the regulatory limits of a core set of values. Also key to the objective of sustainability was an emphasis on ensuring that these objectives were realized through a set of routinely replicable practices that enabled the model to be continually scaled up through the establishment of new peace committees that could quickly and easily learn the values and steps and, through this learning, contribute directly to the safety of their communities.

As discussed in the previous chapter and as we have just reiterated, the focus was more on how to scale up, sustain, and institutionalize the model than on searching for new ways of performing basic functions. We agree with Whande and Nordien (2006), however, that this has meant that there was, to some degree, a tension within the program—as indicated by March's exploitation/exploration dichotomy—between a willingness to constantly improve and develop the model and a reluctance to change it, as it had been working well.

This tension, as March's (1991) discussion makes clear, is a typical state of affairs in operational environments and one that organizations need to carefully manage by walking what is sometimes a fine line between exploration and exploitation. Within this context too a strong emphasis on exploitation will have negative effects on bottom-up learning processes. At the same time, an absence of top-down controls is likely to weaken accountability. Whande and Nordien's (2006) evaluation report in this regard gives a valuable input, as it warns against perceiving the Zwelethemba model as a finished product, and points to the need for further explorations. This tension is something to which the Zwelethemba modelers and those who ran the Community Peace Program were sensitive. Their concern was that if exploration was not reined in but became a constant feature of the model, there would be nothing to "roll out" and the Zwelethemba process would not become a replicable model, but rather a constantly developing set of innovations. What was required, the modelers concluded, was to consciously put a halt to exploration and exploit what had been developed.

## Accountability Through the Market

As we outlined in the first chapter, the payment system that was built into the model enabled committees (and through them members) to earn a monetary payment for every peace gathering held and facilitated according to the code of good practice and the steps—that is, payments were made for acting in ways that were compliant with the model. In taking this position the modelers expressed considerable confidence in the code and steps as vehicles for resolving disputes.

Peace committee members, during the pilot phase, often raised a "free rider" problem. They did so by saying, in effect:

> We do all of this work and the community benefits, but we get no compensation and the members of our households would prefer us to spend the time earning some money instead of doing this work that benefits others without any compensatory benefits to us—we are poor and unemployed and we need to put bread on our tables.

The modelers, and community members involved in the Zwelethemba experiment, were very aware that the obvious solution to the problem—paying participants a salary—was likely to replicate the failures of previous reform programs undertaken by governmental and nongovernmental organizations in South Africa. It was thought, for example, that turning the work into paid jobs was likely to give rise to another layer of "experts," divorced from the community, which might very well create divisive status distinctions. And yet, the modelers recognized the validity of these concerns on both ethical grounds and grounds of sustainability. The Zwelethemba community was, for the most part, an exceptionally poor community, and it was quite simply wrong, in their view, to ask such persons to do voluntary work while all the professionals engaging with them were paid. On grounds of sustainability the modelers realized, through the experience of the experiment itself, that it would not be possible to sustain the involvement of community members in the way the emerging model required, without some form of payment that recognized their work, as well as their worth as people performing a service, that contributed to placing bread on their tables.

The solution developed to respond to this issue recognized the material value of the committees' work to its members and to the community and the costs associated with carrying it out. What was developed was systematic payments for work done, an arrangement that placed very small amounts of money into the pockets of peace committee members. While the amounts were small—these have varied somewhat over the life of the model—they were appreciated both because they recognized the worth of the people involved and their work and because these small amounts indeed made a significant contribution to their tables. In developing this idea the modelers were very aware that this would place an additional demand for funding that would need to be satisfied if the model was to be sustainable.

What was not at the forefront of the modelers' minds when this thinking and experimenting over money was taking place, but that emerged very clearly as a payment system was developed, was that a payment system that was outcome based, and that focused not on the resolution of disputes but on following the procedures of the model, would have very useful regulatory (and hence accountability) implications. Indeed, this payment for work done system emerged, over time, as a central feature of the model's accountability arrangements.

By paying committee members strictly on an outcome basis, modelers sought to blend features of market-based governing mechanisms with what might perhaps be thought of as a Keynesian approach through the use of tax resources from South African governments (both local and national, as well as development aid from foreign governments) to promote economies for enhancing self-direction and the "thickening" of social capital and "collective efficacy" (Sampson, Raudenbush, & Earls, 1997; Sampson, Morenoff, & Earls, 1999; Morenoff, Sampson, & Raudenbush, 2001) within poor communities.

The focus on output was important since the modelers wished to ensure that peacemaking and peace-building processes would be funded by governments who would want an assurance that they were getting what they paid for (value for money) and that processes were in compliance with the standards of the model, that is, that they were normatively compliant. The model was predicated on a "no product, no support" mentality. Peace committee members were to be paid for complying with the basic rules and values of the model. As we have seen, remedial actions were taken when these normative standards were violated and it was discovered that individual members or a whole peace committee were not complying with the model's requirements.

When asked about their motives for joining the Community Peace Program members typically emphasized moral values:

> I liked the idea, that I was going to make a difference to the community, to make it less violent.[19]

> The code of good conduct, I really liked that. The way of mediation, and no judgment.[20]

> I decided to participate to get peace in the community, that was my intention.[21]

Such statements should not be interpreted as an indication that the payment received by peace committees had less or insignificant importance. Members generally earned from 100 to several hundred rands a month, depending on the number of peace gatherings they participated in, and while certainly very little, it had both material and symbolic value. As one member pointed out,

> The income is important to me. In a month I can earn 150 to 240 rands. That is not enough, of course. I always experience money problems.[22]

A productive synergy was accomplished through this complementary set of incentives—normative values combined with material incentives for doing work in accordance with rules and principles. Members also reported that they also saw payments as a token of respect, as an acknowledgment of the importance of the work that they were doing as peacemakers.

There was, however, some concern on the part of peace committee members that they might be criticized for making money out of other people's hardships. Accordingly, some peace committee members reported hiding the fact that they were being paid from fellow residents, fearing that if others knew about these payments it would decrease their legitimacy with some residents (Whande & Nordien, 2006).

An associated use of the incentive scheme that developed over time was its use as a way of limiting the number of committee members who attended gatherings. One of the aims of the model was that it would promote gatherings that residents who were deemed to have the knowledge and capacity to contribute to solutions would attend. This objective was built into several of the steps. Over time it was realized that sometimes committee members would be in a majority. On these occasions they would tend to dominate discussions. While the model encouraged members, as residents, to participate in discussions, it sought to avoid a situation where committee members would establish themselves as experts who would determine action plans.

By paying a single amount per *case* an incentive was created not to have too many members at any one gathering among whom a payment would need to be split. This incentive did not always have the desired outcome, as committee members were often infused with egalitarian values and expressed a desire to attend gatherings and contribute to the discussion even if this would decrease the amount paid to individuals. In Khayelitsha, for instance, it was not unusual to find 10 to 15 members in attendance at a gathering. One member explained his willingness to attend gatherings even if the payment was small.

> The money, it is important. But we are not here to get the money. I had a concern, the community. The members get some money, little payments, it encourages them. But it is difficult to share 200 rands; we are ±20 members. It is a problem with the payment, that we are so many to share, but all persons have a right to participate, we cannot decide who should come and not. It is the code of good practice, we are not to decide.[23]

Here we find an example of how one accountability template with a specific modality (community and solidarity) may interfere with another modality (market and contract work). This draws attention to a feature of the model, namely, its hybridity and redundancy: The model was built on the understanding that its procedures would work together and support each other.

There were, not surprisingly, other consequences associated with the payment mechanism we have outlined that have both pluses and minuses associated with them. The payment system and the concern about normative limits meant that the Community Peace Program had to have sufficient resources to enact the various audit systems that accountability required. This was costly and escalated the cost of running the program in ways that did not always find favor with donors and governments who wanted to see their resources focused primarily on supporting local communities.

In addition, these monitoring requirements led to frequent conflicts between peace committees and the CPP when payments that committees felt were due to them were withheld because, according to the program's auditors, the actions of committee members had not complied with the model's standards. Similarly, there were repeated conflicts around payment delays. Such delays were a particular concern to members who typically depended on payment to meet daily living expenses.

## Conclusion

As indicated by the analysis of a series of peace gatherings, as well as by interviewing both peacemakers and community members, the Zwelethemba modelers succeeded in building a local security practice that was highly regulated and closely in tune with the core principles and values of the model. This is a remarkable achievement, given the context of poverty and despair within which the model operates. In such circumstances there are so many factors that motivate people to look out for themselves or their closest friends or family members, and so many obstacles for collective and accountable governance initiatives to overcome. That it has been possible to build an accountable private security model in this context offers hope of what such dispersed forms of governance have to offer to the state and to society in building a better future for all.

A reason for this success, in our view, has been that the modelers were able to build on new insights offered by a range of accountability scholars as to how to build regulated practices in polycentric environments. They then combined these insights with local knowledge and experiences through an experimental process of model building that enabled principles and practices to emerge gradually through trial and error.

A particular theoretical insight and inspiration in the model-building process was the idea that redundancy in administrative and regulatory practices is desirable. This idea, first explored by Landau (1969) in his seminal paper on redundancy in public administration, has, as we reviewed above, more recently been explored by scholars seeking to use his insights to think about how accountability can be built into more decentered systems of governance (Dowdle, 2006; Scott, 2000; Black, 2008; Baldwin & Black, 2008; Braithwaite, 2006a). The key idea behind this thinking is that redundancy creates robustness and resilience because each of the accountability mechanisms that it is possible to integrate into the governance model works independently. If one accountability modality breaks down, others will still be in place to secure a highly regulated and accountable local practice.

We have in this chapter explored and evaluated the many different accountability mechanisms that the Zwelethemba model sought to integrate to create a highly regulated nonstate security governance system. Some of these accountability modalities are predominantly horizontal structures and are expressed through communal, deliberative, and competitive relations within the local community, while other modalities have been built into more hierarchical structures of oversight and principles for respecting the law and the South African Constitution and its emphasis on human rights. We have explored how the model sought to balance the need for predictability and integrity with the need for constant evolution and learning, and how the modelers sought to combine normative forms of regulation with more material incentive structures that rewarded the peacemakers directly and individually for complying with the principles of the model.

Our most basic interpretation is that each of these modalities, as they operate within the model, tends to support the theory of redundancy; the more accountability mechanisms you can integrate, the more likely it is that you create a robust and regulated system. This does not indicate, however, that Zwelethemba and other governance initiatives attempting to build upon systems of extended accountability measures will not experience their own particular challenges and problems. Our Zwelethemba investigation documented a range of tensions that emerged as a direct consequence of building on a variety of different accountability mechanisms.

One such tension originated, as we have documented, as the conflict between establishing a code of good practice intended to provide a common meaning for all parties involved in dispute cases and coaching peace committee members so that they became experts in understanding the values and principles of the code. This created a need for careful monitoring to ensure that committee members did not start to regard themselves as more important than other participants at the gatherings whose knowledge was as valuable in resolving disputes.

Another tension emerged from the occasional use by peace committee members of the threat of the shadow of the law to encourage disputants to acknowledge their responsibilities and understand the value of coming to an agreement within the confines of the deliberative forums that the model had established. The threat serves as a reminder of the more unpleasant experience that one might undergo if the dispute were to escalate into the state's security net. As we have observed, such a practice in many instances did encourage disputants to admit that they were part of a problem to be resolved. However, it also testifies to the need for constant monitoring to ensure that the "shadow of hierarchy" does not loom too large over proceedings and thus dominate the more communal or deliberative modalities of the model.

A further example of how one accountability template frequently was observed to interfere with another modality was the use of a market mechanism in the form of direct payment to peacemakers depending on their compliance with the rules of the model and how often each of them participated at the gatherings. As illustrated by examples we drew upon in the exploration above, this mechanism, carefully designed as an incentive to reduce the number of peacemakers attending each peace gathering (as this would reduce each peacemaker's share of the pay), tended, in this environment, to interfere with another, more communal modality that underscored equality and the right of all to participate as much as they wanted. Our main interpretation is that the model was able to combine the use of normative values and material incentives in ways that were mostly synergetic from an accountability point of view. As we have outlined above, however, the payment mechanism also tended to produce unforeseen conflicts and consequences that frequently drew heavily on the limited managerial and administrative resources of the model.

The Zwelethemba experiment sought to build an accountable model of security governance built on notions of hybridity and redundancy, integrating a range of accountability mechanisms in the hope that all of them would work together, support each other, and compensate for each other when one of the modalities failed or needed an overhaul. Our observations showed that this hybridity created tensions, but also that such tensions could be managed, even within a model like Zwelethemba, which drew on a very limited amount of administrative and professional resources. The model was not, as we have argued, designed to be perfect, but to build a highly regulated practice of nonstate security that kept local practice within the confines of the model's values and principles. Recent ideas of how to build redundant practices within polycentric systems of governance became a crucial source of inspiration for the modelers in developing their security model. When it comes to building accountable nonstate security in challenging environments, the model does seem to have a lot to offer.

## Endnotes

1. The empirical investigation was designed as a comparative study of three peace committees conducted in April and May 2003; the Nkqubela Peace Committee, located outside Robertson, a town two hours' drive east of Cape Town; the Khayelitsha Peace Committee, located on the Cape Flats; and the Mbekweni Peace Committee, located outside Paarl. The study consisted of eight interviews of individual peace committee members and two peace committee group interviews, eight interviews of disputants and other community members, plus attendance at five peace gatherings. A follow-up study was conducted in March to June 2004, consisting of five interviews of experienced committee members, eight interviews of new recruits, five of whom were interviewed a second time, two peace committee focus group interviews, one interview of a disputant, plus attendance at three gatherings.
2. Member of the Mbekweni Peace Committee (Lonwabo), group interview, May 2003.
3. Member of the Nkqubela Peace Committee, interview, April 2003.
4. Member of the Mbekweni Peace Committee, interview, March 2004.
5. Member of the Nkqubela Peace Committee, interview, April 2003.

6. Member of the Nkqubcla Peace Committee, interview, April 2003.
7. Member of the Khayelitsha Peace Committee, interview, May 2003.
8. Member of the Nkqubela Peace Committee, interview, April 2003.
9. Member of the Mbekweni Peace Committee (Lonwabo), group interview, May 2003.
10. Member of the Khayelitsha Peace Committee, interview, May 2003.
11. Member of SANCO, the local civic organization in Khayelitsha, interview, May 2003.
12. Member of the Khayelitsha Peace Committee, interview, May 2003.
13. Member of the Khayelitsha Peace Committee, interview, May 2003.
14. Participant at the monthly review meeting of the Khayelitsha Peace Committee, May 2003.
15. Member of the Khayelitsha Peace Committee, interview, May 2003.
16. Member of the Mbekweni Peace Committee, interview, March 2004.
17. Member of the Khayelitsha Peace Committee, interview, May 2003.
18. Member of the Nkqubela Peace Committee, interview, April 2003.
19. Member of the Nkqubela Peace Committee, interview, April 2003.
20. Member of the Khayelitsha Peace Committee, interview, May 2003.
21. Member of the Mbekweni Peace Committee (Pola-Park), group interview, May 2003.
22. Member of the Mbekweni Peace Committee (Lonwabo), group interview, May 2003.
23. Member of the Khayelitsha Peace Committee, interview, May 2003.

# Human Rights in Development

5

We now turn our attention to the value of development. In South Africa social and economic development, particularly as it relates to the hope of eradicating poverty, is seen as crucial to the future of the nation, and is often perceived as the goal that trumps all other governmental agendas. Public policies in most areas tend to legitimatize themselves by pointing to the positive effects they are assumed to have for alleviating poverty.[1] A public and scholarly debate on conditions for development in a globalized world, and in particular on the critical role of the institutions and agencies of the South African state, emerged with the transition to democratic rule (see Edigheji, 2010; Bond, 2005, 2006; Maharaj, Desai, & Bond, 2010). The Zwelethemba modelers were very conscious of this debate, realizing that if the security governance model they sought to build were to become a success, it had to face up to the challenge of development in the sense of finding ways for mobilizing resources and enhancing capacities within the local communities where it operated. A particular concern of the modelers, as we have already argued in the previous chapters, was how to support development in a manner that balanced the need for local autonomy and self-directedness with broader cosmopolitan values, in particular the values of universal human rights. In this chapter we explore how the modelers faced this challenge, and the extent to which the practices that unfolded actually can be perceived as having contributed toward development within South Africa. As in the previous chapters, we begin this exploration by first turning to the scholarly debate on development, its perceptions and conditions.

## No Development Without a Strong State

Development, as it has often been conceived, is about how to catch up—how developing nations can close the gap with the developed, "mature," or modernized nations of the world. Looking for conditions for development, the debate has primarily been on the role of the state versus the role of the market (Mjoeset, 2007; Kohli, 2003, 2004; Fukuyama, 2004; Chang, 2003; Reinert, 1999; Osborn & Gaebler, 1993; Friedman, 1953, 2002). This debate has extended more recently to include a discussion of the importance of a vibrant civil society (Opoku-Mensah, Lewis, & Tvedt, 2007; Zuern, 2002; Howell &

Pearce, 2001; Bratton, 1994; O'Donnell & Schmitter, 1986; Putnam, 1993) and on the role of the national (internal state conditions), as in modernization theory (Rostow, 1956, 1960; Apter, 1965; Lipset, 1959; McClelland, 1961), versus the international (the global capitalist system of production and the worldwide system of states), as in dependency theory and world system analysis (Heller, Rueschemeyer, & Snyder, 2009; Wallerstein, 1974, 1980, 2004; Frank & Gills, 1993; Frank, 1967, 1979; Amin, 1976, 1992).

The neoliberal turn of the 1980s and 1990s, while to some extent pinpointing the state as the problem of development (World Bank, 1980, 1981), may more positively be conceived of as a policy not aiming to dismantle the "undeveloped state," but rather as seeking to identify key interventions required to make its government more efficient and less afflicted by factional interests and abuse of power (Hyden, 2005). In practice, however, the structural adjustment policies forwarded by the World Bank and the International Monetary Fund (IMF) became a template for free market-oriented governance, formulated miles away by Western economic bureaucrats with little concern for local context (Greenberg, 1997; Stiglitz, 2002) and surprisingly uninformed about the West's own experience of the importance of autocentric conditions for development (Senghaas, 1982). By the late 1980s, however, international organizations began to admit that structural adjustment policies were worsening the life for the world's poor, and especially so when implemented in countries with limited institutional frameworks or capacity (DeVries, 1996; Mwanza, 1992; Mkandawire & Olukoshi, 1995). The debate on the Asian developmental state (Muscat, 1994; Evans, 1995; Leftwich, 1995; Kulick & Wilson, 1996) and the good governance discourse promoted by the multilaterals from the early 1990s (World Bank, 1992, 1994, 1997; IMF, 1997; see also Woods, 2000) reintroduced the concern for political institutions and restored the central thesis of the development discourse that there can be no development without a state. A strong state, throughout most of the postcolonial period, has been seen as the key to catching up.

## What Is a Strong State?

The literature points to three characteristics that are thought to be essential for a strong state, without which it will not be an efficient mechanism for catching up. First, the state must, as Hobbes (1651/1968) asserted, be a good leviathan. The state must transcend the Machiavellian concern of "how the prince can stay in power" to embrace public rule as enhancing the life and the happiness of the population. Despotic rule in which the state is just an arena for "big man" competition for power or a mechanism for personal enrichment will not do. A national project of improving life and the happiness of the population must be installed (Foucault, 1991, 2008; Lemke, 2001; Dean,

1999; Gordon, 1991; Burchell, Gordon, & Miller, 1991). While it is usually assumed that democracy and democratization are essential to realize such a project, the debate on the Asian development state might indicate that there may be more than one solution to this particular problem (Polidano, 2001; Weiss, 2000; United Nations Development Program (UNDP), 2000; Woo-Cumings, 1999; Leftwich, 1995; Evans, 1995; Johnson, 1982).

Second, the state must have governing capacity. A long scholarly debate concerns what this capacity consists of and how it is developed. Weber (1978) was among the first to understand the importance of the state for development. He focused on the role of its permanent organization, the public administrative system. Weber held the German office model as superior to earlier collegial forms and regarded bureaucracy and a hierarchy of offices as the most rational form of state organization. A central insight of Weber, however, was that bureaucracy also has its potential vicious sides, such as a strong tendency to maintain the status quo and to move beyond its proper borders. Bureaucratic tendencies had to be balanced against opposing forces both within the state, by politics and Parliament, and in society, by private entrepreneurs and civil associations, like the political parties (Weber, 1947). Later research confirmed Weber's emphasis on the important role of the state bureaucracy for development and deepened his insight into the role of scientific knowledge and expertise. It became an accepted fact that expansion of the forms of scientific knowledge a state can draw upon, beyond law, is a key determinant to its capacity for rational and autonomous interventions in society (Albrow, 1970; Skocpol, 1973; Wilson, 1989; Evans, 1995; Woo-Cumings, 1999). A danger, however, is that such knowledge is used to dominate other forms of knowledge and perspectives in society. Scott (1998), in *Seeing Like a State*, documents how (early) modernized states tended to standardize their social environments to facilitate their own centralized rule. He documents the often negative effects of such interventions when they were based on an uncontested faith in the superiority of science and rationality and when the capacity or opportunity of groups in society to oppose such policies was limited.

Jacobsen (1960) suggested that a balanced adherence to different role expectations by state officials—loyalty to the political leadership, equal treatments of clients, and professional autonomy—was crucial to good governance. He revised Weber by arguing that bureaucratic rule orientation is insufficient for development. The state bureaucracy needs to combine "rule of law" virtues with close contacts to its clientele and an active commitment toward its welfare needs (Jacobsen, 1964). With the development of the professionalized state, clients whose interests were not protected by strong, client-oriented professionals would have problems getting their interests acknowledged and managed or regulated by the state in a client-friendly manner (Jacobsen, 1965, 1967). Such groups might be "left behind" in the modernization process, generating poverty and marginalization that sooner or later would become an impediment to further development (Jacobsen, 1967; see also Jacobsen & Eckhoff, 1960).

In a more recent formulation the argument above has been cast as the state having capacity for "embedded autonomy" (Evans, 1995, 1996). As Scott (1998) argues, the medieval state was more or less a blind state, with limited knowledge about its population and their lives. Following the argument above, this will not do for a developmental state; it needs to be "embedded." It requires detailed knowledge about its population and close contacts with private entrepreneurs and other groups in society. However, to the extent that such knowledge is not generated in developmental states due to weak professional knowledge systems that are not granted a degree of autonomy by the political leadership or that have too few or too weak links to the world of its clients, development will be difficult (Appiah, Chimanikire, & Gran, 2004). In addition, the state must have autonomy; it must be able to regulate social relations and develop planning and policies in accordance with long-term development goals, even when this goes against the interests of strong groups in the society. To do this it must have overwhelming power, so that it can enforce its decisions in spite of resistance (Hobbes, 1651/1968). Two arguments are important here. One is that the state bureaucracy must to some extent be insulated from external social pressure and state officials must identify with the developing state and its "catching up" project (Skocpol, 1973; Trimberger, 1978). The debate on the Asian developmental state underscores the virtue of having a coherent cadre of high-status public officials recruited from the best universities who strongly identify with a national project of development (Trimberger, 1978; see also Zamora, 1979; Kim, 1982). Also, the state must have regulatory powers and be able to sanction the free riders that do not adhere to the "rules of the development game." The state must therefore monopolize the legitimate use of force and be willing and able to use it when necessary (Evans, 1995).

The third characteristic of a strong state is that it must have sovereign autonomy in the system of states; it cannot be too dependent on other states. The idea that each state ought to have sovereign rule over its own territory and its own population is an idea that in Europe goes back to the Treaty of Westphalia. The treaty had little effect on the European habit of interstate war making, however, and it was confined to regulating the relation between states on the European continent. The treaty did not assume the same sovereign status to preside in non-European political orders, many of which, as we know, were turned into European colonies. The granting of formal independence and sovereignty to the colonies after World War II did not solve the problem of state autonomy, as the state system still consists of stronger and weaker states, and as other strong global players have emerged. It is therefore still considered to be crucial that a state is able to shape its own policies for development based on its own experiences and conditions and not be dictated to by other states or other external agents like the big corporations or the multilaterals. Dependency theory conceives of this as being a major challenge (Frank, 1967; Amin, 1974, Cardoso & Faletto, 1979). As we indicated in the previous section this approach generally assumes that external conditions, such as a state's position within the system of states or within the capitalist economic system, are more important than internal ones in determining its development prospects. Dependency theory postulated that development is only possible, given the emergence of the global capitalist core of states, where synergistic relations evolve between agriculture and light and heavy industries, while on the periphery capital investments generate enclave industries for exportation of raw materials or consumption goods with weak connections to other sectors of the economy, leading to underdevelopment. For emerging economies, the approach stipulated only one possible solution: disassociation from the international market combined with socialism (Amin, 1976, 1991; Frank, 1979). Contemporary theories building on the dependency approach tend to argue that globalization makes developing states even more trapped in international relations of dependency (Koehler & Tausch, 2002; see also Topik, 1998).

The dependency school has been criticized by scholars who agree that peripherization is a key developmental problem, but who challenge the determinism of the approach. Senghaas (1982), in his work on how Europe in the nineteenth and early twentieth centuries responded to the challenge of catching up with England, which was by far the most advanced capitalist state of the age, observed how different states chose different economic strategies based on their different strengths, contexts, and opportunities. The strategy of opening up the economy for unlimited international economic competition—as the World Bank and the IMF have urged contemporary developing nations to do—was the exception, followed only by Switzerland and the Netherlands. All other states adopted policies of selective engagement, trying to protect key sectors from a too competitive global environment, and only gradually opening sectors up for international competition as producers' abilities to compete increased. Senghaas emphasizes the importance of states' capacities for flexible policy making: moving into international markets when opportunities arise, and changing strategy to a reliance on home markets in periods of international economic deprivation. As such his study confirms the significance of developing states having a capacity for autonomous policy making in international environments. However, Senghaas and other recent commentators (Reinert, 1999; Mjoeset, 2007) clearly document how this capacity relies on both external and internal conditions. A key message is that how the state relates to its own society is significant to its capacity for autonomy even on the international level. The character of sociopolitical domestic relations is crucial. Development states that manage to build synergetic relations with their own societies will also increase their capacity to be strong and autonomous players on the global scene (Evans, 1995, 1996).

Two conclusions are consistent with the exploration above. The first is that, while a strong state is still crucial to development, it cannot do it alone; it is essential that it has the capacity to mobilize resources in society. The second conclusion is that a capacity for development requires that opposing forces within the state and between the state and the society are able to engage in its construction. From these statements a series of critical questions can be derived. Which regulatory functions and forms of service provisions should the state monopolize, and which should it share with or leave to others? What kind of regulatory systems does the state need to put in place that will facilitate a sustained mobilization of social resources for development? What characterizes nonstate forms of governance that have the capacity to assist the developing state in "catching up"? All of these questions indicate that a key to development lies in how relations between state and nonstate actors are structured and the synergies that flow from such arrangements (Evans, 1995, 1996; Ostrom, 1990, 1996). Our main focus in this chapter is how private forms of governance may, within the regulatory limits we explored in the previous chapter, assist in building a strong state and a strong nation for development.

## Development and Human Rights

Recent trends in the development discourse point to a lasting problem of state building. Tilly (1985) has argued that Western state building in its early form might be conceived as a form of organized crime. As Fukuyama (2011) documents in his most recent book, *The Origins of Political Order*, this logic of "the state making war, and war making the state," though not a universal trajectory, was clearly also the driving mechanism behind the earliest state building effort in the world, that of the Chinese. State organizations tended to develop as mechanisms to extract resources from society, to control and police the population, and as war machines to conquer new territories. Through colonization and the concomitant struggles for national independence the state model was generalized into a worldwide system of states. However, as states were "governmentalized" to embrace more calculated ways of governing and fostering human life within their territories (Foucault, 1991, 2008; see also Lemke, 2001; Dean, 1999; Rose, 1999), an essential element of state sovereignty remained. Rational state rule as "the proper disposition of men and things towards a convenient end" (Foucault, 1991, p. 95) continued to define the survival of the state as its most fundamental end. In this sense the state, even as it embraced the enhancement of life as a key development goal, continued to conceive its own survival needs as an even more essential state agenda. This had the effect that the state, even as it was governmentalized and democratized, insisted on having the sovereign right to decide who, within its territory, had the capacity for autonomous and responsible action and could thus be ruled through liberty and who had to be ruled in other ways (Valverde, 1996; Buur, Jensen, & Stepputat, 2007). Whenever the state felt threatened it tended to act to oppress or even exclude the forms of life that threatened it (Agamben, 1998).

Recent trends in the development discourse can be perceived as attempts to regulate state sovereignty in ways that set limits to its space for prioritizing its own survival needs at the possible expense of other human values (Douzinas, 2000; Goodhart, 2003; Echavarri, 2003; Sen, 1981; Haq, 1995; Fukuda-Parr, 2003; Alkire, 2003; Rothschild, 1995). Human rights, human development, and human security are discourses that in different ways attempt to reimagine state rule as a *means* to the flourishing of human life, rather than as an end in itself. The movement in international law, economic development, and the security field has been to shift the emphasis from objectives such as state rights, national growth, and state security to human rights, human development, and human security (Alkire, 2003). In so doing these discourses have in significant ways contributed to a reimagining of how we should conceive of development and how it may be attained. In the remaining parts of this chapter we look at trends in these discourses on human rights and explore how the Zwelethemba modelers responded to the visions and challenges about development that each of them embraces. Our argument is that though the Zwelethemba model was not explicitly designed to function as a human rights nongovernmental organization (NGO), it responds to many of the challenges discussed by human rights scholars and practitioners, and therefore has the capacity to assist toward a development aligned with such values.

## Human Rights

In the 1960s and early 1970s the conventional wisdom was that rapid development and human rights were competing concerns, at least in the short run, and that a too strong emphasis on civil, political, cultural, or economic rights would slow down the rate of economic growth and development (Douzinas, 2000). Such arguments, however, proved to be tragically misguided. During the next decades it was generally acknowledged that human rights and development must be seen as fundamentally complementary and mutually reinforcing in all time frames (Donnelly, 1985).

Discourses on human rights have been conceived as the last grand narrative (Alves, 2000) that cuts across national and cultural contexts, characterized as an international communication about human freedom and dignity that can be thought of as signaling an emergent or "overlapping consensus" about justice and core human values in a world of doctrinal fragmentation and insecurity (Donnelly, 2001). One consequence of this, it has been argued, is that "the language of universal rights has been seized by the oppressed and excluded as a weapon in the fight for freedom and dignity" (Goodhart, 2003, p. 959). This claim is not without its critiques, and many scholars have expressed reservations about the continued value of human rights as a source of freedom, critique, and reinvention (Douzinas, 2000; Guilhot, 2005; Stammers, 1995; Forsythe, 2005).

In *The End of Human Rights* Douzinas (2000) maintains that the human rights discourse has been losing its value as an inspirational source of human emancipation, as it has been used to contribute to a language that strengthens state powers and expert knowledge. Baxi (2002) argues that the human rights discourse is being hijacked by powerful groups and that, as a consequence, it is being uncoupled from the suffering and needs of the poor and the oppressed (see also Twining, 2006). Similarly Guilhot (2005) argues that human rights, through a process of "professionalization" and "technical specialization," have been translated into a language of state administration and institutions. Likewise, Stammers (1995, pp. 506–507) argues that this discourse is now almost exclusively tied to states, so that there is now "little more space for thinking about human rights in any other way." As a consequence, private economic powers often evade human rights protections.

These arguments identify human rights as a resource that can be mobilized in a variety of ways for a variety of purposes. Fitzpatrick (2006, p. 15) notes that the "political" elements of rights inhere, at least partly, from the ability rights have to go beyond their existent content. Rights have shown a capacity to be something other than what they were intended to be. This indeterminate or "abstract" character of rights has made them susceptible to occupation by effective powers (Fitzpatrick, 2006). In making this point Guilhot (2005) documents how the United States, under republican rule, transformed the human rights discourse into a mechanism of domination and aggression, tying it to its foreign policy aim of exporting democracy and American institutions. While human rights used to function as external standards held up against government, especially as a guard against an imperialistic foreign policy, today they have been instrumentalized as weapons to legitimate aggressive interventions. Chandler (2001) underscores how the human rights-based approach to humanitarian aid has undermined earlier humanitarian values such as universality and neutrality and has constructed humanism as an ambiguous concept "capable of justifying the most barbaric of military actions" (p. 698). In a similar vein Forsythe (2005) notes how humanitarian arguments were used by the United States to legitimate the invasion of Iraq.

The challenging question, that these and other observers raise, is how to uphold the critical intent of human rights. Central to this challenge is how human rights as a resource may be mobilized by the poor and the oppressed. The growth and expansion of an international network of human rights NGOs has frequently been interpreted as a quiet revolution spawning the emergence of an international civil society (Otto, 1996). However, Smith, Pagnucco, and Lopez (1998) draw attention to important dividing lines within such networks, as Southern NGOs have to work with substantially less access to resources than Northern ones. Mertus (1999) questions the democratic status of the NGOs themselves and argues that many of them operate in ways that may threaten local autonomy. Guilhot (2005) points out that traditional forms of NGO activism have to a large extent been transformed because, in order to be successful, international networks have increasingly been professionalized through lawyers, political scientists, media specialists, and public relations experts. As Robins (2008, pp. 22–24) argues, two schools of thought have emerged as to how NGOs are conceived, one perceiving them as benevolent agencies providing the solution to human sufferings that markets or states are unwilling or incapable of providing, and the other seeing them as ideological conduits of neoliberal policies and global capital. As Robins indicates, however, such sweeping generalizations about human rights-oriented NGOs in either color do not acknowledge the heterogeneous character of NGOs or the complex and varying contexts within which they operate (p. 23).

According to Donnelly (2001) the key to human rights progress in the coming decades lies in creating more creative and effective efforts by a multitude of agencies—states, citizens, and other national and international actors. Freeman (1994) emphasizes the need to conceptualize human rights in a manner that is flexible enough to allow space for the very human creativity it seeks. Langlois (2002) sees the human rights discourse as a tool for cooperation, providing a forum that will permit multicultural traditions of justice to find expression. The call here is for greater and more varied forms of participation that give life to human rights. Preis (1996) makes the point that underlying the "progressive" assumptions of many human rights texts is the often subterranean assumption that development must emanate from centers of powers, such as states or international interests, through a staged process. What is needed, he argues, is better knowledge of human rights as actual existing practices, which accords priority to an understanding of human rights within everyday life and as embedded in different social practices (pp. 13–15).

By raising issues such as these about participation in human rights critics are pointing to the question of how to contribute to finding the spaces that enable human rights to continue to express emancipatory possibilities. How can the poor and the oppressed better use human rights possibilities to promote their emancipation? As Robins (2008) argues, rights have increasingly become the accepted language of political claims in the new post-apartheid South Africa, and political demands have increasingly been formulated as claims of legally and constitutionally based entitlements. The strategies for using "rights talk" to access donor funds or state resources have varied, though, and not all attempts have been equally successful (pp. 165–174). One conclusion seems to be—as the studies conducted by Robins (2008) in South Africa and Appadurai (2000, 2002, 2004) in India seem to confirm—that the most successful forms of political mobilization have recently come in the form of new partnerships between globally linked NGOs and social movements/community initiatives that combine rights-based approaches with attempts to mobilize solidarity and sociability among marginalized populations. A difference, though, is that Robins's extraordinary success story, the South African-based action and treatment campaign, effectively used litigation as a means to access state resources, while Appadurai's (2002) equally successful Shack/Slum Dwellers International (SDI) has to a large extent refrained from such strategies of claims making and confrontation. Instead, SDI has adopted what is referred to as a "policy of patience" that places major emphasis on building and demonstrating its own capacities as a way of seeking to negotiate with state and other authorities from a position of strength.

The Zwelethemba modelers, while acknowledging that different issues of concern for the poor and disadvantaged might require different strategies, forms of mobilization, and partnerships, developed a strategic position that is closely related to that of the SDI. Their model focuses on concentrating knowledge and capacities in nodes that the poor control and building projects and alliances from such a platform. While the Zwelethemba experiment did not engage in the politics of human rights litigation and claims making, its practice was still informed by human rights values, and it sought to explore human rights concerns through its various practices. Through such practices poor communities were mobilized in a process of dispute resolution that harnessed human rights values, as these were locally conceived, as tools in the construction of peaceful existences. While these processes were not developed explicitly to address human rights-related issues, they were still highly relevant to the application of the model, and—as the following exploration will reveal—the experiment can be read as addressing core concerns of the debates we have just reviewed.

## Reconciling Universal Human Rights With Local Norms

In 1947 the American Anthropological Association issued a statement rejecting the idea that the Declaration of Human Rights had universal application,
asserting that "rights of Man in the Twentieth Century cannot be circum-
scribed by the standards of any single culture" (for a more recent discussion,
see Pollis, 1996). Notwithstanding the influence of this position, a number of
scholars have recently begun to look for ways of rescuing the idea of universal human values. In doing so, the challenge has been to steer a path between
strong versions of both universalism and particularism (Twining, 2006). In
developing this line of thought Perry (1997) and Tilley (2000) distinguish
between different versions of the relativist argument. Tilley demarcates
methodological contextualism (the position that every custom, belief, or
action must be studied in the context of the culture in which it occurs) from
the claim of ethical or moral relativism, which holds that any event or action
can only be properly judged or appraised from within the normative context
of the culture within which it arises. Radical relativism leads to a cascade of
absurdities, such that in the end it is by necessity a wrong or ridiculous act to
morally criticize the norms of one's own culture. In challenging radical relativism he notes how some moral statements, like "torturing children, only
for the fun of hearing them screaming is wrong" (Tilley, 2000, p. 529), are
difficult to reject from any cultural perspective. As Perry argues, claiming
that cultural contexts are relevant "is a far cry from claiming that nothing,
no act or failure to act, is bad and nothing is good for every human being"
(Perry, 1997, p. 482; see also Fields & Narr, 1992, p. 20; O'Manique, 1990,
pp. 482–483).

Freeman (1994), in canvassing this issue, distinguishes between those
who emphasize contingency, construction, and relativity, and those who try
to locate objective foundations for human rights in reason or morality. His
own position is to see human rights as contingent while at the same time
insisting that core human rights values, like well-being and freedom, are not
arbitrary, because they are respected across a wide range of cultures (see also
Donnelly, 2001).

Others have sought to reconceptualize how the universal character of
human rights relates to the particularities of diverse collectivities. Langlois
(2002), for example, argues that the concept of human rights does not make
sense without a reference to universalism. The problem for him is that current discourses are often dominated by moral and political interests embedded in Western concerns. A solution for Langlois would be to understand
human rights as "a proposal for the rules under which people who pursue
diverse goals in a complex, rapidly changing and highly inter-dependent
world might hope to live in dignity and peace" (p. 495).

Many of the concerns explored above are similar to the debates that took place in the formation of the Zwelethemba model. These debates were embodied in a process of trial-and-error experimentation. A major concern of the modelers during this process was, as we have already argued, that many participatory forms of governance within local South African communities have had a checkered history, sometimes producing limited change and sometimes being hijacked for repressive ends (Martin, 2012). In response the modelers developed regulatory structures that drew upon popular understandings of human rights. These understandings look to general human rights values as constraints that would regulate the way in which local knowledge and capacity were mobilized. While local knowledge and capacity should be given precedence in problem solving, they should not, the modelers felt, reign supreme. Central to the regulatory constraints (which we explored in more detail in Chapter 4) that the model embeds are the set of steps (rules) that structure the deliberative processes in ways that give all participants rights to be heard and the set of overarching values (seen as having wide community support) in the form of the code of good practice. Universalism was introduced into this code through a reference to the South African Constitution and South African law. The code requires respect for law and the constitution. Within the model this code embodies, and is seen as embodying, a constitutional framework that guides and limits what takes place locally. It establishes a language and meanings that are used in constituting cases and in developing resolutions. At this level of practice the universal and the local are seen as usually complementary. The universal here is understood, however, not as universal values that South Africans, through the processes that had founded a new South Africa, had embraced. The assumption upon which the Zwelethemba model was built was that there had been and would continue to be deliberative processes at the state level that canvassed and then endorsed proposals for values that would be treated by South Africans as universal in Langlois's (2002) sense. The universal here was seen as a product of a democratic state that had the support of local people and local collectivities. The universal-local distinction was seen as a distinction between multiple deliberative forums, with more general forums both setting the frameworks for and trumping more local ones. What the modelers were saying essentially was that they consented to be bound by deliberative processes that they either participated in or endorsed more indirectly—human rights became a matter of nested democracy.

In the case of this process peace committees constitute themselves deliberately as having no adjudicative or coercive powers—arguing that these were properly powers that belonged only to state processes and state officials. For them, acting in ways that respected the human rights of persons meant respecting state sovereignty in those realms—a classic Hobbesian position. What the processes of the model seek to do is to carve out a space in which human rights endorsed by deliberative forums at the state level can be mobilized effectively to enhance democratic self-direction—local people developing plans for creating peace in their lives that enable the voices of the poor and the marginalized to shape courses of action. Within the Zwelethemba model human rights have meaning within nested deliberative forums that promote self-direction.

## Reconciling Tensions Within the Family of Human Rights

A significant arena of debate within human rights discourses has been the extent to which development—economic, social, and cultural rights—is recognized within the family of universal human rights. Most scholars agree that there has been relatively little practical success in getting these rights included as genuine universal human rights—something incidentally that the South African Constitution formally does. It is indicative that the relation between the human rights discourse and the prestigious Millennium Development Goals project of the UN is described as "ships passing in the night" (Alston, 2005, p. 755). Neither the human rights nor the development communities have embraced this linkage with enthusiasm or conviction (Alston, 2005). Human rights continue to be debated mostly at large international conferences and monitored by the UN's Human Rights Commission, while development policies are still formulated and implemented by completely different institutions (Sano, 2000). Human Rights NGOs, having had a significant voice within the human rights discourse during the last couple of decades, continue to focus almost exclusively on civil and political rights. Skogly (2002) suggests that the main reason that the UN and the human rights community continues to neglect economic and social human rights is that it is poor people that by far most frequently experience violations of these rights. Poor people have been left out in the drafting and implementation of the instruments designed to protect such rights.

A link between development and rights has indeed been forged, but this has taken place through the linkage of aid from wealthy nations to the willingness of host nations to support and promote the established conception of human rights as centered on civil and political rights (Skogly, 1990). This approach to rights has been linked within some of the rights literature to structural adjustment programs promoted by international agencies such as the World Bank and the IMF, as both sets of initiatives prioritize Northern concerns over those of the global South. This has led to arguments from the South that Southern regions should be wary of adopting policies in any arena that do not arise out of and resonate with their own concerns (Udombana, 2000).

Mary Robinson (2004), the UN's high commissioner for human rights from 1997 to 2002, argues that there should be a link between economic, social, and cultural human rights and practices that promote decision-making processes that include the poor and the marginalized. In arguing along these lines Felice (2004) questions the possibility of this happening so long as decisions as to what should count as human rights are left to forums in which states are the principal players. Similarly, Wellman (2000) argues for finding institutional mechanisms that will permit the inclusion of a plurality of actors, knowledge, and institutions that extend beyond states. This will require institutional arrangements at various levels that will facilitate this. In promoting this argument Yamin (2005) proposes a search for innovative strategies in human rights that moves out of the entrenched dichotomy between the public and the private, identifies how power can be devolved to different groups, communities, and individuals through their participation in decision-making forums that provide for an authentic transfer of power from the state, and establishes forms of collaboration between traditional human rights communities and a broad range of other groups and social movements (pp. 1232–1239).

As the development of the Zwelethemba model was motivated by a similar interest in building institutional arrangements outside of state institutions that would promote participatory decision making, we now turn once again to this set of processes and their implications for shifting beyond an understanding of rights that is constructed around political and civil rights.

At the heart of the Zwelethemba model's process is the notion that economic, social, and cultural rights count. Or, put differently, civil and political rights are of value if they are associated with processes that promote economic, social, and cultural values at local levels. Human rights within the logic of the model must be seen to promote not simply individual rights but community well-being. There are several forms of community well-being that the Zwelethemba model promotes—these include the well-being that comes from the construction of peace as a foundational order and the well-being that emerges when self-direction is realized. In addition, the model seeks to put funds that can be used to promote development directly into the hands of peace committees, which are required to dispense these resources in ways that respond to local needs and concerns as measured both through the deliberative processes of peace gatherings and through community surveys and gatherings that bring people together specifically to identify collective needs and concerns. For every dispute that is resolved within the constraints of the regulatory framework a small amount of money is accredited to a peace-building account to support developmental initiatives.

In 2009 alone the peace committees handled 23,943 peacemaking cases, which means that more than R2.3 million was generated as income for the members of the committees and their families. In addition, the same year more than R1.1 million was used for peace-building initiatives by the 241 peace committees then in operation. Committee members were encouraged to develop plans in collaboration with other community members and local service deliverers that use these funds to lever other resources, both financial and in kind. The idea lying behind this is to tie a dispute resolution or peacemaking process that respects individual human rights to a process that promotes economic, social, and cultural well-being through peace-building initiatives. The objective was to relate self-direction to development by establishing the possibility of self-directed development. This focus on peace building means that the emphasis was not simply on disputes, but included broader issues such as public health, food, shelter, waste management, education, recreation, and the like. Peace is extended beyond a Hobbesian focus on the provision of physical security to more general questions of rights to security and development (Wood & Shearing, 2007).

As Roche (2002) argues, one critique of informal justice schemes has consistently been that they fail to address the problems that underlie crimes and offending, such as unemployment, poverty, and family breakdown. Some critiques go even further, arguing that such programs actually compound the problems, by distracting attention from them or transforming potential resistance into "massive non-rebellious normality" (Fitzpatrick, 1988, quoted in Roche, p. 535). A novelty of the Community Peace Program, as Roche sees it, was that it avoided this criticism as it went further than simply addressing individual disputes or crimes, and attempting to address the underlying conditions that cause insecurity and unrest, and prevent development.

As Goodhart (2003) has suggested, one way of thinking about the universality of human rights is as a question of effectiveness in achieving particular values. If this argument is accepted, as we believe it should be, this requires us to distinguish between different ways of structuring processes that we organize to attain such values. Uncoupling values from processes opens a conceptual space that allows one to scrutinize the extent to which such values can be effectively realized through different kinds of institutions and mechanisms (Wood, Shearing, & Froestad, 2011). It is quite possible that justice is delivered and human rights protected through forms of practices that are not explicitly established or normally recognized as promoting such values.

Our aim in this section has been to argue that the Zwelethemba model, while not conceived or referred to as a human rights NGO, in practice promotes a range of such values. We have underscored the capacity of the model to reconcile core tensions in human rights, as conceptualized by scholars and practitioners. The model negotiates a terrain of nested peacemaking and peace-building forums that mobilize local knowledge and norms within the limits of rules and principles associated with universal rights and that allow for a dual approach to civil/political and developmental human rights. What we have argued is that a bottom-up perspective, emphasizing the relevance and potential of local human rights-oriented practices, such as the

Zwelethemba model developed by poor and marginalized communities in South Africa, might have something to offer the human rights discourse and the human rights community. The time seems to be ripe to embrace a nodal approach to human rights. It is becoming more and more obvious that a state-centered focus is insufficient (Leman-Langlois & Shearing, 2010). The future challenge lies in finding new ways of building alliances among a range of actors, knowledge, and capacities in human rights—these are challenges similar to the ones that have emerged with respect to the development of polycentric governance initiatives (Burris, Kempa, & Shearing, 2008).

## Human Development

Adam Smith (1776) held that the wealth of nations depended on the proportion between the income produced and the number of people who consumed it. This concern of Smith is still alive, as indicated, for instance, by the worries that the sinking proportion of the workforce in modern societies will not be able to support the elderly or others who do not work. The use of per capita gross national income (GNI) to stipulate the wealth and borrowing eligibility of national states is another indication of the continued relevance of Smith's original formulation (Echavarri, 2003). Modernization theory in the 1950s and 1960s delved into Smith's core issue of how to increase collective well-being, pinpointing technological advances as the key mechanism to expand the wealth of states and regions. Industrialization through market mechanisms became the dominant thesis of how to stimulate economic growth. Lewis, in his *Theory of Economic Growth* (1955), underscored how growth expanded human choice and freedom. Though scholars like Rostow (1956) emphasized the need for a society to move toward economic modernization through a series of stages, each preparing the society for the next challenges it must face, it was generally assumed that capital investments and introduction of technological knowledge would allow developing countries to speed up their development process. Development became equated with economic growth.

During the latter part of the 1960s the growth = development paradigm met with increasing criticism. In 1969, at the world conference of the Society for International Development, the requirement of enhancing the capacity not only for economic growth, but also for meeting human needs, was promoted. The International Labor Organization boosted a campaign for a new approach to basic human needs (Echavarri, 2003). Rawls (1971), in his *Theory of Justice*, held that a just society would provide its citizens with the broadest access to social goods and argued that principles of distribution ought to favor the worst off. Half a decade later Amartya Sen published his first work on famine and entitlements (Sen, 1976). In this and following contributions Sen argued that famine was caused not by a lack of wealth and resources, as assumed by the economic growth theory, but because poor people could not access available food supplies due to a lack of entitlements (Sen, 1981, 1984, 1986). The first human development report launched by Sen's colleague Mahbub ul Haq in 1990 had the explicit purpose to "shift the focus of development economics from national income accounting to people centered policies" (Haq, 1995, quoted in Fukuda-Parr, 2003, p. 302). This and all the following reports were based on Sen's conceptual framework on capabilities and functionings. Sen also contributed to the construction of a new Human Development Index (HDI) for measuring and ranking regions and countries according to basic human capabilities (to survive, to be healthy, to be knowledgeable, and to enjoy a decent standard of living), rather than according to GNI. The HDI had significant policy impact, provoking new examinations of why some countries such as Costa Rica and Sri Lanka or the Indian state of Kerala managed to achieve higher levels of human development than regions with similar or even higher income levels (Fukuda-Parr, 2003). Sen, in a series of studies conducted in the mid-1980s, used the capability approach to explore differences in HDI dimensions among nations like China and India, demonstrating that these were caused not by differences in gross national product (GNP) per capita, but rather by variations in national public policies (Sen, 1985a, 1985b).[2]

Freedom, as the choice to undertake the actions and activities one has reasons to value, and to be what one wants to be, provides the normative position of Sen's capability approach. Development, so understood, is the process of removing obstacles preventing people from living the kind of lives that they, upon reflection, want to live. While both capabilities and functionings are important in Sen's comprehensive outcome view of development, emphasis is not on what has been realized (functionings), but rather on freedom as to what is effectively possible, that is, what people can choose to do to increase their well-being as defined by what they value.

> A functioning is an achievement, whereas a capability is the ability to achieve. Functionings are, in a sense, more directly related to living conditions, since they are different aspects of living conditions. Capabilities, in contrast, are notions of freedoms, in the positive sense: what real opportunities you have regarding the life you may lead. (Sen, 1987, p. 36)

Sen distinguished his approach both from the basic needs approach, the utilitarian frameworks of welfare or neoliberal economics, and from resource-based normative theories such as those of Rawls (1971) and Dworkin (1981, 2002). Basic needs, though it places people at the center of development, focuses wrongly on a commodity basis in terms of supplying services, rather than on people's capabilities and "agency freedoms." Welfare and neoliberal economics define well-being primarily by utility maximization and, in Sen's view, neglect the importance of rights, free-doms, and agency (Sen & Williams, 1982). Concentration on primary goods is rejected because it neglects the importance of the diversity of human beings, leading to varieties in capabilities and experienced needs (Sen, 1984). The focus therefore needs to be on quality of life, not on the richness and distribution of material resources per se.

Sen's capability approach is genuinely liberal in the sense that it respects individuals' and groups' different ideas of the good life, which is why the emphasis is on advancing capabilities rather than functionings. He refrained from specifying an exact and definite list of functionings or to rank them, deliberately seeking to avoid ending up with an overspecified or prescriptive approach. Sen insisted that capability sets must be context dependent and always in need of "acts of reasoning" to be illuminated (Sen, 1984, 1987).

One kind of critique has repeatedly been leveled against the capabil-ity approach, which is of relevance to our exploration of what development means and requires and how this was reflected in the Zwelethemba experi-ment and the model it has sought to build. This criticism argues that there is both too little individualism in the capability approach and too weak a con-cern for the self and the conditions for individual growth and development.

## Building Individual Capacity

A key idea of liberalism is to conceive of the individual as an autonomous agent, capable of making free and moral choices. As Hindess (1997) has argued, this idea remains an ambiguous presupposition in liberal thought, as it is obvious that such individual capacities need to be fostered and depend for their realization on social circumstances, for instance, on the extent and quality of formal education, as Locke (1693) clearly acknowledged. Sen's approach, in spite of its strong emphasis on individual freedom and choice, has rightly been criticized for lacking attention to self and self-development. As Giri (2000, p. 1004) argues, Sen's concept of well-being lacks a notion of a critically reflective, creative, transformative self, and his notion of capa-bility does not embody the seeking and quest for being and becoming, for self-development and self-realization. Sen takes the self for granted, and the core idea in his concept of freedom seems to be "more choice," which does not facilitate reflection of the need for self-cultivation and self-constraint (Foucault, 1986, 1988), or the conditions under which choice might become oppressive (Gasper, 2000, p. 999). As Giri (2000, p. 1007) maintains,

> Sen's heart lies with the disadvantaged and we cannot but salute this. But the poor and the disadvantaged are not only objects of welfare. The difficulty is that Sen's "functioning" and "capability" does not embody striving for self-development on the part of the poor. Despite Sen's celebration of human

agency, one does not find much of an agent-view of the disadvantaged in his writings and his capability approach to human well-being lacks an objective of self-actualization and self-realization.

A philosopher who explored these issues in some detail was John Dewey. Dewey (1927) emphasized that individuals needed to develop democratic capacities—what he conceived of as stable habits of democratic engagement. He rejected, however, the republican idea of political virtues, assumed to evolve as individuals engage in the free debates in the public sphere. Dewey conceived such an "ethicization" of politics as both elitist and unrealistic, arguing that "man is a consuming and sporting animal as well as a political one" (p. 139). Today, with the increasing value placed on pluralism in society, the idea of reaching agreements in the public sphere on particular political virtues seems even less realistic (Honneth, 1998).

For Dewey, a revival of democracy presupposes a form of ethical life anchored not in political virtues but in the consciousness of social coop- eration in civil society through which it is experienced that common goals are and can be pursued. He thereby pointed to social preconditions of democracy that cannot fully be met by introducing formal rights of citi- zenship. In South Africa the legacy of apartheid still weighs heavily on the prospects of revitalizing democratic life. Unemployment remains a cen- tral obstacle to South Africa's attaining the African National Congress's 1994 promise of a "better life for all." The current rate of unemployment is officially recorded at approximately 25% (Schulze, 2010). This is signif- icantly higher than that of almost any other comparable developing econ- omy. Among young black African South Africans the figure now climbs to over 50%. Families and communities disintegrate, as people migrate in desperate search for jobs and income. Poor people are marginalized, not only from economic life, but from a meaningful participation in society (Terreblanche, 2002). High rates of violence and crime are among the conditions that make it very difficult to initiate and implement new proj- ects in poor communities that seek development through processes of "decision-making by discussion" (Holtmann & Domingo-Swarts, 2008; CSVR, 2009). Opportunities for building habits of democratic engage- ments under such conditions are scarce.

The Zwelethemba experiment was initiated as a response to this situa- tion. The main focus of the modelers was not to equip people with capacities to make better use of their civil and political rights relative to the state, but rather to build social capacities of self-directedness and self-mastery bottom- up, in local communities. In this sense its approach was in alignment with Dewey's focus on essential prepolitical democratic requirements. Inspired by Christie's (1977) idea of "conflicts as property" the experiment sought to use conflicts as a "window of opportunity" to engage people in collective dispute resolution and to transform a past-oriented "blaming habit" to a future-focused "problem-solving habit," thus building local capacities of democratic cooperation. Our interviews with peace committee members and community members indicated that a capacity to govern security democratically did emerge through this practice. The following comments by two committee members are illustrative:

> What I have learned is mostly from myself, taking part, facilitating, by experience. But we also have discussions among PC [peace committee] members. We have a meeting per month, with the coordinator. But often even after the peace gathering we may discuss "why did that happen." We try to show the facilitator, good and bad things. This is very important for getting better.[3]

> I have facilitated approximately 50 cases. One is appointed as a facilitator, we do it in turns. The role of the facilitator is to control that the process goes in accordance with the code of conduct, the PC not taking either side, not taking any decisions. As a facilitator the important thing is to try to share experiences, teach the disputants to solve the problems themselves. I have learned a lot, but not so much as a facilitator. More when I am not facilitating, just participating in the gathering. Then it is easier to come up with things.[4]

Experiences and capacities for collective problem solving were learned individually and collectively and not only at the peacemaking gatherings. Frequently the committees engaged in assessments to discuss what they could learn from a case. When asked how they saw this practice a member of the Khayelitsha Peace Committee commented:

> After the peace gathering we always do an assessment, whereby we get our experience. "What has been good, or not so good?" "What extra questions could we have asked?" Lack of information that we could have reached. Also, if the case is postponed, such an assessment will help us a lot. Assessments are very important, the sharing of ideas. Sometimes we also discuss experiences with other structures, like SANCO [South African National Civic Organization].[5]

Community members who participated in the gatherings were also affected by the process, and the experience of democratic problem solving was thereby diffused throughout the community. A community member stated:

> Many things we manage to solve ourselves, privately. But the PC, it is here to solve the problems we cannot solve ourselves. I have been to the peace gatherings before; I started to see what they are doing. The problems in this community have decreased. Here, we can come no matter what kind of problem. The PC is not defeated, it always finds a solution. For most problems, the PC can solve it. I am free to speak when I am here. I am part of the solution. The

> PC is supported in our community because the problems here, the crime, it is solving them. And it is part of the community, people can speak freely, it is very respected and always available.[6]

In the interviews peacemakers frequently commented how peace gatherings affected participants, as they experienced the process to be a fair and just attempt to solve the dispute. Frequently this made them more willing to contribute to a solution by offering more information.

> The outcome of the process, it very much depends on the disputants, if they are open to us. During the peace gathering process, the picture often changes. New information may be coming up, most often by the disputants themselves. In advance, people might have told them that the PC is going to take sides, when they see that this is not happening, they come up with additional information.[7]

The significance of experiments like Zwelethemba is that individuals are able to see that they can contribute personally and that through their cooperative action they are able to pursue common goals. As Adam Smith (1776) explained, an essential part of having individual capacity is to be able to appear in public without feeling ashamed. Poverty often tends to erode this capacity, as empirical studies have documented (Goldin, 2005). Our interviews convinced us that peacemaking gatherings and associated activities often became occasions for personal growth and enhancement of self-respect. Over time, as cooperative skills and talents grew among participants, individual and collective capacities to identify common agendas and act on them increased. Collective capacities of problem solving were documented and strengthened. As Appadurai (2004) argues, this "capacity to inspire" by demonstrating ability is an essential developmental asset and requirement. It facilitates a transformation of people's self-images, it changes how one conceives of oneself and is conceived by others, and it builds the capacity to engage in the plays of contestation and democratic negotiation within the broader issue networks to which one belongs.

## Reimagining Strategies of Collective Engagement

Another criticism frequently made against Sen and the capability approach argues, contrary to the one referred to above, that it is too individualistic. Evans (2002), for instance, maintains that Sen's analysis focuses on the individuals and their relations to social contexts, but not on collectivities as the necessary link. The approach, in Evans' view, builds upon an implicit acceptance of individual (as opposed to social) preferences as exogenous, while in his view it is the "promotion of a vibrant associational life that enables the less privileged to develop their own distinct preferences and priorities"

(p. 59). Evans is correct that Sen's approach embraces a strong individualism, in the sense of seeking to take into account the uniqueness of each person. Sen insisted that the intrinsic satisfaction that occurs in a life must occur in an individual life (Evans, 2002, p. 85), and he explicitly warned against the tendency of conceiving of individuals merely as members of groups to which they belong, as "nothing more is seen in them." He referred to Marx's insistence in "The Critique of Gotha Program" "on the need to go beyond class analysis, even as one acknowledges the social relevance of class" (p. 81). Sen refused to accept that his approach was based on a "methodological individualism," however, in the sense of conceiving of individuals as separated or detached from their social surroundings, pointing to a number of occasions in which he had tried to demonstrate precisely the opposite, that is, how preferences are socially constructed (p. 80). Even so, it is clear that the notion of collectivities as social actors is given little attention in Sen's work, and his critics typically advance the need to expand the capability approach toward a more sincere exploration of the significance of social power, political economy, and institutional dynamics (Stewart & Deneulin, 2002; Hill, 2003).

A unique strength of the capability approach, however, is its antipaternalistic approach to development, insisting on an "evaluative exercise" to be performed by individuals and society in order to form judgments on the proper paths to development. Making choices and giving priorities are seen as issues to be solved within the society affected and not by outsiders (Stewart & Deneulin, 2002). As Carter (2003) suggests, directly promoting particular functionings means failing to treat people as ends in themselves, because it fails to treat them as points of origins of ends, or as "patients" rather than "agents." The problem with approaches that take needs, commodities, or services as their basis rather than capabilities is by now well acknowledged. As noted by Pritchett and Woolcock (2004), most of these approaches have followed a similar logic of defining poverty as a series of needs to be met (supplied) through public service bureaucracies, frequently with complete lack of attention to what people actually want or with little effort to incorporate local knowledge. As these two scholars rightly conclude, "The old king—that agencies of the nation-state organized through a bureaucracy (in the good sense) civil service were *the* solution, or at least, the instrument for the development solution—is dead, wounded by disappointing experience" (p. 206). Not only is the king dead, but there is no new king to take his place (p. 206). Development professionals should therefore, in their view, try to create conditions "under which genuine experiments to discern the most appropriate local solutions to local problems can be nurtured and sustained" (p. 207).

The capability approach responds to this challenge by the emphasis it puts on democratic participation in the thick sense, and on the right of individuals and local communities to self-determination. Political reforms have increasingly become an important aspect of the human development policy agenda. The human development reports have placed an increasing focus on social and political institutions that would empower the poor and disadvantaged groups. As noted by Fukuda-Parr (2003, p. 313), "A consensus is emerging on the importance of collective action by actors other than the state, notably people and civil society groups, for promoting development."

A focus on building capacities of self-directedness and democratic participation among the poor has clear implications for development thinking and practice. First, state programs and interventions would be required to coordinate themselves with existing purposes and commitments of local communities, so that changes introduced during the development process would seek to build on and enhance existing practices (Alkire & Black, 1997). Second, a state promoting capabilities would be required to take care not to perpetuate the dependency of the poor on state programs, but rather seek to find ways of eliminating such dependency (Hill, 2003). Third, institutional policies would be required to include participatory methodologies for human development. One problem is that many institutions operating within the development field still lack systematic methods for identifying the changes that are valued by the affected communities themselves, and methods to give decision control to the local level (Alkire, 2002, 2003, 2005). A final question is how to identify what constraints will be put on local decision making, that is, how to make developmental initiatives and practices accountable to external standards and values (Williams, 1987). (This was the core question we explored in Chapter 4.)

What the exploration above seems to indicate is a need to reimagine strategies of participation that might work to strengthen the position of the poor and the marginalized, as citizens, receivers, and co-producers of services. A state-centered approach, conceiving of participation fundamentally as attempting to mobilize the poor communities to monitor, evaluate, and advise on public service delivery, has not been a viable strategy. Evidence strongly suggests that participatory forums under such conditions are sidelined by policy processes engaging other stakeholders such as powerful politicians and bureaucrats, corporate interests, and international institutions and donors. A state-focused strategy of participation does not enable poor communities to concentrate resources and become "players" in governance systems consisting of a plurality of networked actors. The global governance deficit cannot be countered by relying on the state alone. Poor and disadvantaged people must seek to develop their own independent platforms. They must concentrate resources in governmental nodes that allow them to interact with more resourceful groups and institutions without being co-opted for policy agendas and projects primarily defined by others and in other places (Wood & Shearing, 2007).

How can new approaches to participation enhance the power of the poor? The way the Zwelethemba modelers sought to respond to this challenge was to assume that if democratic processes are to become more responsive to excluded communities, it is necessary to make use of a host of nodal possibilities, rather than primarily working through conventional democratic mechanisms such as elections or interest group politics. The approach that the modelers adopted requires that one search for strategies that enable the weak, like the strong, to gain, and then maintain, access to nodes of governance—including but not limited to states and their agencies—and that will accord them an influential voice in governance (Wood & Shearing, 2007). We will now turn our attention to an experiment initiated to explore the capacity of the model to fulfill this requirement in a somewhat different environment from the pilot sites where it was developed, and that will serve to illustrate this point.

## The McGregor Experiment

A significant feature of the Zwelethemba experiment is the observation of the inventiveness that was released once people were enabled to get together in deliberative forums they controlled themselves. A new project initiated in 2006 sought to extend the model that the program had developed from urban to rural sites. The selection of poor farm-based communities close to McGregor, a small agricultural and tourist town in the Western Cape Province, South Africa, provided for pilot sites particularly suited to experimentation and development of the model in this new context. Two peace committees were established.

The establishment of peacemaking and peace-building forums tended to alter the language of communication between farm workers and the farmers in the area. Traditionally the relationship between workers and farmers had been experienced as exceptionally unequal—a relationship of subservience. Following the establishment of peace committees, workers began to shift the nature of this relationship as they felt increasingly empowered as they assumed the identity of a member of a committee. Workers experienced that approaching the farmers as members of a PC, as a representative of a collective, was far more advantageous to them. As one member commented,

> We have been able to talk to the farmer, to change things, to feel that we make a difference. It is different when you talk to the farmer as a PC member, different from approaching him individually. Also, if you talk to him individually, and nothing happens, one can go back to the PC and take it from there.[8]

One relationship with a farmer in the district had proved to be particularly difficult for workers over many years. The problem with this farmer, as the members of the PC saw it, was that he had "no manners," so that communication with him was fraught with difficulties. As one member noted, "We can't talk to him, there is no point he has no respect." One issue they had tried to raise with him over many years was to have running water installed in their houses and in particular to connect this to their toilets. Members of the PC engaged in discussions on how to approach the problem of the disrespectful farmer. One member commented, "What we have been thinking is that we should all go to the farmer and talk to him, as a PC."

Another member responded, "Maybe one of us should go to him first and ask for a meeting. If that does not work, maybe the coordinator should go, if that does not work, the development worker (a professional working in the area)."

It was agreed that one of the members of the PC, who had an additional job as a painter in the town and was generally held to be courageous, would approach the farmer on behalf of the whole group. He would arrange with the farmer for them to meet him, as a group. In advising this representative one member said: "If he says no, ok, be polite. Then, next step."

This and similar observations indicated how the PCs functioned as deliberative forums that encouraged poor communities to stretch their imagination of how to govern more effectively, how to act to solve collective problems. This enabled them to identify and formulate more sophisticated strategies of how to deal with conflicts not only within their communities, but also more generally. Typically such strategies consisted of a plan of action that proposed a graduated strategy that sought to escalate incentives (an approach advanced by Ayres and Braithwaite, 1992, and by Braithwaite in many of his later publications; see Braithwaite, 2002, 2004, 2006b, 2008). These strategies were combined with a focus on the future and long-term goals, instead of following more immediate and short-term strategies that might antagonize an opponent and lead to less optimal outcomes in the long run.

By mobilizing local knowledge, technical competence, and "symbolic capital" in peace committees, poor communities can concentrate power in governmental nodes under their direct control. In this way peace committees used local knowledge to resolve conflicts and establish and implement local development projects. Other actors, frequently strong ones, typically sought to access this knowledge and capacity to realize their own agendas. Local knowledge and capacity became bargaining chips poor people could use in negotiations with stronger actors.

The PCs in McGregor used their local knowledge and networking skills to build partnerships that could be drawn upon in developing their activities and responding to challenges. Partners included Adult Basic Educational Training (ABET), South African Police Service (SAPS), Community Police Forum, the Farmers Union, schools, religious organizations, guest houses, the municipality, and community leaders. The PCs in McGregor continuously engaged in networking with other organizations in the community that were dealing with root causes of many of the problems experienced in the community. Within the McGregor community a particularly important root cause proved to be alcoholism. In response, the PCs organized a series of gatherings to develop a plan of action for tackling alcoholism. In the course of seeking solutions to alcoholism and its effects the PCs had developed a partnership with an NGO, Dopstop (*dop* refers to drinking), an organization focused on alcoholism and its causes in rural areas. Links had also been established with local churches and with farmers in an attempt to develop a more coordinated plan of action to reduce the consumption of alcohol on the farms. Based on discussions between PC members, farm workers, and the coordinator in the area, the work of the PCs had increasingly come to be focused on alcohol abuse—which was seen as the key challenge. As commented by the coordinator,

> Almost any problem coming up is related to drinking. Solutions are almost always that people apologize. But then things stay the same. People monitor (the plan of action agreed to at the peacemaking gathering), but people go on drinking in the weekends.

Over time the PCs adopted a strategy based on the assumption that an effective approach to alcohol consumption should be multidimensional and make use of the knowledge and the capacities of multiple actors. The challenge was to identify mechanisms that might work together to create synergies between different kinds of interventions and between different capacities as represented by different actors. A problem of the contemporary situation was that different organizations operating in the area approached the problem from different angles, with little coordination or coherence. So a new strategy was formulated by the PCs in the area, assisted by the coordinator and the Community Peace Program. The strategy attempted to build a coherent approach to the problem of alcohol and drug abuse around four elements: provide factual information, construct incentive systems, support victims and increase security, and create new opportunities.

It is clear from these observations that the PCs had become a voice of the farm workers in the area, a mechanism through which they learned to speak and act collectively. However, frequently a condition for being heard is to broaden the circle; more governmental nodes need to be involved to identify and implement possible solutions. This led the PCs to establish nodal assemblages with other governmental nodes in the district, as they sought to enroll the resources of these nodes to support their development agenda of enhancing the power and self-directedness of poor communities.

What the McGregor experiment illustrates is how important it is that the interests and conceived perceptions of poor groups have a voice and the power to influence key decisions in processes of development and knowledge formation. The still dominant tendency, however, as observed by Briggs and Sharp (2004, p. 661), is that

> local knowledge continues to be drawn into development by both theorists and development institutions in a very limited way, failing to engage with other ways of perceiving development, and thus missing the possibilities of devising more challenging alternatives.

The capability approach, with its emphasis on local self-determination and the requirement to ground evaluative practices in affected communities, poses a normative challenge to this practice. To increase its political and normative challenge, however, it needs to attend more seriously to the question of how poor groups can expand both their voice and their power in processes of development. The Zwelethemba model was carefully designed to explore this question. The position it adopted was that poor and disadvantaged groups seeking to expand their power base must concentrate knowledge and resources in institutions they directly control, and from such a position of strength seek to engage others in the nodal play of contestation and enrollment. Our observations indicate that the model on this basis has a capacity to contribute to human development, on both an individual and a group level.

## Human Security

There are several reasons why human security has come to the fore in the human rights and human development discourses during recent decades. For one thing, it became increasingly clear that Sen's approach to famine offered too narrow an economic explanation (entitlement collapse) that overlooked famine mortality as a consequence of social and political processes. As observed by Duffield, most recent famines were triggered by political instability or civil war, or by a lethal combination of war plus drought (Devereux, 2001). An overview stated that 21 out of 32 major twentieth-century famines had adverse politics at the local, national, or international level as a principal cause (Duffield, 1993, in Devereux, 2001, p. 256). The human security concept can be seen as a response to the acknowledgment of a close connection between poverty, famine, and insecurity. For this reason Ikpe (2007) argues that state ability had to be related not only to its capacity to facilitate economic growth, but also to its resilience and its ability to forge a stable and peaceful relation with civil society, thus preventing conflicts.

Another reason that human security is seen as an appropriate focus of attention in our time has to do with changes in the nature of security threats. The nature of many conflicts has shifted from inter- to intrastate violence, often with higher incidents of civilian casualties. In addition, the stable configuration of mostly state-related security threats associated with the Cold War has radically transformed as new insecurities have proliferated in many other fields, such as increased immigration; human trafficking and other forms of international criminal activity; the spread of HIV/AIDS, drug-resistant diseases, and global epidemics; financial and economic collapse; and global warming and other ecological threats. The 1994 human development report of the UNDP set the tone for all subsequent definitions and articulations of the human security concept, articulating a universal, preventive, people-centered approach to security. Kofi Annan, in his 2000 report to the United Nations, gave the following description on human security:

> Human security in its broadest sense embraces far more than the absence of violent conflict. It encompasses human rights, good governance, access to education and health care and ensuring that each individual has opportunities and choices to fulfill his or her own potential ... freedom from want, freedom from fear and the freedom of the future generations to inherit a healthy natural environment—these are the interrelated building blocks of human, and therefore national, security. (Quoted in Alkire, 2003, p. 14)

From then on the human security concept was embraced by an increasing number of international, regional, and national governments (World Bank, 2001; Narayan et al., 2000a, 2000b), including the New Partnership for African Development (Alkire, 2003, p. 20). Promoting security has come to be conceived as a substantial part of what is meant by societal progress (Smoljan, 2003). A key contemporary concern is therefore how to achieve the virtuous nexus of more inclusive development, better security, and more development (Stewart, 2004). The concept of human security has contributed to the contemporary "extended security" thinking that extends the national security concept downwards, from a concern with states and nations to a concern with the security of individuals; upwards from the security of nations to the security of supra-national physical security or the concern for "environmental security" of protecting the earth systems all humans depend upon; and horizontally, to all sorts of insecurities beyond the threats of aggressive states. Such thinking diffuses the responsibility for ensuring human security in all directions from national states to international institutions, regional and local governments, and communities (Rothschild, 1995).

Scholarly debates have been inspired by and have also contributed to the human security discourse. Scholars within development studies, poverty research, and peace studies have come to regard poverty, peace building, and socioeconomic development as closely related phenomena. In academic debates development has increasingly been "securitized" (Marenin, 2005, p. 7), as peace and safety have increasingly come to be perceived as preconditions for desirable developments (Bayley, 2006). Scholars have also moved away from paradigms that identify states as the primary sources of security. Taylor and Jennings (2005, p. 32ff), for example, argue that a state focus makes it difficult to conceive of the wide plurality of issues that affect human security. A focus on the governance of security, rather than the government of security, shifts empirical and theoretical attention to all the means and processes by which security can be accomplished (Marenin, 2005, p. 17).

Most African states have limited will and capacity to govern security justly and efficiently. The public police are often perceived as indifferent, inept, brutal, and corrupt. Extensive documentation also exists of the African police engaging in extra-judicial killings, using excessive force against civilians, conducting arbitrary arrests, and colluding with criminals (Berg, 2005a, 2005b, 2005c; Bertelsen, 2007). Partly due to this, there has been an enormous growth recently of different private security arrangements in Africa: mob justice, vigilantes, religious police, ethnic/clan police, political party militia groups, civil defense groups, as well as informal and especially the formal commercial security sectors. Some of these private forms of policing adhere to the law, some are unregulated or lawless, some are spontaneous, some permanent (Baker, 2008). In addition, international donors—government development agencies, international organizations, human rights groups, peace support operations, NGOs, and large international private sector companies—play increasingly significant roles in security and justice delivery in many developmental states (OECD, 2006, p. 32). A key implication of this is that conventional notions of policing and security have lost theoretical credibility and policy relevance as distinctions between public and private (and domestic and transnational) policing are increasingly blurred. Sometimes integral to the state apparatus and sometimes decoupled from it, contemporary African security governance, especially in the cities, is polycentric (or nodal), involving state, private sector, civil society, and international institutions. Some security nodes operate primarily as auspices of security, financing, or authorizing the delivery done by others; some are primarily providers (Bayley & Shearing, 2001). In many contexts a complicated mix of competition, cooperation, and parallel provision of security (or insecurity) has developed on the security landscape. As Baker (2004a) points out:

> As people move about their daily business, or as the time of the day changes, so they move from the sphere of one policing agency to which they would naturally look for protection, to another or be faced at times with a choice of agency to be made in terms of personal experience, preference for mentality (surveillance or punishment), cost or communal status.

Many citizens of weak or fragile states experience justice and security in terms of "what is available," "what works best," and "what I can afford," rather than in terms of legal authority, mandate, and accountability (Baker, 2004a).

Despite the realities of the security situation, most African states continue to rely on the public police to govern security, not least in urban spaces. This has to some extent been a donor-driven policy development, as Western experts have offered European state-centered solutions to African problems (Rosingaunet, 2007). Several decades of assistance, however, have failed to establish Western styles of policing, and African state policing remains poorly resourced, trained, and managed, and frequently it is still blatantly corrupt and violent (UNIS, 2005).

To increase service delivery and promote more accountable practices in security and justice it is often essential to reform the African state police. In the new security environments, however, an exclusive focus on the public police is insufficient. Good security governance, in our time, in Africa and elsewhere, depends fundamentally on finding better ways to mobilize and coordinate diverse capacities and a range of governing nodes operating in the security landscape, particularly so in urban spaces. It is necessary to "imagine security" governance (Wood, 2006) in new ways.

There are clear resemblances between the human security concept and its insistence on moving beyond paradigms that identify security solely with the state, and the thinking that the Zwelethemba modelers adopted and which now underlies the model and associated practices. A common concern, that also includes the human rights discourse more generally, is the need to mend the divide in the generations of human rights. Zwelethemba, while using security as a window of opportunity to engage people in local capacity governance, has the same broad freedom from want and freedom from fear agenda that also underlies the human security approach. Both approaches acknowledge that in promoting this agenda, one needs to use a broad range of governing mechanisms and institutions (Alkire, 2003, p. 40), which includes security provision and security regulation to ensure respect for human security in the sense that "whatever their primary objective may be, all actors, whether institutional or individual, must ascertain that their actions do not foreseeably albeit unintentionally, threaten human security" (p. 30).

This emphasis on adopting a range of governance mechanisms to some extent differentiates both of these approaches from the human rights discourse, which still has a narrower focus on legal instruments. Another resemblance is the strong, preventative, risk- and future-oriented mentality that both approaches seek to realize. Human security seeks to protect human beings, in an equal manner, from critical and pervasive threats, underscoring the need for preventive and proactive interventions (Alkire, 2003, pp. 3, 13), in a manner that reconciles short- and long-term concerns. This is empha-sized by Alkire, the senior researcher of the Human Security Commission: "People's lives must not only be protected per se; they must be protected in a manner that is consistent with their long-term good" (Alkire, 2003, p. 4). As such, the human security approach, to a larger extent than is usu-ally acknowledged in the human rights discourse, recognizes the possibility of a conflict between short- and long-term goods or between different cat-egories of goods. It is quite possible, for instance, that "growth with equity," which has been conceived as the core agenda of the human development discourse, will increasingly be seen to be in conflict with the human secu-rity right of being protected against environmental disasters. Alkire (p. 39) therefore suggests that "specifying human security does entail the explicit, open-ended prioritization of freedoms and rights that current human rights theories studiously avoid." In a similar manner the Zwelethemba modelers deliberately sought to move the governance of security from a backward and short-sighted orientation characterized by blaming and punishment toward a future-oriented concern in which reducing the likelihood of further viola-tions of human integrities is paramount. In so doing it has sought to build local capacity for identifying plans of action in dispute resolution, and com-munity projects for development, that in a practical manner identify human needs and wants, and that engage people in trying to reconcile and, when necessary, make collective prioritizations among them. This also points to a final similarity between Zwelethemba and the concept of human security, as emphasized by a number of scholars, in that the range of actors is expanded beyond the state alone (Galtung, 2003/2004). As Braithwaite (2002, pp. 177, 185) argues,

> Social engineers of statist diplomacy do not have enough local knowledge to understand what are the real conflicts. The conflicts on the ground are always more complex than their reifications.... Mediation among elites is not enough. Peacemaking must be democratized; it must heal whole peoples, preparing the soil of popular sentiments for peace and democracy.

In a similar manner Alkire (2003) maintains that the human secu-rity approach gains coherence when it specifies carefully what it is trying to protect and insists that elements of human security or responses to human security threats take their shape not from medical manuals or committee conclusions but rather "from people's reflections, on the basis of their own experience and knowledge, of their values and needs" (p. 25). In so arguing Alkire draws on the principle of subsidiarity as developed by the German Jesuit lawyers in order to protect workers from alienating labor conditions. The implication of the principle for human security is that it assumes that the most local organizations capable of protecting human values should also have the main responsibility for doing so. However, Alkire also warns that the principle introduces an array of procedural concerns that must be taken into account (p. 31). (This is a theme we explored in the previous chapter.)

The bottom-up orientation to human security as mobilizing and empowering people on the ground, as well as the need for a careful regulation of such practices, accords well with the kind of thinking that has inspired the Zwelethemba experiment. In attempting to reimagine forms of polycentric governance that are both more thoroughly democratic and more effective, the model has sought to build on the Hayekian (1944) idea that *local knowledge and local capacity* are crucial to good governance. In addressing dimensions of local knowledge, the Zwelethemba model builders realized that (1) dispersed knowledge, capacity, and resources are mobilized through effective and efficient arrangements, and (2) these arrangements promote public as well as legitimate collective and private interests such as, specifically, the protection of human rights and human security.

Before we leave this exploration on the human security discourse and how the Zwelethemba modelers sought to respond to its way of conceiving development, one form of criticism against the thinking that underlies it must be addressed. This criticism argues that human security and practices that are based upon or inspired by it in reality often end up being handmaidens to the security concerns of more hegemonic Western states.

## Zwelethemba—Mobilizing the Savages to Fight the Barbarians?

As Abrahamsen (2001) argues, Western donor policies, associated with phrases such as "basic needs," "structural adjustment," or "good governance," have frequently, contrary to their stated intent, played a central role in the genesis of internal conflicts in many sub-Saharan African countries. She sees the new discourse on fragile or failed states as a search for new policy prescriptions that construe African problems as having primarily internal causes, and which construct rich countries as the problem solvers and protectors of democracy. Abrahamsen (p. 98), like Duffield (2005), links human security to a new barbarism thesis, building on Foucault's attention to the emergence of the figures of the savage and the barbarian in eighteenth-century historic and political discourse.

> There can be no barbarian unless an island of civilization exists somewhere, unless he lives outside it, and unless he fights it. And the barbarian's relationship with that speck of civilization—which the barbarian despises, and which he wants—is one of hostility and permanent warfare.... He does not make his entrance into history by founding a society, but by penetrating a civilization, setting it ablaze and destroying it.... What is more, and unlike the savage,

the barbarian is not a vector for exchange.... The savage is a man who has in his hands, so to speak, a plethora of freedom which he surrenders in order to protect his life, his security, his property, and his goods. The barbarian never gives up his freedom. (Foucault, 2003, pp. 195–196)

The savage, in exchange for security and development, is now expected to support the regime and defend society against barbarian attacks. Building on Agamben (1998), Buur et al. (2007) see the recent merger of security and development as but one concrete instance of the production and reproduction of political communities. The human security discourse implies that development is being "radicalized" in its civilizing mission. Inequalities and ensuing violence are dangers from which the wealthy part of the world must protect itself (Duffield, 2001, p. 7). A key concern in such protective measures is to distinguish friends from foes by, for example, mobilizing the savages to fight the barbarians.

Clearly such concerns are currently reflected in many Western national security policies seeking new defense strategies against the "dark" transborder networks of crime and terrorism (Raab & Milward, 2003). The 2001 report of the Hart-Rudman Commission on U.S. National Security, for instance, advocated investment in education and increases in material well-being for those living outside the boundaries of the United States as part of the national security strategy:

There are no guarantees against violence and evil in the world. We believe, nonetheless, that the expansion of human rights and basic material well-being constitutes a sturdy bulwark against them. (United States, 2001, p. 5)

As stated by the Development Assistance Committee of the Organization for Economic Cooperation and Development (OECD), development assistance has "an important role to play in helping deprive terrorists of popular support and addressing the conditions that terrorist leaders feed on and exploit" (OECD, 2003, quoted in Duffield, 2005, p. 154). Within the new security terrain homeland security is increasingly seen to rely upon securing all that is autonomous, unpredictable, and threatening in the global borderland (p. 157). One problem with this logic, as Alkire (2003, pp. 33–34) notes, is that interest in human security, from a state security point of view, swiftly ceases if more cost-effective terrorism prevention mechanisms are discovered. Proponents of "offensive realism" in the United States and other Western nations have frequently legitimized actions that counter human security if they are perceived as increasing national power and protection (p. 34). A clear message in Lasswell's (1941) classic notion of the "garrison state" and in Agamben's (1998) analysis of "sovereign power and bare life" is that dangers evolve when security becomes the basic principle of state activity and political legitimization. Galtung (2003/2004), in commenting on human security and the war in Iraq, asks a timely question of what the legitimization of the word *security* might lead to when it is given the connotation *human*.

Bearing in mind these critics of the potential dangers embedded in the notion of human security, especially as it might link up with concerns for national security or with international structures of domination and control, what might this imply for private forms of security governance like Zwelethemba or collaborative forms of public-private security governance? Does it imply that Zwelethemba, its community members, and its police partners were mobilized as agents who disciplined and normalized the poor and deprived potential terrorists of popular support, all in the interests of global institutions that have Western security concerns as their core agenda? Was the Community Peace Program turned into a mechanism that used the space of the community to order the interface between poor citizens and global institutions in ways that strengthened Western dominance in the world? Our data indicate that the opposite is true. Although the project was supported by the Finnish embassy over a number of years and was committed to liberal and cosmopolitan ideas on democracy and human rights, it does not seem fair to interpret Zwelethemba as a handmaiden of global capital or Western liberal or strategic interests. Too much concern was built into the model to ensure that the peace committees were not turned into implementation agencies for security policies defined by others. Our observations on the associated activities of peacemaking and peace building do not lead to the conclusion that these practices directly or indirectly normalized poor people in accordance with globally defined security agendas. To the contrary, the data points unanimously to a genuine strengthening of local autonomy and self-directedness.

## Conclusion

Contributions to the postmodern critique of development (Ferguson, 1990; Escobar, 1995; Hobart, 1993) tend to stress that development can only be an instrument of domination, that is, an instrument for the production and reproduction of relations of social inequality. This postmodern critique has itself come under fire, however, for its preoccupation with discourse, its insufficient attention to development as localized practices and relationships, its radical assumption about incommensurability between local and scientific forms of knowledge (Pottier, 2003), and more normatively, giving no answer to the question of "What can you offer instead?" (Diawara, 2000, p. 365). The position we have sought to defend in this chapter is that development is possible: It is a matter of human choice. Development crucially depends on building synergetic relations between state and nonstate actors, and aligning collective efforts closely with human rights.

The contemporary trajectory toward a global knowledge economy creates new requirements for learning and innovation in development, increasing the demands on the state for its ability to facilitate a mobilization of resources and capacities in society. The old model of governing through and by professions in the state—using scientific expertise to gather detailed knowledge about clients and processes in different policy sectors and then steering "at close range" from a center by the help of this knowledge—has become insufficient. Neoliberalism potentially created a more balanced relationship between state and society, allowing for greater inputs from civil society in policy. But even this model might now be approaching its limits, as it prefers to conceive of mobilization as being limited to policy implementation and tends to keep the formulation of policy as an internal state affair. Embedded engagement, in Evans's (1995) more radical formulation, implies that the state supports, engages with, and directly participates in dense social networks that cross institutional borders to support the development processes. As Crane and Swilling (2008, p. 266) argue, "Development only works when the experiences and ideas that are deeply embedded in dense networks of lived social relations are directly tapped and mobilised to animate development processes." But this, they argue, does not suggest that these ideas can be directly extracted from the networks, from the outside. That no longer works, which is why the old model of steering by and through professional knowledge systems is insufficient (though still important). The developmental state must therefore seek to rule in more collaborative ways than states traditionally have been doing, allowing a range of actors to contribute not only to the rowing but to the steering of policy.

As Braithwaite (1998) emphasizes, the relation between the state and society in development is not a zero-sum play. A state seeking to build a capacity for designing and implementing developmental interventions that work needs to foster a strong civil society, and itself be nurtured by it. This, however, is not how most states tend to operate the "developmental play." Hill (2003), building on Fraser (1989), argues that advances of individual freedom rest on collective efforts for greater self-determination by persons sharing similar interests, and she denounces the tendency of the state to preempt such processes. Ostrom and colleagues (Ostrom, 1999, 2000; Dietz, Ostrom, & Stern, 2003) make similar observations regarding the tendency of the state to take control and "crowd out citizenship" in common pool natural resource governance systems, which frequently leads to worsening environmental problems. In making this argument relevant to South African developments, Miraftab (2004, p. 90) offers an analysis of the national housing subsidy scheme, which in his view failed to meet the needs of the poor for shelter through three-part partnership. The government abdicated its role of leveling the playing field for all partners, preventing the Homeless Federation, the People's Dialogue, and their allied NGOs from playing a more assertive role in the policy process. In conclusion, Miraftab argues that positive outcomes of partnerships and broadened participation rely critically on how grassroots and disadvantaged communities can be supported to exert and sustain their interests in the development process.

Our aim in this chapter has been to illustrate how the Zwelethemba project responded to developmental challenges in ways that might assist the state in its efforts to tackle the challenges in line with human rights. The model seeks to reconcile universal human rights with local cultures and norms, and to reconcile political and civil rights more closely with economic, social, and cultural rights. Achieving this balance is frequently posed as the big challenge by scholars or practitioners in human development discourse. Our observations clearly indicate that the model fosters individual and collective capacities for democratic engagement, aligning itself with many of the ideas that underlie the capability approach. The Zwelethemba experiment also sought to respond to the challenges associated with the broad concept of human security, underscoring the need for preventative, proactive, and future-oriented responses to support freedom from want and freedom from fear for all humans.

The Zwelethemba model and the McGregor experiment illuminate the conclusion that many practitioners and researchers in the development field have reached: Local group formation and local institutions have great potential to empower poor people and raise their incomes (Thorp, Stewart, & Heyer, 2005; Olowu, 1989). What is needed is for the South African state to acknowledge the opportunities that are offered by the Zwelethemba model and similar experiments in private security governance, and how, by supporting and genuinely engaging with such experiments, it will be able to build its own capacity for development.

## Endnotes

1. See the "National Development Plan: Vision for 2030" of the South African National Planning Commission, where this is a message that clearly comes through.
2. The capability approach also became influential for development thinking on the African continent. Trevor Manuel, in the foreword to the newly released South African National Development Plan, and on behalf of the National Planning Commission, states: "At the core of this plan is a focus on capabilities, the capabilities of people and of our country and of creating the opportunities for both."
3. Member of the Nkqubela Peace Committee, interview, April 2003.
4. Member of the Khayelitsha Peace Committee, interview, May 2003.
5. Member of the Khayelitsha Peace Committee, interview, May 2003.

6. Community member in Nkqubela, interview, April 2003.
7. Member of the Nkqubela Pace Committee, interview, April 2003.
8. This quote and those to follow are based on interviews with members of the peace committees in McGregor conducted in November 2006.

# Conclusion
## Zwelethemba's Hope

# 6

Hope is directed to a future good which is hard but not impossible to attain.

—Thomas Aquinas (*Summa Theologica*, circa 1270)

In preceding chapters we have traced a journey to develop a set of robust and sustainable processes—a model—designed to enable poor communities to contribute to the accomplishment of effective and legitimate security governance.[1] As we come to the end of this journey—a journey that we have examined through the lens of four ideals of good governance—we return to where we began, namely, to the period immediately after South Africa's first democratic elections and to a small energetic, committed, and hopeful group of people drawn from a desperately poor suburb in the town of Worcester, who joined together with a small, and equally enthusiastic, group of professionals from the University of the Western Cape—our modelers.

Unlike today, a little over 15 years later, when almost daily service delivery protests express the anger and frustration of millions of people at the failure of the South African government to provide basic services, our modelers were full of hope that post-1994 their lives would be better. Indeed for many, and perhaps most, Zwelethembians, realizing the new South Africa they hoped for would, they believed, require their participation not simply as voters, but as nation builders. They had directly participated in the struggle against apartheid that had enabled them to vote for the first time in their lives and they expected that building a new South Africa would also require their active involvement. For the people of Zwelethemba, and most certainly our modelers, this was a time to contribute to building an effective, democratic, and just country. The desire for "payback" that has become so much a part of the politics of South Africa today—a desire that was emblematically expressed in a statement by a government official who observed that "we did not participate in the struggle to be poor"—while certainly present, did not imply that one should simply "sit back" and wait for delivery.

What the modelers hoped to discover was a set of pathways for engagement that would enable ordinary South Africans to participate actively, in ways that were consistent with the values set out in the constitution, in reshaping their neighborhoods so that they would become safe places in which they and their children could live, work, and play. The modelers were looking for ways in which micro, grassroots processes could be established that would enable South Africans, particularly poor South Africans living in informal settlements, to participate and contribute to their own, their families', and their neighbors' safety. At the heart of this thinking was the idea that ordinary South Africans had much to offer in building a new South Africa and that ways needed to be found to involve them.

J. Bradford DeLong (1999) nicely captured this participatory sensibility in a review of James C. Scott's *Seeing Like a State* (1998), a book that was published at precisely the same time as our modelers were working:

> The bureaucratic planner with a map does *not* know best, and can *not* move humans and their lives around the territory as if on a chessboard to create utopia, that the local, practical knowledge possessed by the person-on-the-spot *is* important and *must* remain with those who have the craft to understand the situation; that any system that functions *at all* must create and maintain a space for those on the spot to use their local, practical knowledge. (DeLong, 1999, p. 245)

This sensibility, as DeLong makes clear, has deep theoretical roots that stretch back to Frederick Hayek and the Austrian economic school of which he was a part, and to Adam Smith. Indeed, this line of thinking has roots that extend beyond economics to American pragmatism and political thinkers like John Dewey, whose work we cited earlier. It was this sensibility that inspired the modelers and the people of Zwelethemba as they stepped forward into a new South Africa.

What the modelers sought to discover were pathways for participation in governance that would ensure that the capacity and knowledge of ordinary South Africans were recognized and used in the promotion of safety. What the previous chapters have attempted to do is to examine how the modelers sought to do this and how well they did so, from the perspective of four values—justice, democracy, accountability, and human rights.

We have argued that although the achievements of the modelers were modest, the experiences of those who adopted the Zwelethemba model can be mined for lessons that others, who see value in the utilization of local knowledge in governance, might find useful. With this in mind, we now turn to a review of some of the lessons we have identified in the preceding chapters.

The first set of lessons we discussed arose out of our attempts to comprehend what was being celebrated by those who attended gatherings when, as the gatherings came to an end, they held hands, offered prayers, and sang songs of appreciation and thanks. These celebrations drew upon established cultural repertoires that have come to be associated, especially among Xhosa and Zulu speakers, with symbolic gestures that signify a sense of unity—a unity that is encapsulated in the term *ubuntu*, which we have already discussed. *Ubuntu*, Desmond Tutu (1999) argues, signifies that, as humans, we become who we are through others—"a person is a person through other people.... I am human because I belong, I participate, I share" (p. 35).

We have argued that what was being celebrated, at the conclusion of the gatherings, was the accomplishment of a credible plan of action—a plan to govern security more effectively. However, we argued further, these celebrations should be read as referencing much more than this. What was also being celebrated, we suggested, was the ability of ordinary people to contribute to their governance through shaping solutions to their own problems. We went on to suggest further that these celebrations had an even more expansive significance, as they recognized a sense of justice that arose, not from a backward-looking balancing of harms, but from a forward-looking creation of a better future.

The Zwelethemba experiment reminds us of Polanyi's idea that justice itself might be an ideal one can only hope to approach by means of a gradual trial-and-error process in collective problem solving (Polanyi, 1951). Polanyi believed that attempts to impose morality by a central authority would be unlikely to succeed (Polanyi, 1951; see also Aligica & Tarko, 2012). The Zwelethemba project also attests to Hayek's insight that justice is something that may be progressively discovered as people learn about the possibility of peaceful coexistence (Hayek, 1973, discussed in Thomson, 1991, p. 89).

What was being celebrated at the gatherings was the accomplishment of an alternative future that either had not been visible or had remained unrealized. This conception of justice helps explain the sense of injustice that so many South Africans feel today as they recognize how little has changed in their lives since 1994.

This provides, we argued, for the possibility of a conception of justice that is applicable to routines of security governance that look to the future as a way of providing a just closure to past events. What was being celebrated, we argued, was this closure, and with it, the opening up of a new tomorrow. A crucial lesson here is that justice should not be understood as the preserve of processes, like those of criminal justice, that are focused on identifying and punishing a blameworthy offender.

The second set of lessons we identified had to do with democracy, which is perceived by many to be the core value of a good society, but is also regarded by social theorists to be one of the most essentially contested concepts in political thought (Gallie, 1956; Connolly, 1974; Gray, 1978; Mason, 1990). We pointed to the tendency in contemporary Western political culture to conflate democracy with the representative institutions of the state and how such a perception of democracy as "one assembly of men" contained its own internal conflict of ideas—for instance, between the idea of an unconstrained demos and the contrary need for fostering a range of self-regulatory systems seen as vital for the constitution of such a demos in the first place. We argued for the need to embrace a broader concept of democracy as an ongoing practical accomplishment of actors engaging in "problem-solving through discussion." Such a definition provides for the possibility that local publics may participate in democratic governance in, and through, many different forums.

We pointed to the perception by many scholars that we are witnessing a widening democratic deficit, understood as a broadening gap between democratic ideals and practices. One dominant interpretation, often associated with the cosmopolitans, relates this development to globalization, which displaces politics from established democratic institutions and therefore undermines them. While there are certainly good reasons to question the effects of globalization on established political institutions, we argued that a danger with defining displacement of politics as wrong is that it tends to function as "democratic blackmail" that severely constrains our ability to explore the potential for new political experiences and to use them to reimagine what democracy might mean. As an alternative we pointed to John Dewey's (1927) argument that displacement of politics from established institutions is an important democratic mechanism that enables concerned publics to search for new political and democratic solutions.

We recognized that the Zwelethemba experiment may be conceived as a displacement of security governance from what has conventionally been seen as its natural place within the agencies of the state, such as the public police. A core concern of the Zwelethemba model, however, was to seek to align representative and more direct forms of democracy by producing outcomes that would nurture both—by creating local deliberative assemblies that confirmed state sovereignty. The concern of the modelers in this regard was to identify principles of appropriate conduct, and proper procedural constraints, so as to avoid the danger that a displacement might be exploited by dominant local elites—something that had proved to be a very real danger previously with grassroots dispute resolution forums of popular justice. The question this raised was: Would the new local publics established as part of the experiment work to strike a balance between democratic self-governance, sensitive to local cultural values and goals, and the constraints of more broadly defined democratic values and principles? Our observations led us to conclude that the local publics had indeed managed to balance these concerns fairly well.

Did the Zwelethemba experiment function to deepen democracy in South Africa? We concluded that it is reasonable to answer this question in the affirmative. This, we admit, is related to our own conceptualization of democracy as an essentially contested concept. Those who perceive of democracy in terms of the idea of one assembly of men might well disagree.

We have proposed a conception of democracy—located within a tradition of thinking that stretches from Tocqueville (1835/2003), through

Polanyi (1951), to Vincent and Elinor Ostrom and the Bloomington School—as a decentered, polycentric pattern of nested democratic forums (see Aligica & Boettke, 2009). A key idea, of such an arrangement, is that while general rules within cover all subunits, how these rules are applied may vary considerably (Aligica & Tarko, 2012, p. 18).

Adherence to general rules determines if subunits, like the peace committees of the Zwelethemba model, define themselves (and are defined by others) as belonging to a particular polycentric order. A key principle of the experiment was to work within the confines of the South African law and constitution, and not to challenge the state's monopoly of the legitimate use of force. In that sense the model clearly defined itself as belonging to the polity established by the new democratic South African state. On the other hand, the experiment also insists upon its democratic right to establish its own particular rules for how to govern security locally, adhering to a set of principles and values that radically deviates from the criminal justice system. In this way the model both accepts the sovereignty of the state and insists on its right to explore an alternative, and potentially more democratic way of governing security.

In a democracy conceived as a nested set of democratic institutions influences should in principle be allowed to flow both ways, from the law to local practices and from local practices to laws and policies. Hayek (1973) argued that the law would, and in his opinion also should, mostly give expression to rules that had already proven their value as embodied in local practices. Our observations give reasons to hope that the processes that unfolded within the Zwelethemba model strengthened and generalized the values of democratic inquiry and peaceful problem solving. The model's practices enabled public values to emerge from an informal, nonadjudicative process outside state institutions. Norms were produced bottom-up that may gradually have had an influence on the shaping of formal law and policies. The model deepens democracy by creating local forums that enhance the self-directedness of poor communities in the governance of their own security, and by allowing them to become a voice in the broader democratic forums of the state.

A third set of lessons we explored related to a core concern of the modelers: to design a model that would allow for local autonomy and creativity and give space for contextually informed problem solving, but that at the same time would keep local practice within the limits. The modelers recognized that building a model that would be robust, sustainable, and legitimate would be crucial to the success or failure of their project. They also acknowledged that the shift from government to governance, from monocentric to more polycentric governing—a shift they in one sense contributed to themselves—threw them into an ambivalent and unfamiliar conceptual landscape, as the predominant discussion about accountability has been about how to hold states and their political authorities, agencies, and officials to account.

A concern of many contemporary scholars, contemplating the effects of developments such as privatization and globalization, as well as changes in the modalities of state rule, has been that a crisis in political accountability may be emerging. The lesson that the Zwelethemba modelers drew from debates about how to respond to this crisis and from their own experiments was that it was necessary to reimagine accountability within contemporary polycentric realities. The challenge they confronted was: Would it be possible to build a strongly regulated set of private security practices by using a variety of accountability mechanisms embedded in different nodes and operating at different scales of governance?

Building upon the experiences and knowledge that had emerged from the ongoing experiments in Zwelethemba the modelers concluded that a redundancy of independent accountability mechanisms was crucial in building robust and accountable local practices. Our argument has been that each of the accountability modalities built into the Zwelethemba model, some operating on a horizontal and others on a vertical accountability axis, worked to realize this ideal of redundancy. A lesson from the project was that the more such mechanisms you are able to build into polycentric systems of governance, the more likely that you will succeed in creating a well-regulated practice. Our observations showed that such a design is not without challenges of its own, because a range of tensions emerged as a direct result of building a hybridity of different accountability modalities into the model. However, the experiment also indicated that such tensions could be successfully managed.

The Zwelethemba experiment supports the idea that multilevel and multimodal arrangements of accountability may display a built-in capacity for self-correction. The viability of the model depended on its ability to align rules and incentives.

A fourth and final lesson we have identified is that successful development requires an effective mobilization of organizational and institutional resources within the state and in society. As argued by Swilling (2008), this requires a "capability approach" operationalized at two levels: first through an approach that builds public sector institutional capacity, and second via the creation of multiple spaces for effective participation by a range of civil society organizations in governance. It was the second challenge that was a particular concern of the Zwelethemba modelers. They knew that if their project was to succeed, they had to find ways of mobilizing resources and enhancing capacities within the local communities with which they engaged. The pathway they identified was to use security as a window of opportunity to build a governance model that would eventually go beyond a focus on security. As the modelers came to focus on security as a catalyst for development, they did not, as we have argued, see this as building a project in competition with the South African state. The understanding of the modelers was that they would build a project focusing on the governance of security and broader development issues in a way that would complement and offer to assist the state in building a safer and more prosperous society.

As the modelers sought to extract model-building principles from the ongoing trial-and-error experiments in Zwelethemba, as well as from the scholarly literature they engaged with, a further understanding that emerged was that the project had to align itself closely with human rights. Human rights discourses emerged as a rich repertoire of ideas for the modelers as they sought to identify the broader cosmopolitan values and principles that would inform and constrain the practices of the local peace committees. The human development discourse also became a source of information as the modelers reflected on how they were to conceive of human freedom and human capabilities while they sought to enhance the autonomy and self-directedness of the communities in which they worked. Further, human security discourses also became a source of inspiration as the modelers sought to develop a governance model that would embrace a range of human needs and seek to combine intervention in disputes (peacemaking) with proactive and preventative measures to reduce the likelihood of such disputes arising in the first place (peace building).

While the Zwelethemba project was not developed explicitly to address human rights, a lesson from this exploration has been that the processes that have emerged do in fact address core concerns of these discourses. We have argued that the model offers insight for the many scholars who currently pose the question of how the poor and the oppressed could better use human rights possibilities to promote their emancipation. The model has developed a strategic position in this regard that is closely related to what other community organizations, such as the Slum Shack Dwellers International, have come to realize. To gain the position and the powers to realize human rights and human development, a principal challenge for poor communities is to concentrate knowledge and capacities in nodes that the poor control and then to build projects and alliances from such a platform.

In poor communities the opportunities for building habits of democratic engagement and collective problem solving are, for many reasons, rare; nonetheless, a lesson supported by many of our observations has been that it is possible, through projects like Zwelethemba, to build local practices with what Appadurai (2004) has called a "capacity to inspire"—the ability to facilitate individual and collective growth. These observations have led us to conclude that the model, though its contribution may be modest, does have the capacity to contribute to human development, on both an individual and a group level.

The Zwelethemba project was built upon the assumption that governance is constituted through nodes. A crucial developmental question is: Who has access to governing nodes (Burris, Drahos, & Shearing, 2005)? A lesson to draw from our explorations is that key to a successful development "game," seen from a poor community's point of view, is how poor people can gain access to governmental nodes like the peace committees that facilitate a concentration of knowledge and resources under their direct control, and how they thereby can enhance their leverage by enrolling other nodes within wider systems of governance. The Zwelethemba project attests to the soundness of the argument by Burris, Drahos and Shearing (2005, p. 55) that good nodal governance consists of governance arrangements that draw upon neglected capacities and knowledge in ways that deepen democracy, and promote development.

The Zwelethemba project was built on the assumption that poor communities are a significant source of untapped capacity that, if mobilized, could have a considerable impact, for the common good, within security and the broader development agenda. We can now conclude that while this proved to be a challenging task, it is also clear that this was, and is, possible.


## A Road Block and Beyond?

With our review complete we turn to what has become of, and what might become of, this small experiment in security governance. As we noted in the first chapter, at the end of 2009 the funding that the Community Peace Program (CPP) had relied upon to facilitate the operation of peace committees in over 240 schools and surrounding communities in the Western Cape came to an abrupt end. This followed a significant shift in power within the African National Congress (ANC), along with a shift in the fortunes of senior politicians associated with the established order. This seismic shift within the ANC began with its 52nd national conference at the end of 2007. Thabo Mbeki, the president of South Africa, was ousted as the president of the ANC by a majority of members who had rallied behind Jacob Zuma. Zuma immediately became the president of the ANC.

Mbeki remained president of South Africa until he resigned under a cloud on September 24, 2008, following a court judgment that suggested that Mbeki had improperly interfered with the workings of the National Prosecuting Authority. The deputy president, Kgalema Motlanthe, became president of South Africa on September 25, 2008. He remained president of the country until March 9, 2009, when Jacob Zuma, after a vote in Parliament, replaced him as president. During this period of change at the national level, in May 2009, the Democratic Alliance won a majority of seats in the Western Cape legislature—a province that had been under the political control of the ANC since 1994.

As a result of these developments 2009 proved to be an important year for the CPP, as the political leaders who had championed the work of peace committees within the national government during the Mbeki era were moved from the center of the political stage to its periphery, and indeed in some cases were removed from the stage entirely.

Just before Christmas 2009 all funding for the CPP was terminated, and both the program and the peace committees they supported lost their operating budget. This not only meant that the work of peace committees came to an abrupt end, but that an anticipated expansion of peace committees across the rest of the country was stillborn.

While anyone who had been paying careful attention to unfolding political events might not have been surprised by this, for the peace committees this was a completely unexpected event—a "black swan" event to use Taleb's (2007) phrasing—for which they were completely unprepared. The response was shock followed immediately by anger. This led to a flurry of letters of protest, supported by the CPP, from the committees and the schools with which they were associated to the Office of the Presidency. Nothing came of this. As we write there has been no further funding for peace committees.

What remain are the lessons that can be drawn from this experiment—lessons that we have explored in this book. A crucial question that needs to be considered, by anyone who is attracted by the Zwelethemba model, is why, given the model's considerable local support, it was so easy for the national government to stop supporting it. How was it possible for the government to so easily make a decision that undid a process that had taken over a decade to develop, and was successfully enhancing safety and providing paid work in over 250 schools and surrounding neighborhoods? How was it possible for a government that had spoken so loudly about improving safety and supporting poor communities to take such a cavalier decision?

For an answer to these questions—and it is an answer that many readers will already have identified—we turn to a conversation that one of us had with a police commissioner in the South African Police Service after it was clear that the national government would no longer be funding the CPP. After a meeting with a number of foreign dignitaries, the commissioner asked if we would like to know why the Zwelethemba process had not survived. In response to an affirmative nod he replied: "Because they [the CPP] did not make us [the South African Police] central to the model."

The commissioner was correct. If the police had been central to the Zwelethemba process the funding situation would very likely have been entirely different. Had the South African Police championed the Zwelethemba process, it is most unlikely that any government would have been able to cut off the flow of funds to the program so easily.

This wise response was no surprise. The CPP had been well aware from the model's inception that one way it could secure the program would be to encourage a powerful government agency, like the police, to take ownership of it. And indeed, as we have noted, there were attempts to involve the police in the process, though without making them central to it. But herein lies a catch-22 situation. If a police agenda had driven the process, the model would perhaps have still been in operation today. However, any model driven by such an agenda would in essence be a different model.

Once donor funding came to an end, after a robust model had been developed, the decision to seek funding through political champions who were outside the national government's security cluster was in part a function of opportunity, but it was also attractive because it meant that the model's integrity would be preserved. Associated with this was the decision to focus on schools. Had political support continued, it was hoped that the source of funding could be shifted from funds under the control of the Office of the Presidency to budget lines within the Departments of Education. But government support came to an end before this shift had taken place.

Had events unfolded differently the fortunes of the Zwelethemba model may have been very different. Should different decisions have been made? It is hard to tell. Catch-22 conundrums are by their very nature difficult. Further, after-the-fact counterfactual imaginings are also fraught with difficulties. Had the program's champions remained in positions of influence for another couple of years things may well have been different and the Zwelethemba model might have been operating in schools around the country with support from Departments of Education.

Irrespective of what might have happened, the lessons are clear. Any program of governance, whether it be within the state, civil, or private sectors, that does not become embedded within a well-established organizational and institutional context with secure funding streams will, by definition, be vulnerable. The literature on the relevance of path dependency in social and political development supports this conclusion (Stinchcombe, 1968; Krasner, 1984, 1988; Steinmo, Thelen, & Longstreth, 1992; Putnam, 1993; Page, 2006; Streeck & Thelen, 2005). As Unger (1996) has argued, such mechanisms of path dependency tend to be self-strengthening in the sense that they enhance an institutional fetishism that makes us believe that institutions that have been good at solving problems in the past should also be the ones that we rely on for solving our future problems. How the circle of innovation that seeks to develop processes outside of conventional boxes might be squared is no easy matter. The fact that some innovations survive and sometimes flourish certainly provides evidence that there are occasions when conditions coalesce to provide for the sustainability of new innovations. But, as with evolution more generally, the main variable here is often chance rather than planning.

Braithwaite and Drahos (2000) have shown that models, like Zwelethemba, that are located at a periphery rather than a center are less likely to be adopted and to survive than those that come from a center. This does not auger well for the Zwelethemba model. When governments in developing countries like South Africa look for models they typically turn to more powerful countries for inspiration. There is considerable evidence for this in South Africa (for a recent example, see Froestad, Shearing, Herbstein, & Grimwood, 2012).

At this moment in the history of the life of the Zwelethemba model it looks very much as if the strong—epitomized perhaps by the wise, clear-thinking, and steely senior policeman we quoted—are very much in the ascendancy. The weak—the peace committee members and those they serviced in their neighborhoods—are not. Nonetheless, as we write these words there is at least one bright spot on the horizon. Some of the modelers, playing the role of "model missionaries" (Braithwaite & Drahos, 2000), have been working with a South African provincial government to use the design principles of the Zwelethemba model to rethink the way in which the province governs security (Cartwright & Shearing, 2012). As these missionaries move forward they have been mindful of the lessons that we have canvassed. Only time will tell how successful they will be in applying those lessons. Whatever the outcome of the provincial project, however, it is an indication that the governance mentality that the project developed lives on and adds to the "institutional diversity" that Elinor Ostrom (2005) reminds us is so crucial to maintain and expand.

## Endnotes

1. For a recent statement, among many, of the importance of both enhancing the security of South Africans and enabling a variety of constituencies to contribute to this objective, see the National Planning Commission's Final Report (2011).

# References

Aars, J., & Fimreite, A.L. (2005). Local government and governance in Norway: Stretched accountability in network politics. *Scandinavian Political Studies, 28*(3), 239–256.

Abers, R. (2000). *Inventing local democracy: Grassroots politics in Brazil.* Boulder, CO: Lynne Rienner Publishers.

Abrahamsen, R. (2001). Development policy and the democratic peace in sub-Saharan Africa. *Conflict, Security and Development, 1*(3), 79–103.

Abrahamsen, R., & Williams, M. (2011). *Security beyond the state: Private security in international politics.* New York: Cambridge University Press.

Agamben, G. (1998). *Homo sacer: Sovereign power and bare life.* Stanford, CA: Stanford University Press.

Albrow, M. (1970). *Bureaucracy.* London: MacMillan.

Aligica, P.D., & Boettke, P.J. (2009). *Challenging institutional analysis and development. The Bloomington School.* London: Routledge.

Aligica, P.D., & Tarko, V. (2012). Polycentricity: From Polanyi to Ostrom, and beyond. *Governance: An International Journal of Policy, Administration and Institutions, 25*(2), 237–62.

Alkire, S. (2002). Dimensions of development. *World Development, 30*(2), 181–205.

Alkire, S. (2003). *A conceptual framework for human security.* Working Paper 2. Center for Research on Inequality, Human Security and Ethnicity (CRISE), Queen Elisabeth House, University of Oxford.

Alkire, S. (2005). *Valuing freedoms. Sen's capability approach and poverty reduction.* Oxford: Oxford University Press.

Alkire, S., & Black, R. (1997). A practical reasoning theory of development ethics: Furthering the capabilities approach. *Journal of International Development, 9*(2), 263–279.

Alston, P. (2005). Ships passing in the night: The current state of the human rights and development debate seen through the lens of the millennium development goals. *Human Rights Quarterly, 27*, 755–829.

Althusser, L. (1971). Ideology and ideological state apparatuses. In L. Althusser (Ed.), *Lenin and philosophy and other essays.* London: New Left Books, 127–186.

Alves, J. (2000). The declaration of human rights in postmodernity. *Human Rights Quarterly, 22*(2), 478–500.

Amin, S. (1974). *Accumulation on a world scale.* New York: Monthly Review Press.

Amin, S. (1976). *Unequal development: An essay on the social formation of peripheral capitalism.* New York: Monthly Review Press.

Amin, S. (1991). The ancient world-system versus the modern capitalist world-system. *Review, 14*(3), 349–385.

Amin, S. (1992). *Empire of chaos.* New York: Monthly Review Press.

Anderson, B. (1991). *Imagined communities: Reflections on the origins and spread of nationalism.* London: Verso.

Appadurai, A. (2000). Grassroots globalization and the research imagination. *Public Culture, 12*(1), 1–19.

Appadurai, A. (2002). Deep democracy: Urban governmentality and the horizon of politics. *Public Culture, 14,* 21–47.

Appadurai, A. (2004). The capacity to aspire: Culture and the terms of recognition. In V. Rao and M. Walton (Eds.), *Culture and public action: A cross-disciplinary dialogue on development policy,* pp. 59–84. Stanford, CA: Stanford University Press.

Appiah, F., Chimanikire, D., & Gran, T. (Eds.). (2004). *Professionalism and good governance in Africa.* Oslo: Abstrakt Forlag.

Apter, D. (1965). *The politics of modernization.* Chicago: University of Chicago Press.

Atkinson, M., & Coleman, W. (1992). Policy networks, policy communities and the problems of governance. *Governance, 5*(2), 154–180.

Ayling, J., Grabosky, P., & Shearing, C. (2006). Harnessing resources for networked policing. In J. Fleming & J. Wood (Eds.), *Fighting crime together: The challenges of policing and security networks.* Sydney: University of New South Wales Press.

Ayres, I., & Braithwaite, J. (1992). *Responsive regulation: Transcending the deregulation debate.* Oxford: Oxford University Press.

Bachrach, P., & Baratz, M. (1970). *Power and poverty.* New York: Oxford University Press.

Baiocchi, G. (2005). *Militants and citizens: The politics of participatory democracy in Porto Alegre.* Stanford, CA: Stanford University Press.

Baker, B. (2002). Living with non-state policing in South Africa. The issues and dilemmas. *Journal of Modern African Studies, 40*(1), 29–53.

Baker, B. (2004a, July). Post-conflict policing: Lessons from Uganda 18 years on. *Journal of Humanitarian Assistance.* Retrieved from http://sites.tufts.edu/jha/archives/16

Baker, B. (2004b). Protection from crime: What is on offer for Africans? *Journal of Contemporary African Studies, 22,* 165–88.

Baker, B. (2008). *Multi-choice policing in Africa.* Uppsala: Nordiska Afrikainstitute.

Baker, B. (2009). *Security in post-conflict Africa: The role of nonstate policing.* London: CRC Press.

Baker, B. (2010). Grasping the nettle of nonstate policing. *Journal of International Peacekeeping, 14*(3–4), 276–300.

Baker, B., & Scheye, E. (2007). Multi-layered justice and security delivery in post-conflict and fragile states. *Conflict, Security and Development, 7*(4), 503–528.

Baker, B., & Scheye, E. (2009). Access to justice in a post-conflict state: Donor-supported multidimensional peacekeeping in southern Sudan. *International Peacekeeping, 16*(2), 171–185.

Baldwin, R., & Black, J. (2008). Really responsive regulation. *Modern Law Review, 71*(1), 59–94.

Bansal, P., & Roth, K. (2000). Why companies go green: A model of ecological responsiveness. *Academy of Management Journal, 43*(4), 717–737.

Barber, B. (1984). *Strong democracy: Participatory politics for a new age.* Los Angeles: University of California Press.

Barrientos, S., Conroy, M.E., and Jones, E. (2007). Northern social movements and fair trade. In L.T. Raynolds, D.L. Murray, & J. Wilkinson (Eds.), *Fair trade: The challenges of transforming globalization.* London: Routledge.

Barry, A., Osborne, T., & Rose, N. (Eds.). (1996). *Foucault and political reason.* Chicago: University of Chicago Press.

Baxi, U. (2002). *The future of human rights.* Dehli: Oxford University Press.

Bayley, D. (2006). *Changing the guard: Developing democratic police abroad.* Oxford: Oxford University Press.

Bayley, D. (2011). The morphing of peacekeeping: Competing approaches to public safety. *International Peacekeeping, 18,* 52–63.

Bayley, D., & Shearing, C. (1996). The future of policing. *Law and Society Review, 30*(3), 585–606.

Bayley, D., & Shearing, C. (2001). *The new structure of policing.* Washington, DC: National Institute of Justice, U.S. Department of Justice.

Bazemore, G., & Walgrave, L. (1999). Restorative juvenile justice: In search of fundamentals and an outline for systemic reform. In G. Bazemore & L. Walgrave (Eds.), *Restorative juvenile justice: Repairing the harm of youth crime.* Monsey, NY: Willow Tree Press.

Beck, U. (1997). *The reinvention of politics: Rethinking modernity in the global social order* (P. Ritter & M. Ritter, Trans.). Cambridge: Polity Press.

Beck, U. (2002). *Macht und Gegenmacht in Globalen Zeitalter: Neue Weltpolitische Ökonomie.* Frankfurt am Main: Suhrkamp Verlag.

Beck, U. (2005). *Power in the global age.* Cambridge: Polity Press.

Berg, J. (2005a). *Overview of plural policing oversight in select Southern African Development Community (SADC) countries.* Institute of Criminology, University of Cape Town.

Berg, J. (2005b). *Audit of police oversight in the East African region.* Institute of Criminology, University of Cape Town.

Berg, J. (2005c). *Police accountability in Southern African commonwealth countries.* Institute of Criminology, University of Cape Town.

Bertelsen, B. (2007). Violence, sovereignty and tradition. Understanding death squads and sorcery in Chimoio, Mozambique. In A. Guedes & M. Lopes (Eds.), *The state and traditional law in Angola and Mozambique.* Coimbra, Portugal: Almedina.

Bhattacharya, C., Sen, S., & Korschun, D. (2011). *Leveraging corporate social responsibility: The stakeholder route to business and social value.* Cambridge: Cambridge University Press.

Bittner, E. (1979). *The functions of the police in modern society.* Cambridge, MA: Oelgeschlager Gunn & Hain.

Black, J. (2001). Decentring regulation: Understanding the role of regulation and self regulation in a "post-regulatory world." *Current Legal Problems, 54,* 103–147.

Black, J. (2003). Enrolling actors in regulatory processes. Examples from UK financial service regulation. *Public Law,* 62–90.

Black, J. (2007). Tensions in the regulatory state. *Public Law,* 58–73.

Black, J. (2008). Constructing and contesting accountability in polycentric regulatory regimes. *Regulation and Governance, 2*(2), 137–164.

Blagg, H. (1997). A just measure of shame? Aboriginal youth conferencing in Australia. *British Journal of Criminology, 37,* 481–501.

Blagg, H. (2001). Aboriginal youth and restorative justice: Critical notes from the frontier. In A. Morris & G. Maxwell (Eds.), *Restorative justice for juveniles: Conferencing, mediation and circles.* Oxford: Hart Publishing.

Blau, P. (1956). *Bureaucracy in modern society.* New York: Random House.

Bohman, J. (1996). *Public deliberation: Pluralism, complexity, and democracy.* Cambridge, MA: MIT Press.

Boltanski, L., & Chiapello, E. (1999). *Le Nouvel Esprit du Capitalisme.* Paris: Gallimard.

Bond, P. (2005). *Elite transition: From apartheid to neoliberalism in South Africa.* London: Pluto.

Bond, P. (2006). *Talk left, walk right: South Africa's frustrated global reforms* (2nd ed.). Pietermaritzburg: University of KwaZulu-Natal Press.

Börzel, T., & Risse, T. (2010). Governance without a state—Can it work? *Regulation and Governance, 4*(2), 1–22.

Bourdieu, P., & Wacquant, L.D. (1992). *An invitation to reflexive sociology.* Chicago: University of Chicago Press.

Bowden, B. (2009). *The empire of civilization: The evolution of an imperial idea.* Chicago: University of Chicago Press.

Braithwaite, J. (1989). *Crime, shame and reintegration.* Cambridge: Cambridge University Press.

Braithwaite, J. (1993). Responsive regulation for Australia. In P. Grabosky & J. Braithwaite (Eds.), *Business regulation and Australia's future.* Canberra ACT: Australia Institute of Criminology.

Braithwaite, J. (1998). Institutionalizing trust: Enculturating distrust. In V. Braithwaite & M. Levi (Eds.), *Trust and governance.* New York: Russel Sage.

Braithwaite, J. (1999a). Accountability and governance under the new regulatory state. *Australian Journal of Public Administration, 58*(1), 90–94.

Braithwaite, J. (1999b). Restorative justice: Assessing optimistic and pessimistic accounts. In Michael Tonry (Ed.), *Crime and justice: A review of research* (Vol. 25, pp. 1–127). Chicago: University of Chicago Press.

Braithwaite, J. (2000a). The new regulatory state and the transformation of criminology. *British Journal of Criminology, 40*, 222–236.

Braithwaite, J. (2000b). *Regulation, crime, freedom.* Aldershot, UK: Ashgate.

Braithwaite, J. (2002). *Restorative justice and responsive regulation.* Oxford: Oxford University Press.

Braithwaite, J. (2004). Methods of power for development: Weapons of the weak, weapons of the strong. *Michigan Journal of International Law, 26*(1), 298–330.

Braithwaite, J. (2006a). Accountability and responsibility through restorative justice. In M. Dowdle (Ed.), *Public accountability: Designs, dilemmas and experiences.* Cambridge: Cambridge University Press, p. 33–51.

Braithwaite, J. (2006b). Responsive regulation and developing economies. *World Development, 34*(5), 884–898.

Braithwaite, J. (2008). *Regulatory capitalism: How it works, ideas for making it better.* Cheltenham, UK: Edward Elgar.

Braithwaite, J., Braithwaite, V., Cookson, M., & Dunn, L. (2010). *Anomie and violence: Non-truth and reconciliation in Indonesian peacebuilding.* Canberra, Australia: ANU E Press.

Braithwaite, J., & Drahos, P. (2000). *Global business regulation.* Cambridge: Cambridge University Press.

Bratton, M. (1994). Civil society and political transitions in Africa. In J. Harbeson, D. Rothchild, & N. Chazan (Eds.), *Civil society and the state in Africa.* Boulder, CO: Lynner Rienner Publishers.

Briggs, J., & Sharp, J. (2004). Indigenous knowledges and development: A postcolonial caution. *World Quarterly*, *25*(4), 661–676.

Briggs, X. (2008). *Democracy as problem solving*. Cambridge, MA: MIT Press.

Brodeur, J.-P. (2010). *The policing web*. Oxford: Oxford University Press.

Brunsson, N. (1989). *The organization of hypocrisy: Talk, decisions, and actions in organizations*. Chichester, UK: John Wiley.

Burchell, G., Gordon, C., & Miller, P. (Eds.). (1991). *The Foucault effect: Studies in governmentality*. Chicago: University of Chicago Press.

Burris, S. (2004). Governance, microgovernance and health. *Temple Law Review*, *77*(2), 335–361.

Burris, S., Drahos, P., & Shearing, C. (2005). Nodal governance. *Australian Journal of Legal Philosophy*, *30*, 30–58.

Burris, S., Kempa, M., & Shearing, C. (2008). Changes in governance: A cross-disciplinary review of current scholarship. *Akron Law Review*, *4*(1), 1–66.

Buur, L., Jensen, S., & Stepputat, F. (Eds.). (2007). *The security-development Nexus: Expressions of sovereignty and securitization in Southern Africa*. Cape Town: HSRC Press.

Buzan, B., & Hansen, L. (2009). *The evolution of international security studies*. Cambridge: Cambridge University Press.

Buzan, B., Wæver, O., and De Wilde, J. (1997). *Security: A new framework for analysis*. Boulder, CO: Lynne Rienner Publishers.

Cardoso, F., & Faletto, E. (1979). *Dependency and development in Latin America*. Berkeley: University of California Press.

Carter, I. (2003, September 7–9). *Functionings, capabilities and the value of freedom*. Paper presented at the 3rd International Conference on the Capability Approach, University of Pavia, Italy.

Cartwright, J., & Shearing, C. (2012). *Where's the chicken? Making South Africa safe*. Cape Town: Burnet Media.

Cashore, B. (2002). Legitimacy and the privatization of environmental governance: How non-state market driven (NSMD) governance systems gain rule-making authority. *Governance*, *15*(4), 503–529.

Cashore, B., Auld, G., Newsom, D., & Egan, E. (2009). The emergence of non-state environmental governance in European and North American forest sectors. In M. Schreurs, H. Selin, & S.D. VanDeveer (Eds.), *Transatlantic environment and energy politics: Comparative and international perspectives*. Aldershot, UK: Ashgate, 209–230.

CSVR (Center for the Study of Violence and Reconciliation). (2009, April 7). *Why does South Africa have such high rates of violent crime?* Supplement to the final report of the study on the violent nature of crime in South Africa, produced for the Justice, Crime Prevention and Security (JCPS) cluster. Submitted to the Minister of Safety and Security. Retrieved from http://www.csvr.org.za/docs/study/7.unique_about_SA.pdf

Chambers, C. (2003). Nation-building, neutrality and ethnocultural justice: Kymlicka's liberal pluralism. *Ethnicities*, *3*(3), 295–319.

Chambers, C. (2008). *Sex, culture, and justice: The limits of choice*. University Park, PA: Penn State University Press.

Chandler, D. (2001). The road to military humanitarianism: How the human rights NGOs shaped a new humanitarian agenda. *Human Rights Quarterly, 23,* 678–700.

Chandler, D. (2003). New rights for old? Cosmopolitan citizenship and the critique of state sovereignty. *Political Studies, 51,* 332–349.

Chang, H.-J. (2003). *Globalisation, economic development and the role of the state.* London: Zed Books.

Christensen, T., & Lægreid, P. (1998). Administrative reform policy: The case of Norway. *International Review of Administrative Sciences, 64*(3), 457–475.

Christensen, T., & Lægreid, P. (2001). *New public management. The transformation of ideas and practice.* Aldershot, UK: Ashgate.

Christensen, T., & Lægreid, P. (2009). *Transcending new public management. The transformation of public sector reforms.* Aldershot, UK: Ashgate.

Christie, N. (1977). Conflicts as property. *British Journal of Criminology, 17*(1), 1–15.

Clear, T.R. (2007). *Imprisoning communities: How mass incarceration makes disadvantaged neighborhoods worse.* New York: Oxford University Press.

Cohen, J. (1989). Deliberative democracy and democratic legitimacy. In A. Hamlin & P. Pettit (Eds.), *The good polity.* Oxford: Blackwell.

Cohen, J., & Sabel, C. (1997). Directly-deliberative polyarchy. *European Law Review, 3*(4), 313–342.

Connolly, W.E. (1974). Essentially contested concepts in politics. In W.E. Connolly (Ed.), *The terms of political discourse.* Lexington: Heath.

Consedine, J. (1999). *Restorative justice: Healing the effects of crime.* Lyttelton, New Zealand: Ploughshares Publications.

Consedine, J. (2005). Is there a place for forgiveness in restorative justice? *Journal of South Pacific Law, 9*(1). Retrieved from http://www.paclii.org/journals/fJSPL/vol09no1/6.shtml

Considine, M. (2002). The end of the line? Accountable governance in the age of networks, partnerships, and joined-up services. *Governance, 15*(1), 21–40.

Cooke, B., & Kothari, U. (2001). *Participation: The new tyranny.* London: Zed Books.

Cooperrider, D., & Srivastva, S. (1987). Appreciative inquiry in organizational life. *Research in Organizational Change and Development, 1,* 129–169.

Courville, S. (2006). Understanding NGO-based social and environmental regulatory systems: Why we need new models of accountability. In M. Dowdle (Ed.), *Public accountability: Designs, dilemmas and experiences.* Cambridge: Cambridge University Press.

Crane, W., & Swilling, M. (2008). Environment, sustainable resource use and the Cape Town functional region—An overview. *Urban Forum, 19,* 263–287.

Crawford, A., & Clear, T.R. (2003). Community justice: Transforming communities through restorative justice? In E. McLauglin, R. Fergusson, G. Hughes, & L. Westmarland (Eds.), *Restorative justice. Critical issues,* pp. 215–29. London: Sage/The Open University.

Crawford, A., & Newburn, T. (2003). *Youth offending and restorative justice. Implementing reform in youth justice.* Cullompton, Devon: Willan Publishing.

Cronin, T. (1989). *Direct democracy: The politics of initiative, referendum and recall.* Cambridge, MA: Harvard University Press.

Cunneen, C. (2002). Restorative justice and the politics of decolonization. In H. Strang & J. Braithwaite (Eds.), *Restorative justice and civil society*, pp. 32–49. Cambridge: Cambridge University Press.

Dahl, R. (1961). *Who governs? Democracy and power in an American city*. London: Yale University Press.

Dahl, R. (1989). *Democracy and its critics*. New Haven, CT: Yale University Press.

Dahl, R. (1998). *On democracy*. New Haven, CT: Yale University Press.

Dalton, R. (2004). *Democratic challenges, democratic choices: The erosion of political support in advanced industrial societies*. Oxford: Oxford University Press.

Davis, M. (2006). *Planet of slums*. London: Verso.

Deal, T.E., & Kennedy, A.A. (1982). *Corporate cultures: The rites and rituals of corporate life*. London: Penguin Books.

Dean, M. (1999). *Governmentality: Power and rule in modern society*. London: Sage.

DeLong, J.B. (1999). Seeing one's intellectual roots: A review essay on James Scott's "Seeing Like a State." *Review of Austrian Economics, 12*(2), 245–255.

Devereux, S. (2001). Sen's entitlement approach: Critiques and counter-critiques. *Oxford Development Studies, 29*(3), 245–263.

DeVries, B.A. (1996). The world bank's focus on poverty. In J.M. Griesgraber & B.G. Gunter (Eds.), *The world bank: Lending on a global scale*. London: Pluto Press.

Dewey, J. (1916). *Democracy and education*. New York: The MacMillian Company.

Dewey, J. (1927). *The public and its problems*. Chicago: Swallow Press.

Dewey, J. (1938a). *Experience and education*. New York: Macmillan.

Dewey, J. (1938b). *Logic: The theory of inquiry*. New York: Holt, Rinehart and Winston.

Dewey, J. (1962). From absolutism to experimentalism. In G. Adams & W. Pepperell Montague (Eds.), *Contemporary American philosophy: Personal statements* (pp. 13–27). New York: Russell and Russell.

Diawara, M. (2000). Globalisation, development politics and local knowledge. *International Sociology, 15*(2), 361–371.

Dietz, T.E., Ostrom, E., & Stern, P.C. (2003). Review: The struggle to govern the commons. *Science, 12*, 1907–1912.

Dixon, B. (2004). In search of interactive globalization: Critical criminology in South Africa's transition. *Crime, Law and Social Change, 41*, 359–384.

Donnelly, J. (1985). Human rights and development: Complementary or competing concerns? In G.W. Shepherd & V.P. Nanda (Eds.), *Human rights and third world development* (pp. 27–55). Westport, CT: Greenwood Press.

Donnelly, J. (2001). *The universal declaration of human rights: A liberal defense*. Working Paper 12. Human Rights and Human Welfare.

Dorf, M.C., & Sabel, C.F. (1998). A constitution of democratic experimentalism. *Columbia Law Review, 98*, 267–473.

Douglass, M., & Friedmann, J. (Eds.). (1998). *Cities for citizens: Planning and the rise of civil society in a global age*. New York: John Wiley.

Douzinas, C. (2000). *The end of human rights*. Oxford: Hart Publishing.

Dowdle, M.W. (2006). Public accountability: Conceptual, historical, and epistemic mappings. In M.W. Dowdle (Ed.), *Public accountability, designs, dilemmas and experiences* (pp. 1–29). Cambridge: Cambridge University Press.

Drahos, P. (2005). An alternative framework for the global regulation of intellectual property rights. *Journal für Entwicklungspolitik, XXI*(4), 44–68.

Drahos, P., & Braithwaite, J. (2002). *Information feudalism: Who owns the knowledge economy*. London: Earthscan.

Drucker, P. (1994, November). The age of social transformation. *Atlantic Weekly*, 53–80.

Dryzek, J.S. (1996). Political inclusion and the dynamics of democratization. *American Political Science Review, 90*(1), 475–487.

Dryzek, J.S. (2002). *Deliberative democracy and beyond: Liberals, critics, contestations*. Oxford: Oxford University Press.

Dryzek, J.S. (2010). *Foundations and frontiers of deliberative governance*. Oxford: Oxford University Press.

Dryzek, J.S., & Dunleavy, P. (2009). *Theories of the democratic state*. Basingstoke, UK: Palgrave Macmillan.

Dryzek, J.S., & Niemeyer, S. (2008). Discursive representation. *American Political Science Review, 102*(4), 481–493.

Duff, R.A. (1992). Alternatives to punishment—or alternative punishments? In W. Craigg (Ed.), *Retributivism and its critics* (pp. 43–68). Stuttgart: Franz Steinter.

Duffield, M. (1993). NGOs, disaster relief and asset transfer in the horn: Political survival in a permanent emergency. *Development and Change, 24*, 131–157.

Duffield, M. (2001). *Global governance and the new wars: The merging of development and security*. London: Zed Books.

Duffield, M. (2005). Getting savages to fight barbarians: Development, security and the colonial present. *Conflict, Security and Development, 5*(2), 141–159.

Dunn, J. (1999). Democracy and development? In I. Shapiro & C. Hacker-Cordón (Ed.), *Democracy's value* (pp. 132–140). Cambridge: Cambridge University Press.

Dupont, B., Grabosky, P., and Shearing, C. (2003). The governance of security in weak and failing states. *Criminal Justice: An International Journal of Policy and Practice, 3*(4), 331–349.

Dworkin, R. (1981). What is equality? Part 2. Equality of resources. *Philosophy and Public Affairs, 10*(4), 283–345.

Dworkin, R. (2002). *Sovereign virtue: The theory and practice of equality*. Cambridge, MA: Harvard University Press.

Echavarri, R.A. (2003, September 7–9). *Development theories and development as social capability expansion*. Paper presented at the 3rd International Conference on the Capability Approach, University of Pavia, Italy.

Edigheji, O. (2010). *Constructing a democratic developmental state in South Africa*. Cape Town: Human Science Research Council Press.

Elster, J. (Ed.). (1998). *Deliberative democracy*. Cambridge Studies in the Theory of Democracy. Cambridge: Cambridge University Press.

Erdèlyi, P. (2008). Noortje Marres on the materiality of publics. Retrieved from http://erdelyi.wordpress.com/2008/02/11/noortje-marres-on-the-materiality -of-publics/

Ericson, R., & Haggerty, K. (1997). *Policing the risk society*. Toronto: University of Toronto Press.

Escobar, A. (1995). *Encountering development: The making and unmaking of the third world*. Princeton, NJ: Princeton University Press.

Etzioni, A. (1993). *The spirit of community. The reinvention of American society*. New York: Simon & Schuster and Crown Publishers.

Evans, P. (1995). *Embedded autonomy: States and industrial transformation*. Princeton, NJ: Princeton University Press.

Evans, P. (1996). Government action, social capital and development: Reviewing the evidence on synergy. *World Development, 24*(6), 1119–1132.

Evans, P. (2002). Collective capabilities, culture, and Amartya Sen's development as freedom. *Studies in Comparative International Development, 37*(2), 54–60.

Falk, R. (1992). Democratizing, internationalizing and globalizing: A collage of blurred images. *Third World Quarterly, 13*(4), 627–640.

Falk, R. (1999). *Predatory globalization: A critique*. Cambridge: Polity Press.

Felice, W. (2004). *Respecting, protecting and fulfilling economic and social rights: A UN Security Council?* Working Paper 12. Human Rights and Human Welfare.

Ferguson, J. (1990). *The anti-politics machine. "Development" and bureaucratic power in Lesotho*. Cambridge: Cambridge University Press.

Fields, A.B., & Narr, W.-D. (1992). Human rights as a holistic concept. *Human Rights Quarterly, 14*, 1–20.

Fishkin, J. (1995). *The voice of the people: Public opinion and democracy*. New Haven, CT: Yale University Press.

Fitzpatrick, P. (1988). The rise and rise of informalism. In R. Matthews (Ed.), *Informal justice?* (pp. 178–98). London: Sage.

Fitzpatrick, P. (2006). *Is humanity enough? The secular theology of human rights*. Working Paper 32. Human Rights and Human Welfare.

Forsythe, D.P. (2005). *International humanitarianism in the contemporary world: Forms and issues*. Working Paper 22. Human Rights and Human Welfare.

Foucault, M. (1978). *The history of sexuality: Vol. 1: An introduction*. New York: Pantheon Books.

Foucault, M. (1986). *Care of the self*. New York: Pantheon.

Foucault, M. (1988). An aesthetics of existence. In M. Foucault (Ed.), *Politics, philosophy, culture: Interviews and other writings, 1977–1984*. London: Routledge.

Foucault, M. (1991). Governmentality. In G. Burchell, C. Gordon, & P. Miller (Eds.), *The Foucault effect: Studies in governmentality*. Chicago: University of Chicago Press, p. 87–104.

Foucault, M. (2003). *Society must be defended. Lectures at the College De France 1975–1976*. New York: Picador.

Foucault, M. (2008). *The birth of biopolitics. Lectures at the College de France 1978–1979*. New York: Palgrave Macmillan.

Frank, A.G. (1967). *Capitalism and underdevelopment in Latin America: Historical studies of Brazil and Chile*. New York: Monthly Review Press.

Frank, A.G. (1979). *Dependent accumulation and underdevelopment*. London: Macmillan.

Frank, A.G. (1998). *Reorient: Global economy in the Asian age*. Los Angeles: University of California Press.

Frank, A.G., & Gills, B. (Eds.). (1993). *The world system: Five hundred or five thousand years*. London: Routledge.

Fraser, N. (1989). *Unruly practices*. Minneapolis: University of Minnesota Press.

Freeman, J. (2006). Extending public accountability through privatization: From public law to publicization. In M.W. Dowdle (Ed.), *Public accountability: Designs, dilemmas and experiences*. Cambridge: Cambridge University Press, p. 83–114.

Freeman, J., & Farber, D.A. (2005). Modular environmental regulation. *Duke Law Journal, 54*, 795–909.

Freeman, M. (1994). The philosophical foundation of human rights. *Human Rights Quarterly, 16,* 491–514.

Frenkiel, E. (2011, December 28). Democracy: Bridging the representation gap. *Books and Ideas.*

Friedman, M. (1953). *Essays in positive economics.* Chicago: University of Chicago Press.

Friedman, M. (2002). *Capitalism and freedom.* Chicago: University of Chicago Press.

Friedmann, J. (1998). The new political economy of planning: The rise of civil society. In M. Douglass & J. Friedmann (Eds.), *Cities for citizens: Planning and the rise of civil society in a global age* (pp. 19–37). New York: John Wiley.

Friedmann, J. (2002). *The prospect of cities.* Minneapolis: University of Minnesota Press.

Froestad, J. (2005a). Environmental health problems in Hout Bay: The challenge of generalising trust in South Africa. *Journal of Southern African Studies, 31*(2), 333–356.

Froestad, J. (2005b). *The incapacitating impact of distrust: Observations from the health sector.* Aldershot, UK: Ashgate.

Froestad, J., & Shearing, C. (2005). Prática da Justiça—O Modelo Zwelethemba de Resolução de Conflitos [Practicing justice—The Zwelethemba model of conflict resolution]. In C. Slakmon, R. Campos, & R. Sócrates Gomes Pinto (Eds.), *Justicia restaurativa* (pp. 79–123). Brasília, D.F.: Ministério da Justiça do Brasil e Programa das Naçaões Unidas para o Desenvolvimento–Brasil.

Froestad, J., & Shearing, C. (2007a). Conflict resolution in South Africa: A case study. In G. Johnstone & D. van Ness (Eds.), *Handbook of restorative justice* (pp. 534–556). Cullompton, Devon: Willan Publishing.

Froestad, J., & Shearing, C. (2007b). Beyond restorative justice—Zwelethemba, a future-focused model of local capacity conflict resolution. In R. Mackay, M. Bošnjak, J. Deklerck, et al. (Eds.), *Images of restorative justice theory* (pp. 16–34). Frankfurt: Verlag für Polizeiwissenschaft.

Froestad, J., & Shearing, C. (2007c). Effecting security and deepening democracy through peace making and peace building forums: A South African rural experiment. In R. Southall (Ed.), *Conflict and governance in South Africa. Moving towards a more just and peaceful society.* Johannesburg: Lyttelton: The Conflict and Governance Facility, p. 312–333.

Froestad, J., & Shearing, C. (2007d). The Zwelethemba model—Practicing human rights through dispute resolution. In S. Parmentier & E. Weitekamp (Eds.), *Crime and human rights* (Vol. 9 in the Series Sociology of Crime, Law and Deviance, Part II: Human Rights and Justice). Oxford: Elsevier Press, p. 534–556.

Froestad, J., & Shearing, C. (2011). Re-imagining justice from the bottom up. In M. Carnelley & S. Hoctor (Eds.), *Law, order and liberty: Essays in honour of Tony Matthews.* Scottsville, South Africa: University of Kwa-Zulu Natal Press, 237–250.

Froestad, J., Shearing, C., Herbstein, H., & Grimwood, S. (2012). City of Cape Town solar water heater bylaw: Barriers to implementation. In A. Cartwright, S. Parnell, G. Oelofse, & S. Ward (Eds.), *Climate change at the city scale: Impacts, mitigation and adaptation in Cape Town.* London: Earthscan, 244–262.

Fry, L.W., Keim, G.D., and Meiners, R.E. (1982). Corporate contributions: Altruistic or for profit? *Academy of Management Journal, 25*(1), 94–106.

Fukuda-Parr, S. (2003). The Human Development Program: Operationalizing Sen's ideas on capabilities. *Feminist Economics, 9*(2–3), 301–317.

Fukuyama, F. (1992). *The end of history and the last man.* New York: Free Press.

Fukuyama, F. (2004). *State-building: Governance and world order in the 21st century.* Ithaka, NY: Cornell University Press.

Fukuyama, F. (2011). *The origins of political order. From prehuman times to the French Revolution.* London: Profile Books.

Fung, A. (2001). Accountable autonomy: Toward empowered deliberation in Chicago schools and policing. *Political Sociology, 29*(1), 73–103.

Fung, A. (2003). Associations and democracy: Between theories, hopes and realities. *Annual Review of Sociology, 29,* 515–539.

Fung, A. (2004). *Empowered participation: Reinventing urban democracy.* Princeton, NJ: Princeton University Press.

Fung, A., & Wright, E.O. (2001). Deepening democracy: Innovations in empowered participatory governance. *Politics and Society, 29*(1), 5–41.

Fung, A., & Wright, E.O. (Eds.). (2003). *Deepening democracy: Institutional innovations in empowered participatory governance.* London: Verso.

Furger, F. (1997). Accountability and systems of self-governance: The case of the maritime industry. *Law and Policy, 19*(4), 445–476.

Galanter, M. (1981). Justice in many rooms: Courts, private ordering and indigenous law. *Journal of Legal Pluralism, 19,* 1–47.

Gallego, A. (2007). *Inequality in political participation: Contemporary patterns in European countries.* CSD Working Papers. Center for the Study of Democracy, University of California, Irvine.

Gallie, W.B. (1956). Essentially contested concepts. *Proceedings of the Aristotelian Society, 6*(23), 167–198.

Galtung, J. (2003/2004). *Human needs, humanitarian intervention, human security and the war in Iraq.* Keynote, Sophia University/ICU, Tokyo, December 14, 2003, and Regional Studies Association, Tokyo, January 10, 2004. Retrieved from http://www.transnational.org/SAJT/forum/meet/2004/Galtung_HumanNeeds.html

Gardner, J.A. (1996). Shut up and vote: A critique of deliberative democracy and the life of talk. *Tennessee Law Review, 63,* 624–651.

Garland, D. (1996). The limits of the sovereign state: Strategies of crime control in contemporary society. *British Journal of Criminology, 36*(4), 445–471.

Gasper, D. (2000). Development as freedom: Taking economics beyond commodities—The cautious boldness of Amartya Sen. *Journal of International Development, 12,* 989–1001.

Gastil, J. (2000). *By popular demand: Revitalizing representative democracy through deliberative elections.* Berkeley: University of California Press.

Gellner, E. (1983). *Nations and nationalism.* Oxford: Blackwell.

Giri, A.K. (2000). Rethinking human well-being: A dialogue with Amartya Sen. *Journal of International Development, 12,* 1003–1018.

Gladwell, M. (2002). *The tipping point: How little things can make a big difference.* New York: Back Bay Books.

Gobodo-Madikizela, P. (2003). *A human being died that night: A story of forgiveness.* Cape Town: David Philips Publishers.

Goldin, J. (2005). Pre-packed trust and the water sector. In S. Askvik & N. Bak (Eds.), *Trust in public institutions in South Africa.* Aldershot, UK: Ashgate, 137–152.

Goldstein, H. (1979). Improving policing: A problem-oriented approach. *Crime and Delinquency, 25*(2), 236–258.

Goodhart, M. (2003). Origins and universality in the human rights debates: Cultural essentialism and the challenge of globalization. *Human Rights Quarterly*, *25*, 935–964.

Gooding-Williams, R. (1998). Race, multiculturalism, and democracy. *Constellations*, *5*, 18–41.

Gordon, C. (1991). Governmental rationality: An introduction. In G. Burchell, C. Gordon, & P. Miller (Eds.), *The Foucault effect: Studies in governmentality*. Chicago: University of Chicago Press, 1–51.

Gordon, D. (2006). *Transformation and trouble: Crime, justice, and participation in democratic South Africa*. Ann Arbor: University of Michigan Press.

Gray, J. (1978). On liberty, liberalism and essential contestability. *British Journal of Political Science*, *8*(4), 385–402.

Greenberg, J.B. (1997). A political ecology of structural-adjustment policies: The case of the Dominican Republic. *Culture and Agriculture*, *19*(3), 85–93.

Griesgraber, J.M., & Gunter, B. (1996). *The World Bank: Lending on a global scale*. London: Pluto Press.

Groenewegen, J. (2010). Review of Paul Dragos Aligica and Peter J. Boettke's *Challenging institutional analysis and development: The Bloomington School*, London and New York: Routledge, 2009. *Erasmus Journal of Philosophy and Economics*, *3*(1), 108–113.

Guijt, I. (2010). Accountability and learning: Exploring the myth of incompatibility between accountability and learning. In J. Ubels, N. Acquaye-Baddoo, & A. Fowler (Eds.), *Capability development in practice*. London: Earthscan.

Guilhot, N. (2005). *The democracy makers*. New York: Columbia University Press.

Gunningham, N., Grabosky, P., & Sinclair, D. (1998). *Smart regulation: Designing environmental policy*. Oxford: Clarendon Press.

Gunningham, N., Holley, C., and Shearing, C. (2012). *The new environmental governance*. London: Earthscan.

Gunningham, N., & Rees, J. (1997). Industry self-regulation: An institutional perspective. *Law and Policy*, *19*(4), 363–414.

Haas, P. (1990). Obtaining international environmental protection through epistemic consensus. *Millennium Journal of International Studies*, *19*(3), 347–363.

Haas, P. (1992). Introduction: Epistemic communities and international policy coordination. *International Organization*, *46*(1), 1–35.

Haas, P. (2004). Addressing the global governance deficit. *Global Environmental Politics*, *4*(4), 1–15.

Habermas, J. (2001). The postnational constellation and the future of democracy. In J. Habermas, *The postnational constellation: Political essays* (M. Pensky, Trans. & Ed.). Cambridge: Polity Press, 58–112.

Hammer, M., & Lloyd, R. (2011). *Pathways to accountability II. 2011 revised global accountability framework*. London: One World Trust. Retrieved from http://www.oneworldtrust.org

Hampton, J. (1992). An expressive theory of retribution. In W. Cragg (Ed.), *Retributivism and its critics*. Papers of the Special Nordic Conference held at the University of Toronto, June 25–27, 1990. Stuttgart: Steiner, 29.

Haq, M. (1995). *Reflection on human development*. New York: Oxford University Press.

Haraway, D.J. (1988). Situated knowledges: The science question in feminism and the privilege of partial perspectives. *Feminist Studies*, *14*(3), 575–599.

Harrington, C., & Turem, Z.U. (2006). Accounting for accountability in neoliberal regulatory regimes. In M.W. Dowdle (Ed.), *Public accountability, designs, dilemmas and experiences*. Cambridge: Cambridge University Press.

Haskell, J. (2001). *Direct democracy or representative government? Dispelling a populist myth*. Boulder, CO: Westview Press.

Hayek, F. (1944). *The road to serfdom*. London: Routledge.

Hayek, F. (1973). *Law, legislation and liberty: Rules and order* (Vol. 1). London: Routledge & Kegan Paul.

Heclo, H. (1978). Issue networks and the executive establishment. In A. King (Ed.), *The new American political system*. Washington, DC: American Enterprise Institute for Public Policy Research, 87–124.

Held, D. (1995). Democracy and the new international order. In D. Archibugi & D. Held (Eds.), *Cosmopolitan democracy*. Cambridge: Polity Press, 96–120.

Held, D. (1999). The transformation of political community: Rethinking democracy in the context of globalisation. In I. Shapiro & C. Hacker-Cordon (Eds.), *Democracy's edges*. Cambridge: Cambridge University Press. 84–111.

Held, D. (2000). The changing contours of political community: Rethinking democracy in the context of globalisation. In B. Holden (Ed.), *Global democracy*. London: Routledge, 17–31.

Held, D. (2003). *Cosmopolitanism: A defence*. Cambridge: Polity Press.

Held, D. (2005). Principles of the cosmopolitan order. In G. Brock & H. Brighouse (Eds.), *The political philosophy of cosmopolitanism*. Cambridge: Cambridge University Press, 10–27.

Held, D., & Koenig-Archibugi, M. (2005). *Global governance and public accountability*. Oxford: Blackwell.

Held, D., & Moore, H.L. (Eds.). (2008). *Cultural politics in a global age: Uncertainty, solidarity, and innovation*. London: Oneworld Publications.

Held, D., McGrew, A., Goldblatt, D., & Perraton, J. (1999). *Global transformations: Politics, economics and culture*. Stanford, CA: Stanford University Press.

Heller, P., Rueschemeyer, D., & Snyder, R. (2009). Dependency and development in a globalized world. *Comparative International Development* (special issue), 44(4).

Heymann, P. (Ed.). (1992). *Towards peaceful protest in South Africa: Testimony of prevention of public violence and intimidation*. Pretoria: HSRC.

Hill, M.T. (2003). Development as empowerment. *Feminist Economics, 9*(2–3), 117–135.

Hindess, B. (1997). Democracy and disenchantment. *Australian Journal of Political Science, 32*(1), 79–92.

Hobart, M. (1993). *An anthropological critique of development: The growth of ignorance*. London: Routledge.

Hobbes, T. (1968). *Leviathan* (C.B. Macpherson, Ed.). London: Penguin Books. (Original work published 1651)

Hobson, C. (2008). Revolution, representation and the foundations of modern democracy. *European Journal of Political Theory, 7*(4), 449–471.

Hobson, J.M. (2000). *The state and international relations*. Cambridge: Cambridge University Press.

Holtmann, B., & Domingo-Swarts, C. (2008). Current trends and responses to crime in South Africa. In A. van Niekerk, S. Suffla, & M. Seedat (Eds.), *Crime, violence and injury prevention in South Africa: Data to action*. Medical Research

Council–University of South Africa Crime, Violence and Injury Lead Program, 105–129. Retrieved from http://www.mrc.ac.za/crime/cvi_second_review_ ch1_3.pdf.

Honneth, A. (1998). Democracy as reflexive cooperation: John Dewey and the theory of democracy today. *Political Theory, 26*(6), 763–783.

Hood, C. (1999). *Regulation inside government: Waste watchers, quality police and sleazebusters*. Oxford: Oxford University Press.

Hood, C. (2000). Regulation of government: Has it increased, is it increasing, should it be diminished? *Public Administration, 78*(2), 283–304.

Hood, C., & Scott, C. (1996). Bureaucratic regulation and new public management in the United Kingdom: Mirror image developments? *Journal of Law and Society, 23*(3), 321–345.

Howell, L., & Pearce, J. (2001). *Civil society and development: A critical exploration*. Boulder, CO: Lynne Rienner Publishers.

Hudson, B. (2003). *Justice in the risk society: Challenging and re-affirming justice in late modernity*. London: Sage Publications.

Hutchens, A. (2009). *Changing big business: The globalisation of the fair trade movement*. Cheltenham, UK: Edward Elgar Publishers.

Hutchings, K., & Dannreuter, R. (Eds.). (1999). *Cosmopolitan citizenship*. Basingstoke, UK: Macmillan.

Hyden, G. (2005). *African politics in comparative perspective*. Cambridge: Cambridge University Press.

Ikpe, E. (2007). Challenging the discourse on fragile states. *Conflict, Security and Development, 7*(1), 85–124.

IMF. (1997). *Good governance: The IMF's role*. Washington, DC: International Monetary Fund.

Independent Commission on Policing for Northern Ireland. (1999). *A new beginning: Policing in Northern Ireland*. Retrieved from http://cain.ulst.ac.uk/issues/police/ patten/patten99.pdf

International IDEA (Institute for Democracy and Electoral Assistance). (2002). *Voter turnout since 1945: A global report*. Stockholm: IDEA.

International IDEA (Institute for Democracy and Electoral Assistance). (2008). *Direct democracy: The International IDEA handbook*. Stockholm: International IDEA.

Jacobsen, K.D. (1960). Lojalitet, nøytralitet og faglig uavhengighet i sentraladminis-trasjonen [Loyalty, neutrality and professional autonomy in the central public administration]. *Tidsskrift for Samfunnsforskning, 1*, 231–248.

Jacobsen, K.D. (1964). *Teknisk hjelp og politisk struktur* [Technical assistance and political structure]. Oslo: Universitetsforlaget.

Jacobsen, K.D. (1965). Informasjonstilgang og Likebehandling I den Offentlige Virksomhet [Access to information and equal treatment in public policy]. *Tidsskrift for Samfunnsforskning, 6*(2), 147–160.

Jacobsen, K.D. (1967). Politisk Fattigdom [Political poverty]. *Kontrast, 3*(1), 6–9.

Jacobsen, K.D., & Eckhoff, T. (1960). *Rationality and responsibility in administrative and judicial decision making*. Copenhagen: Munksgaard.

Johnson, C. (1982). *MIT and the Japanese miracle*. Stanford, CA: Stanford University Press.

Johnston, L. (1996). What is vigilantism? *British Journal of Criminology, 36*(2), 220–236.

Johnston, L., & Shearing, C. (2003). *Governing security: Explorations in policing and justice*. London: Routledge.

Johnstone, G. (2007). Critical perspectives on restorative justice. In G. Johnstone & D.W. van Ness (Eds.), *Handbook of restorative justice* (pp. 598–614). Cullompton, Devon: Willan Publishing.

Jordan, G., & Schubert, K. (1992). Policy networks. *European Journal of Political Research* (special issue), *21*, 1–2.

Jordana, J., & Levi-Faur, D. (Eds.). (2004). *The politics of regulation: Institutions and regulatory reforms for the age of governance*. Cheltenham, UK: Edward Elgar.

Kaldor, M. (2003). *Global civil society: An answer to war*. Cambridge: Polity Press.

Kaldor, M. (2007). Democracy and globalisation. In M. Albrow, H.K. Anheier, M. Glasius, et al. (Eds.), *Global civil society 2007/8: Communicative power and democracy*. London: London School of Economics/Sage Publications.

Kant, I. (1987). *Critique of judgement* (W.S. Pluha, Trans.). Indianapolis: Hackett. (Original work published 1790)

Karkkainen, B. (2004). Post-sovereign environmental governance. *Global Environmental Politics*, *4*(1), 72–96.

Kaufman-Osborn, T.V. (1985). Pragmatism, policy science, and the state. *American Journal of Political Science*, *29*(4), 827–849.

Kempa, M., Stenning, P., & Wood, J. (2004). Policing communal spaces: A reconfiguration of the "mass private property" hypothesis. *British Journal of Criminology*, *44*, 562–581.

Kim, Q.-Y. (1982). Review of revolution from above: Military bureaucrats and development in Japan, Turkey, and Peru. *Social Forces*, *60*(4), 1201–1203.

Klingemann, H.-D., & Fuchs, D. (Eds.). (1995). *Citizens and the state*. New York: Oxford University Press.

Koehler, G., & Tausch, A. (2002). *Global Keynesianism: Unequal exchange and global exploitation*. Huntington, NY: Nova Science.

Kohli, A. (2003). *States, markets and just growth*. Tokyo: United Nations University Press.

Kohli, A. (2004). *State-directed development: Political power and industrialization in the global periphery*. Cambridge: Cambridge University Press.

Konig, K. (1996). Public administration—Post-industrial, post-modern, post-bureaucratic. In European Group of Public Administration, *New trends in public administration and public law*. Budapest: University of Economic Sciences, Center for Public Affairs Studies.

Konig, K. (1997). Entrepreneurial management or executive administration. In W.J.M. Kickert (Ed.), *Public management and administrative reforms in Western Europe*. Cheltenham, UK: Edward Elgar, 217–236.

Krasner, S. (1984). Approaches to the state. Alternative conceptions and historical dynamics. *Comparative Politics*, *16*, 223–246.

Krasner, S. (1988). Sovereignty: An institutional perspective. *Comparative Political Studies*, *21*(1), 66–94.

Krasner, S. (1999). *Sovereignty: Organized hypocrisy*. Princeton, NJ: Princeton University Press.

Krasner, S. (2001). *Problematic sovereignty: Contested and political possibilities*. New York: Columbia University Press.

Krasner, S. (2002, January-February). Sovereignty. *Foreign Policy*, 20–29.

Kulick, E., & Wilson, D. (1996). *Time for Thailand. Profile of a new success.* Bangkok: White Lotus Press.

Kymlicka, W. (1991). *Liberalism, community and culture.* Oxford: Oxford University Press. (Original work published 1989)

Landau, M. (1969). Redundancy, rationality and the problem of duplication and over-lap. *Public Administration Review, 29*(4), 346–358.

Langlois, A.J. (2002). Human rights: The globalisation and fragmentation of moral discourse. *Review of International Studies, 28,* 479–496.

Lasswell, H.D. (1941). The garrison state. *American Journal of Sociology, 46*(4), 455–468.

Latour, B. (2005). *Reassembling the social: An introduction to actor-network theory.* Oxford: Oxford University Press.

Latour, B. (2007). Turning around politics: A note on Gerard de Vries' paper. *Social Studies of Science, 37*(5), 811–820.

Law Commission of Canada. (2006). *In search of security: The future of policing in Canada.* Report by the Law Commission of Canada. Ottawa. Retrieved from http://www.policecouncil.ca/reports/LCC2006.pdf

Leftwich, A. (1995). Bringing politics back in: Towards a model of the development state. *Journal of Development Studies, 31*(3), 400–427.

Leman-Langlois, S., & Shearing, C. (2004). Repairing the future: The South African Truth and Reconciliation Commission at work. In G. Gilligan & J. Pratt (Eds.), *Crime, truth and justice: Official enquiry, discourse, knowledge.* Cullompton, Devon: Willan Publishing, 222–242.

Leman-Langlois, S., & Shearing, C. (2008). Transition, forgiveness and citizenship: The TRC and the social construction of forgiveness. In F. du Bois & A. Pedain (Eds.), *Justice and reconciliation in post-apartheid South Africa.* Cambridge: Cambridge University Press, 206–228.

Leman-Langlois, S., & Shearing, C. (2010). *Social control and human rights. Contributors to: The widening web of control: A human rights analysis of public policy responses to crime, social problems and deviance.* Draft report. Geneva: International Council on Human Rights.

Lemke, T. (2001). The birth of bio-politics: Michael Foucault's lectures at the College de France on neo-liberal governmentality. *Economy and Society, 30*(2), 190–207.

Lessig, L. (1999). *Code and other laws of cyberspace.* New York: Basic Books.

Levi-Faur, D. (2005). The rise of regulatory capitalism: The global diffusion of a new order. *Annals of the American Academy of Political and Social Sciences, 598*(1), 12–32.

Levi-Faur, D. (2006). Varieties of regulatory capitalism: Sectors and nations in the making of a new global order. *Governance* (special issue), *19*(3).

Levrant, S., Cullen, F.T., Fulton, B., & Wozniak, J.F. (1999). Reconsidering restorative justice: The corruption of benevolence revisited? *Crime and Delinquency, 45*(1), 3–27.

Lewis, A. (1955). *The theory of economic growth.* Homewood, IL: Irwin.

Lindblom, C.L. (1965). *The intelligence of democracy: Decision making by mutual adjustment.* New York: Free Press.

Lipset, S.M. (1959). Some social requisites of democracy: Economic development and political legitimacy. *American Political Science Review, 53*(1), 69–105.

Loader, I., & Walker, N. (2004). State of denial? Rethinking the governance of security. *Punishment and Society*, *6*(2), 221–228.

Loader, I., & Walker, N. (2007). *Civilizing security*. Cambridge: Cambridge University Press.

Locke, J. (1693). *Some thoughts concerning education*. London: A. and J. Churchill.

Louw, A., Shaw, M., Camerer, L., & Robertshaw, R. (1998). *Crime in Johannesburg: Results of a city victim survey*. Monograph 18. Pretoria: ISS.

Lowi, T. (1969). *The end of liberalism*. New York: W.W. Norton.

Lowi, T. (1999, October/November). Frontyard propaganda. *Boston Review*, 24. Retrieved from http://bostonreview.net/BR24.5/lowi.html, 62.

Lukes, S. (1974). *Power: A radical view*. London: Macmillan.

Maharaj, B., Desai, A., & Bond, P. (Eds.). (2010). *Zuma's own goal: Losing South Africa's "war on poverty."* Trenton, NJ: Africa World Press.

Maitland, F. (1972). *Justice and police*. London: Macmillan. (Original work published 1885)

Majone, G. (1994). The rise of regulatory state in Europe. *West European Politics*, *17*(3), 77–101.

Majone, G. (1997). From the positive to the regulatory state—Causes and consequences from changes in the modes of governance. *Journal of Public Policy*, *17*(2), 139–167.

Majone, G. (1999). The regulatory state and its legitimacy problems. *West European Politics*, *22*(1), 1–24.

Manin, B., Goode, J., & Hawthorn, G. (1997). *The principles of representative government*. Cambridge: Cambridge University Press.

Mansbridge, J. (1992). A deliberative theory and interest representation. In M. Patracca (Ed.), *The politics of interests: Interests transformed*. Boulder, CO: Westview.

Mansbridge, J. (2003). Rethinking representation. *American Political Science Review*, *97*(4), 515–528.

March, J. (1986). How we talk and how we act: Administrative theory and administrative life. In T.J. Sergiovanni & J.E. Corbally (Eds.), *Leadership and organizational culture. New Perspectives on administrative theory and practice*. Urbana and Chicago: University of Illinois Press, 18–35.

March, J. (1991). Exploration and exploitation in organizational learning. *Organizational Science*, *2*(1), 71–87.

Marenin, O. (2005). *Restoring policing systems in conflict torn nations: Process, problems, prospects*. Geneva Center for the Democratic Control of Armed Forces (DCAF) Occasional Paper 7. Retrieved from http://www.isn.ethz.ch/isn/Digital-Library/Publications/Detail/?ots591=cab359a3-9328-19cc-a1d2-8023e646b22c&lng=en&id=14076

Marks, G., Scharpf, F.W., & Schmitter, P.C. (1996). *Governance in the European Union*. London: Sage.

Marks, M., & Bradley, D. (2008, May 26–28). *Nexus policing: Reflections and imaginings: On the "holy" alliance between police practitioners and academic researchers* (unpublished paper). Paper presented at the Nexus Policing: Binding Research to Practice conference, Melbourne Exhibition and Convention Center, Melbourne, Victoria.

Marks, R.B. (2002). *The origins of the modern world: A global and ecological narrative*. Lanham, MD: Rowman & Littlefield.

Marres, N.S. (2005). No issue, no public: Democratic deficits after the displacement of politics. Doctoral thesis, University of Amsterdam. Retrieved from http://dare.uva.nl/document/17061

Marsh, D., & Rhodes, R.A.W. (1992). *Policy networks in British government*. Oxford: Clarendon.

Marshaw, J.L. (2006). Accountability and institutional design: Some thoughts on the grammar of governance. In M.W. Dowdle (Ed.), *Public accountability, designs, dilemmas and experiences*. Cambridge: Cambridge University Press, 115–156.

Martin, J. (2012). Informal security nodes and force capital. *Policing and Society, 22*(1).

Mason, A. (1990). On explaining political disagreement: The notion of an essentially contested concept. *Inquiry: An Interdisciplinary Journal of Philosophy, 33*(1), 81–98.

McClelland, D. (1961). *The achieving society*. Princeton, NJ: Van Nostrand.

McDermott, D. (2001). The permissibility of punishment. *Law and Philosophy, 20*, 403–432.

McGinnis, M.D. (Ed.). (1999a.) *Polycentric governance and development: Readings from the Workshop in Political Theory and Policy Analysis*. Ann Arbor: University of Michigan Press.

McGinnis, M.D. (1999b). *Polycentricity and local public economies: Readings from the Workshop in Political Theory and Policy Analysis*. Ann Arbor: University of Michigan Press.

Menkel-Meadow, C. (2003). *Dispute processing and conflict resolution: Theory, practice and policy*. Burlington, VT: Ashgate/Dartmouth.

Menkel-Meadow, C., Love, J.P., Schneider, A.K., & Sternlight, J.R. (2004). *Dispute resolution: Beyond the adversarial model*. New York: Aspen Publishers.

Mertus, J.A. (1999). Doing democracy differently: The transformative potential of human rights NGOs in transnational civil society. *Third World Legal Studies*, 205–234.

Mika, H. (1992). Mediation interventions and restorative justice: Responding to the astructural bias. In H. Messmer & H. Otto (Eds.), *Restorative justice on trial: Pitfalls and potentials of victim-offender mediation: International research perspectives*. Dordrecht: Kluwer Academic Publishers, 559–568.

Mika, H., & Zehr, H. (2003). A restorative framework for community justice practice. In K. McEvoy & T. Newburn (Eds.), *Criminology, conflict resolution and restorative justice*. New York: Palgrave Macmillan, 135–152.

Miller, P., & Rose, N. (1990). Governing economic life. *Economy and Society, 19*(1), 1–31.

Miller, P., & Rose, N. (2008). *Governing the present: Administering economic, social and personal life*. Cambridge: Polity Press.

Milovanovic, D. (2006). Diversity, law and justice: A Deluzian semiotic view of criminal justice. *International Journal for the Semiotics of Law, 20*, 55–79.

Miraftab, F. (2004). Public-private partnerships: The Trojan horse of neoliberal development? *Journal of Planning Education and Research, 24*(1), 89–101.

Mjoeset, L. (2007). An early approach to the varieties of world capitalism: Methodological and substantive lessons from the Senghaas/Menzel-project. *Comparative Social Research, 24*, 123–176.

Mkandawire, T., & Olukoshi, A.O. (1995). *Between liberalisation and oppression: The politics of structural adjustment in Africa*. Dakar, Senegal: CODESRIA Book Series.

Monbiot, G. (2003). *The age of consent: A manifesto for a new world order*. London: Harper Perennial.

Montesquieu, C. (1766). *The spirit of laws*. London: J. Nourse and P. Vaillant.

Moran, M. (2001). The rise of the regulatory state in Britain. *Parliamentary Affairs, 54*, 19–34.

Moran, M. (2002). Review article. Understanding the regulatory state. *British Journal of Political Science, 32*, 391–413.

Morenoff, J.D., Sampson, R.J., & Raudenbush, S.W. (2001). *Neighborhood inequality, collective efficacy, and the spatial dynamics of urban violence*. Research Report 00-451 (revised March 2001). University of Michigan, Population Studies Center.

Morgan, B. (2006). Technocratic v. convivial accountability. In M.W. Dowdle (Ed.), *Public accountability: Designs, dilemmas and experiences*. Cambridge: Cambridge University Press.

Morris, A., & Maxwell, G. (2001). *Restorative justice for juveniles: Conferencing, mediation and circles*. Oxford: Hart Publishing.

Mouffe, C. (2000). For an agonistic model of democracy. In C. Mouffe, *The democratic paradox*. London: Verso, 80–107.

Murray, D., Raynolds, L., & Taylor, P. (2003). *One cup at a time: Poverty alleviation and fair trade coffee in Latin America*. Fort Collins, CO: Colorado State University.

Muscat, R. (1994). *The fifth tiger: A study of Thai development*. Armonk, NY: M.E. Sharpe.

Mwanza, A.M. (Ed.). (1992). *Structural adjustment programmes in SADC: Experiences and lessons from Malawi, Tanzania, Zambia and Zimbabwe*. Harare, Zimbabwe: SAPES Books.

Nakano, T. (2006). A critique of Held's cosmopolitan democracy. *Contemporary Political Theory, 5*(1), 33–51.

Narayan, D., Chambers, R., Shah, M.K., et al. (2000a). *Voices of the poor: Can anyone hear us?* New York: Oxford University Press for the World Bank.

Narayan, D., Chambers, R., Shah, M.K., et al. (2000b). *Voices of the poor: Crying out for change*. New York: Oxford University Press for the World Bank.

National Planning Commission. (2011). National development plan: Vision for 2030. Pretoria: National Planning Commission.

Nicholls, A., & Opal, C. (2004). *Fair trade: Market-driven ethical consumption*. London: Sage.

Nina, D. (2001). Popular justice and the "appropriation" of the state monopoly on the definition of justice and order: The case of anti-crime communities. In W. Scharf & D. Nina (Eds.), *The other law: Non-state ordering in South Africa*. Cape Town: Juta.

North, D.C. (1990). *Institutions, institutional change and economic performance*. Cambridge: Cambridge University Press.

Nye, J. (1997). *Why people don't trust government*. Cambridge, MA: Harvard University Press.

Nygren, A. (1999). Local knowledge in the environment-development discourse: From dichotomies to situated knowledges. *Critique of Anthropology, 19*(3), 267–288.

O'Donnell, G. (1999). Horizontal accountability in new democracies. In A. Schedler, L. Diamond, & M. Platter (Eds.), *The self-restraining state: Power and accountability in new democracies*. Boulder, CO: Lynne Rienner, 29–52.

O'Donnell, G., & Schmitter, P. (1986). *Transitions from authoritarian rule: Tentative conclusions about uncertain democracies*. Baltimore: Johns Hopkins University Press.

O'Malley, P. (1992). Risk, power and crime prevention. *Economy and Society, 21*, 252–275.

O'Malley, P. (1996a). Indigenous governance. *Economy and Society, 25*(3), 310–326.

O'Manique, J. (1990). Universal and inalienable rights: A search for foundations. *Human Rights Quarterly, 12*, 465–485.

OECD. (2003). *A development co-operation lens on terrorism prevention: Key entry points for action*. Paris: Development Assistance Committee.

OECD. (2006). Enhancing the delivery of justice and security in fragile states. Contribution by the DAC Network on Conflict, Peace and Development Co-operation (CPDC) to the Fragile States Group (FSG) workstream on service delivery. *OECD Journal on Development, 3*.

Olowu, D. (1989). Local institutions and development: The African experience. *Canadian Journal of African Studies, 23*(2), 201–231.

Olsen, J.P. (1983). *Organised democracy*. Bergen, Norway: Universitetsforlaget.

Olsen, J.P. (2006). Maybe it is time to rediscover bureaucracy. *Journal of Public Administration Research and Theory, 16*(1), 1–24.

Olsen, J.P. (2007). *Europe in search of political order. An institutional perspective on unity/diversity, citizens/their helpers, democratic design/horizontal drift, and the coexistence of orders*. Oxford: Oxford University Press.

Olsen, J.P. (2010). *Governing through institution building. Institutional theory and recent European experiments in democratic organization*. Oxford: Oxford University Press.

Opoku-Mensah, P., Lewis, D., & Tvedt, T. (Eds.). (2007). *Reconceptualising NGOs and their roles in development: NGOs, civil society and the international aid system*. Aalborg, Denmark: Aalborg University Press.

Osborne, D., & Gaebler, T. (1992). *Reinventing government: How the entrepreneurial spirit is transforming the public sector*. New York: Penguin Books.

Ostrom, E. (1990). *Governing the commons: The evolution of institutions for collective action*. Cambridge: Cambridge University Press.

Ostrom, E. (1996). Crossing the great divide: Coproduction, synergy, and development. *World Development, 24*(6), 1073–1087.

Ostrom, E. (1999). Coping with tragedies of the commons. *Annual Review of Political Science, 2*(1), 493–535.

Ostrom, E. (2000). Crowding out citizenship. *Scandinavian Political Studies, 23*(1), 3–16.

Ostrom, E. (2005). *Understanding institutional diversity*. Princeton, NJ: Princeton University Press.

Ostrom, V. (1972, September 5–9). *Polycentricity*. Workshop Working Paper Series, Workshop in Political Theory and Policy Analysis. Presented at the Annual Meeting of the American Political Science Association.

Ostrom, V., & Ostrom, E. (1961). A behavioral approach to the study of intergovernmental relations. *Annals of the American Academy of Political and Social Science Review, 55*, 135–146.

Ostrom, V., Tiebout, C.M., & Warren, R. (1961). The organization of government in metropolitan areas: A theoretical inquiry. *American Political Science Review, 55*(4), 831–842.

Otto, D. (1996). Nongovernmental organizations in the United Nations system: The emerging role of international civil society. *Human Rights Quarterly, 18,* 107–141.

*Oxford English Dictionary* online. Retrieved from http://oxforddictionaries.com

Page, S.E. (2006). Essay: Path dependence. *Quarterly Journal of Political Science, 1,* 87–115.

Parsons, T. (1960). *Structure and process in modern societies.* Glencoe, IL: Free Press.

Parsons, T., & Smelser, N. (1956). *Economy and society.* Glencoe, IL: Free Press.

Pateman, C. (1970). *Participation and democratic theory.* Cambridge: Cambridge University Press.

Pavlich, G. (2005). *Governing paradoxes of restorative justice.* London: Glasshouse Press.

Perry, M.J. (1997). Are human rights universal? The relativist challenge and related matters. *Human Rights Quarterly, 19,* 461–509.

Peters, T.J., & Waterman, R.H. (2004). *In search of excellence: Lessons from America's best-run companies.* London: Profile Books Ltd.

Pierre, J. (Ed.). (2000). *Debating governance—Authority, steering and democracy.* Oxford: Oxford University Press.

Pierson, P. (2000). Increasing returns, path dependence, and the study of politics. *American Political Science Review, 94*(2), 251–267.

Pierson, P., & Skocpol, T. (2002). Historical institutionalism in contemporary political science. In I. Katznelson & H.V. Milner (Eds.), *Political science: State of the discipline.* New York: W.W. Norton, 693–721.

Pitkin, H.F. (1967). *The concept of representation.* Berkeley: University of California.

Pitkin, H.F. (2004). Representation and democracy: Uneasy alliance. *Scandinavian Political Studies, 27*(3), 335–342.

Polanyi, M. (1951). *The logic of liberty.* Chicago: University of Chicago Press.

Polidano, C. (2001). Don't discard state autonomy: Revisiting the East Asian experience of development. *Political Studies, 49*(3), 513–527.

Pollis, A. (1996). Cultural relativism revisited: Through a state prism. *Human Rights Quarterly, 18,* 316–344.

Pollit, C., & Bouckaert, G. (2004). *Public management reform.* Oxford: Oxford University Press.

Porter, M.E., & Kramer, M.R. (2002). The competitive advantage of corporate philanthropy. *Harvard Business Review, 80,* 56–68.

Porter, M.E., & Kramer, M.R. (2011, January/February). Creating shared value. How to reinvent capitalism—and unleash a wave of innovation and growth. *Harvard Business Review,* 4–17.

Pottier, J. (2003). Negotiating local knowledge: An introduction. In J. Pottier, A. Bicker, & P. Sillitoe (Eds.), *Negotiating local knowledge. Power and identity in development.* London: Pluto Press, 1–29.

Power, M. (1997). *The audit society: Rituals of verification.* Oxford: Oxford University Press.

Preis, A.-B.S. (1996). Human rights as cultural practice: An anthropological critique. *Human Rights Quarterly, 18,* 286–315.

Pritchett, L., & Woolcock, M. (2004). Solutions when the solution is the problem: Arraying the disarray in development. *World Development, 32*(2), 191–212.

Project Group Vision on Policing. (2006). *The police in evolution. Vision on policing.* Hague: Board of Chief Commissioners. Retrieved from http://www.politie.nl/ImagesLandelijk/visienotaeng_tcm31-21(8509).pdf

Putnam, R. (1993). *Making democracy work: Civil traditions in modern Italy.* Princeton, NJ: Princeton University Press.

Putnam, R. (1995a). Bowling alone: America's declining social capital. *Journal of Democracy, 6*(1), 65–78.

Putnam, R. (1995b). Tuning in, tuning out: The strange disappearance of social capital in America. *Political Science and Politics, 28,* 664–683.

Putnam, R. (2000). *Bowling alone: The collapse and revival of American community.* New York: Simon & Schuster.

Putnam, R. (Ed.). (2002). *Democracies in flux: The evolution of social capital in contemporary society.* Oxford: Oxford University Press.

Putnam, R. (2007). *E pluribus unum*: Diversity and community in the twenty-first century—The 2006 Johan Skytte Prize. *Scandinavian Political Studies, 30*(2), 137–174.

Putnam, R., & Feldstein, L.M. (with D. Cohen). (2003). *Better together: Restoring the American community.* New York: Simon & Schuster.

Raab, J., & Milward, H.B. (2003). Dark networks as problems. *Journal of Public Administration Research and Theory, 13*(4), 413–439.

Rawls, J. (1971). *A theory of justice.* Oxford: Oxford University Press.

Rawls, J. (1982). The basic liberties and their priority. In S.M. McMurrin (Ed.), *The Tanner lectures on human values III.* Salt Lake City: University of Utah Press, 1–88.

Rawls, J. (1995). Political liberalism: Reply to Habermas. *Journal of Philosophy, 92*(3), 132–180.

Raynolds, L.T. (2009). Mainstreaming fair trade coffee: From partnership to traceability. *World Development, 37*(6), 1083–1093.

Raynolds, L.T., Murray, D., & Taylor, P.L. (2004). Fair trade coffee: Building producer capacity via global networks. *Journal of International Development, 16*(8), 1109–1121.

Reed, D. (2009). What do corporations have to do with fair trade? Positive and normative analysis from a value chain perspective. *Journal of Business Ethics, 86,* 3–26.

Reinert, E.S. (1999). The role of the state in economic growth. *Journal of Economic Studies, 26*(4/5), 268–326.

Rhodes, R.A.W. (1997). *Understanding governance: Policy networks, governance, reflexivity and accountability.* Buckingham, UK: Open University Press.

Robins, S.L. (2008). *From revolution to rights in South Africa. Social movements, NGOs and popular politics after apartheid.* Rochester, NY: James Currey.

Robinson, M. (2004). Advancing economic, social, and cultural rights: The way forward. *Human Rights Quarterly, 26*(4), 866–872.

Robinson, M., & White, G. (Eds.). (1998). *The democratic developmental state— Political and institutional design.* Oxford: Oxford University Press.

Roche, D. (2002). Restorative justice and the regulatory state in South African townships. *British Journal of Criminology, 42,* 514–533.

Roche, D. (2003). *Accountability in restorative justice.* Oxford: Oxford University Press.

Rose, N. (1996). Governing "advanced" liberal democracies. In A. Barry, T. Osborn, & N. Rose (Eds.), *Foucault and political reason.* Chicago: University of Chicago Press.

Rose, N. (1999). *Powers of freedom: Reframing political thought.* Cambridge: Cambridge University Press.

Rose, N., & Miller, P. (1992). Political power beyond the state: Problematics of government. *British Journal of Sociology, 42*(2), 173–205.

Rosenau, J. (1992). Governance, order and change in world politics. In J.N. Rosenau & E.-O. Czempiel (Eds.), *Governance without government: Order and change in world politics.* Cambridge: Cambridge University Press, 1–29.

Rosenau, J. (1999). Towards an ontology for global governance. In M. Hewson & T.J. Sinclair (Eds.), *Approaches to global governance theory.* Albany: State University of New York.

Rosingaunet, N. (2007). *Post apartheid security policies in South Africa. The prospect for equitable and democratic security governance.* Master's thesis, University of Bergen.

Ross, R. (1996). *Returning to the teachings: Exploring aboriginal justice.* Toronto: Penguin Books.

Rostow, W.W. (1956). Take-off into self-sustained growth. *Economic Journal, 53,* 202–212.

Rostow, W.W. (1960). *The stages of economic growth: A non-Communist Manifesto.* Cambridge: Cambridge University Press.

Rothschild, E. (1995). What is security? *Daedalus, 124*(3), 53–98.

Rubin, E. (2006). The myth of non-bureaucratic accountability and the anti-administrative impulse. In M.W. Dowdle (Ed.), *Public accountability: Designs, dilemmas and experiences.* Cambridge: Cambridge University Press, 52–82.

Sabel, C., Fung, A., & Karkkainen, B. (1999). Beyond backyard environmentalism. *Boston Law Review, 24*(5), 1–17.

Sabel, C., Fung, A., & Karkkainen, B. (2000). *Beyond backyard environmentalism* (in a democracy forum with Theodore Lowi, Cass Sunstain, and others). Boston: Beacon Press, 3–48.

Sampson, R.J., Morenoff, J., & Earls, F. (1999). Beyond social capital: Spatial dynamics of collective efficacy for children. *American Sociological Review, 64,* 633–660.

Sampson, R.J., Raudenbush, S., & Earls, F. (1997). Neighborhoods and violent crime: A multilevel study of collective efficacy. *Science, 277,* 918–924.

Sano, H.-O. (2000). Development and human rights: The necessary, but partial integration of human rights and development. *Human Rights Quarterly, 22,* 734–752.

Santos, B. de S. (1998). Participatory budgeting in Porto Alegre: Toward a redistributive democracy. *Politics and Society, 4,* 461–510.

Saward, M. (2008). Representation and democracy: Revisions and possibilities. *Sociology Compass, 2,* 1000–1013.

Schacter, M. (2000). *When accountability fails: A framework for diagnosis and action.* Policy Brief 9. Ottawa: Institute on Governance, University of Ottawa.

Scharf, W., & Nina, D. (Eds.). (2001). *The other law: Non-state ordering in South Africa.* Cape Town: Juta.

Scharpf, F.W. (1999). *Governing in Europe. Effective and democratic?* Oxford: Oxford University Press.

Scharpf, F.W. (2010). *Community and autonomy. Institutions, policies and legitimacy in Multilevel Europe.* Publication series of the Max Planck Institute for the Study of Societies. Frankfurt/New York: Campus.

Schattschneider, E.E. (1960). *The semisovereign people*. Hinsdale, IL: Dryden Press.

Scherer, A.G., & Palazzo, G. (2011). The new political role of business in a globalized world: A review of new perspectives on CSR and its implications for the firm, governance and democracy. *Journal of Management Studies, 48*(4), 899–931.

Schulze, C. (2010, November 17). *Research and policy brief: Unemployment's statistical illusion*. South African Institute of Race Relations online. Retrieved from http://www.sairr.org.za/sairr-today-1/research-and-policy-brief-unemployments-statistical-illusion-17th-november-2010/?searchterm=unemployment

Scott, C. (2000). Accountability in the regulatory state. *Journal of Law and Society, 21*(1), 38–60.

Scott, C. (2004). Regulation in the age of governance: The rise of the post-regulatory state. In J. Jordana & D. Levi-Faur (Eds.), *The politics of regulation*. Cheltenham, UK: Edward Elgar.

Scott, C. (2006). Spontaneous accountability. In M.W. Dowdle (Ed.), *Public accountability, designs, dilemmas and experiences* (pp. 1–29). Cambridge: Cambridge University Press.

Scott, J. (1998). *Seeing like a state: How certain schemes to improve the human condition have failed*. New Haven, CT: Yale University Press.

Sen, A. (1976). Famines as failures of exchange entitlements. *Economic and Political Weekly, 11*, 1273–1280.

Sen, A. (1981). *Poverty and famines*. Oxford: Clarendon Press.

Sen, A. (1984). *Resources, values and development*. Oxford: Basil Blackwell.

Sen, A. (1985a). *Commodities and capabilities*. Amsterdam: North-Holland.

Sen, A. (1985b). Well-being, agency and freedom. *Journal of Philosophy, LXXXII*(4), 169–221.

Sen, A. (1986). Food, economics and entitlements. *Lloyds Bank Review, 160*, 1–20.

Sen, A. (1987). The standard of living. In G. Hawthorn (Ed.), *The standard of living*. Cambridge: Cambridge University Press.

Sen, A., & Williams, B. (1982). Introduction. In A. Sen & B. Williams (Eds.), *Utilitarianism and beyond*. Cambridge: Cambridge University Press.

Senghaas, D. (1982). *Von Europa Lernen: Autozentrierte entwicklung und zivilisiering*. Frankfurt am Main: Suhrkamp.

Shapiro, I. (1999a). *Democratic justice*. New Haven, CT: Yale University Press.

Shapiro, I. (1999b). Enough of deliberation: Politics is about interest and power. In S. Macedo (Ed.), Deliberative Politics: *Essays on democracy and disagreement*. New York: Oxford University Press, 28–38.

Shearing, C. (2006). Reflections on the refusal to acknowledge private governments. In J. Wood & B. Dupont (Eds.), *Democracy, society and the governance of security*. Cambridge: Cambridge University Press, 11–32.

Shearing, C. (2010). Independent policing commission.

Shearing, C., & Ericson, R. (1991). Culture as figurative action. *British Journal of Sociology, 42*(4), 481–506.

Shearing, C., & Foster, D. (2007). Back to the future in South African security: From intentions to effective mechanisms. *Acta Juridica*, 156–70.

Shearing, C., & Froestad, J. (2010). Nodal governance and the Zwelethemba model. In H. Quirk, T. Seddon, & G. Smith (Eds.), *Regulation and criminal justice: Innovations in policy and research* (pp. 103–133). Cambridge: Cambridge University Press.

Shearing, C., & Johnston, L. (2005). Justice in the risk society. *Australian and New Zealand Journal of Criminology*, 38(1), 25–38.

Shearing, C., & Marks, M. (2011). Being a new police in the liquid 21st century. *Policing: A Journal of Policy and Practice*, 5(2), 1–9.

Shearing, C., & Stenning, P.C. (1981). Modern private security: Its growth and implications. In M. Tonry & N. Morris (Eds.), *Crime and justice: An annual review of research*. Chicago: University of Chicago Press, 193–245.

Shearing C., & Wood, J. (2003a). Governing security for common goods. *International Journal of the Sociology of Law*, 31(3): 205-225.

Shearing, C., & Wood, J. (2003b). Nodal governance, democracy, and the new "denizens." *Journal of Law and Society*, 30(3), 400–419.

Skocpol, T. (1973). A critical review of Barrington Morre's social origins of dictatorship and democracy. *Politics and Society*, 4(1), 1–34.

Skocpol, T., & Fiorina, M. (1999). *Civic engagement in American democracy*. Washington, DC: Brookings Institution Press.

Skogly, S.I. (1990). Human rights reporting: The "Nordic" experience. *Human Rights Quarterly*, 12, 513–528.

Skogly, S.I. (2002). Is there a right not to be poor? *Human Rights Law Review*, 2, 59–80.

Smith, A. (1776). *An inquiry into the nature and causes of the wealth of nations*. London: W. Strahan and T. Cadell.

Smith, J., Pagnucco, R., & Lopez, A. (1998). Globalizing human rights: The work of transnational human rights NGOs in the 1990s. *Human Rights Quarterly*, 22, 379–412.

Smoljan, J. (2003). The relationship between peace building and development. *Conflict, Security and Development*, 3(2), 233–250.

Sørensen, E., & Torfing, J. (2003). Network politics, political capital and democracy. *International Journal of Political Administration*, 26(6), 609–634.

Sørensen, E., & Torfing, J. (2005). The democratic anchorage of governance networks. *Scandinavian Political Studies*, 28(3), 195–218.

Sørensen, E., & Torfing, J. (2007). *Theories of democratic network governance*. Basingstoke, UK: Palgrave Macmillan.

Stammers, N. (1995). A critique of social approaches to human rights. *Human Rights Quarterly*, 17, 488–508.

Steinmo, S., Thelen, K., & Longstreth, F. (Eds.). (1992). *Structuring politics: Historical institutionalism in comparative analysis*. New York: Cambridge University Press.

Stenning, P., Shearing, C., Addario, S., & Condon, M. (1990). Controlling interests: Two conceptions of order in regulating a financial market. In M.L. Friedland (Ed.), *Securing compliance: Seven case studies*. Toronto: University of Toronto Press, 88–119.

Stewart, F. (2004). Development and security. *Conflict, Security and Development*, 4(3), 261–288.

Stewart, F., & Deneulin, S. (2002). Amartya Sen's contribution to development thinking. *Studies in Comparative International Development*, 37(2), 61–70.

Stiglitz, J. (2002). *Globalization and its discontent*. London: Penguin Books.

Stinchcombe, A. (1968). *Constructing social theories*. New York: Harcourt, Brace and World.

Strange, S. (1996). *The retreat of the state: The diffusion of power in the world economy.* Cambridge: Cambridge University Press.

Streeck, W., & Thelen, K. (2005). *Beyond continuity: Institutional change in advanced political economies.* Oxford: Oxford University Press.

Sturm, S., & Gadlin, H. (2007). Conflict resolution and systemic change. *Journal of Dispute Resolution, 2007*(1), 1–63.

Sun, W. (2010). *How to govern corporations so they serve the public good: A theory of corporate governance emergence.* New York: Edwin Mellen.

Swilling, M. (2008). Tracking South Africa's elusive developmental state. *Administratio Publico, 16*(1), 1–29.

Taleb, N.N. (2007). *The black swan. The impact of the highly improbable.* London: Allen Lane.

Tan, A.C. (1997). Party change and party membership decline. *Party Politics, 3*(3), 363–377.

Taylor, M., & Jennings, K.M. (2005). *In search of strategy: An agenda for applied research on transition from conflict.* Fafo Report 480. Oslo: Fafo.

Terreblanche, S. (2002). *A history of inequality in South Africa, 1652–2002.* Pietermaritzburg: University of Natal Press.

Teubner, G. (1987). Juridification, concepts, aspects, limits, solutions. In G. Teubner (Ed.), *Juridification of social spheres: A comparative analysis of the areas of labor, corporate antitrust and social welfare law.* Berlin: Walter de Gruyter, 3–48.

Thibaut, J., & Walker, L. (1975). *Procedural justice: A psychological analysis.* Hillsdale, NJ: Lawrence Erlbaum Associates.

Thompson, D.F. (1980). Moral responsibility of public officials: The problem of many hands. *American Political Science Review, 74*(4).

Thomson, A. (1991). Taking the right seriously: The case of F.A. Hayek. In P. Fitzpatrick (Ed.), *Dangerous supplements: Resistance and renewal in jurisprudence.* Durham, NC: Duke University Press.

Thorp, R., Stewart, F., & Heyer, A. (2005). When and how far is group formation a route out of chronic poverty? *World Development, 33*(6), 907–920.

Tilley, J.J. (2000). Cultural relativism. *Human Rights Quarterly, 22,* 501–547.

Tilly, C. (1985). War making and state making as organized crime. In P. Evans, D. Rueschemeyer, & T. Skocpol (Eds.), *Bringing the state back in.* Cambridge: Cambridge University Press, 169–191.

Tilly, C. (1994). *Big structures, large processes, huge comparisons.* New York: Russell Sage Foundation.

Tocqueville, A. de. (2003). *Democracy in America* (G. Bevan, Trans.). London: Penguin. (Original work published 1835)

Topik, S. (1998). Dependency revisited: Saving the baby from the bathwater. *Latin American Perspectives, 25*(6), 95–99.

Trimberger, E.K. (1978). *Revolutions from above: Military bureaucrats and development in Japan, Turkey, Egypt and Peru.* New Brunswick, NJ: Transaction Books.

Truth and Reconciliation Commission (South Africa). *Truth and Reconciliation Commission of South Africa Report* (Vol. 1, 5, para. 13–28). Retrieved from http://www.justice.gov.za/trc/report/finalreport/Volume%201.pdf

Tully, J. (1999). The agonic freedom of citizens. *Economy and Society, 28*(2), 161–82.

Tutu, D. (1999). *Without forgiveness, there is no future.* London: Rider Books, Random House.

Tutu, D., & Allen, J. (1997). *The essential Desmond Tutu*. Cape Town: David Philip Publishers.

Twining, W. (2006). Human rights: Southern voices. Francis Deng, Abdullahi An-Na'im, Yash Ghai, and Upendra Baxi. *Review of Constitutional Studies, 11*, 203–279.

Tyler, T.R. (1988). What is procedural justice? Criteria used by citizens to assess the fairness of legal procedures. *Law and Society Review, 22*(1), 103–135.

Tyler, T.R. (2005). *Readings in procedural justice*. Burlington, VT: Ashgate.

Udombana, N.J. (2000). The third world and the right to development: Agenda for the next millennium. *Human Rights Quarterly, 22*, 753–787.

Unger, R.M. (1996). *What should legal analysis become?* London: Verso.

UNDP (United Nations Development Program). (1994). *Human development report*. New York: Oxford University Press.

UNDP (United Nations Development Program). (2000). *Overcoming human poverty: UNDP poverty report (2000)*. New York: United Nations Publications.

UNIS (United Nations Information Service). (2005). *African leaders urged to tackle crime, insecurity and corruption. In order to promote development: A programme of action*. Vienna: UNIS/CP518.

United States. (2001). *United States Commission on National Security/21st Century*.

U.S. Commission on National Security/21st Century. (2001). *Road map for national security: Imperative for change*. Hart-Rudman Report. Retrieved from http://www.fas.org/irp/threat/nssg.pdf

Utting, K. (2009). Assessing the impact of fair trade coffee: Towards an integrative framework. *Journal of Business Ethics, 86*, 127–149.

Valverde, M. (1996). "Despotism" and ethical liberal governance. *Economy and Society, 25*, 357–372.

Van Zyl Smit, D. (2004). Swimming against the tide: Controlling the size of the prison population in the New South Africa. In B. Dixon & E. van der Spuy (Eds.), *Justice gained? Crime and crime control in South Africa's transition*. Cape Town: UCT Press/Willan Publishing, 227–258.

Von Hirsch, A. (1976). *Doing justice: The choice of punishments*. New York: Hill & Wang.

Walgrave, L., & Bazemore, G. (1999). Reflections on the future of restorative justice for juveniles. In G. Bazemore & L. Walgrave (Eds.), *Restorative juvenile justice: Repairing the harm of youth crime*. Monsey, NY: Willow Tree Press.

Wallerstein, I. (1974). *The modern world system. Capitalist agriculture and the origins of the European world-economy in the 16th century*. New York: Academic Press.

Wallerstein, I. (1980). *The modern world system II: Mercantilism and the consolidation of the European world-economy, 1600–1750*. New York: Academic Press.

Wallerstein, I. (1983). *Historical capitalism*. London: Verso.

Wallerstein, I. (2004). World-system analysis. In G. Modelski (Ed.), *Encyclopedia of life support systems (EOLSS)*. Developed under the auspices of UNESCO. Oxford: Eolss Publishers.

Walzer, M. (1994). *Thick and thin: Moral argument at home and abroad*. Loyola Lectures in Political Analysis. Notre Dame: University of Notre Dame Press.

Wardle, H. (2009). *Cosmopolitics and common sense*. University of St. Andrews, Working Paper Series. Open Anthropology Cooperative Press. http://www.openanthcoop.net/press.

Warren, M., & Castiglione, D. (2004). The transformation of democratic representation. *Democracy and Society, 2*(I), 5, 20–22.

Wattenberg, M. (2002). *Where have all the voters gone?* Cambridge, MA: Harvard University Press.

Weber, M. (1946). Politics as a vocation. In *From Max Weber: Essays in sociology* (H.H. Gerth & C.W. Mills, Trans. & Eds.). Oxford: Oxford University Press, 77–128.

Weber, M. (1947). *The theory of social and economic organization* (A.M. Henderson & T. Parsons, Trans.). London: Collier Macmillan Publishers.

Weber, M. (1978). *Economy and society* (G. Roth & C. Wittich, Eds.). Berkeley: University of California Press.

Weiss, L. (2000). Development states in transition: Adapting, dismantling, innovating, not "normalising." *Pacific Review, 13*(1), 621–644.

Wellman, C. (2000). Solidarity, the individual and human rights. *Human Rights Quarterly, 22,* 639–657.

Whande, U., and Nordien, J. (2006). *Internal evaluation report of the Community Peace Foundation.* Commissioned by the government of Finland. Unpublished.

White, R. (1994). Shame and reintegration strategies: Individuals, state power and social interests. In C. Alder & J. Wundersitz (Eds.), *Family conferencing and juvenile justice. The way forward or misplaced optimism?* Australian Studies in Law, Crime and Justice Series. Canberra: Australian Institute of Criminology, 181–196.

Williams, B. (1987). The standard of living: Interests and capabilities. In G. Hawthorn (Ed.), *The standard of living.* Cambridge: Cambridge University Press.

Williams, C. (2006). *Leadership accountability in a globalizing world.* London: Palgrave Macmillan.

Williams, M. (2000). The uneasy alliance of group representation and deliberative democracy. In W. Kymlicka & W. Norman (Eds.), *Citizenship in diverse societies.* Oxford: Oxford University Press, 124–154.

Wilson, J.Q. (1989). *Bureaucracy: What government agencies do and why they do it.* New York: Basic Books.

Wilson, W. (1887). The study of administration. *Political Science Quarterly, 2*(2), 197–222.

Woo-Cumings, M. (1999). *The development state.* Ithaca, NY: Cornell University Press.

Wood, J. (1996, April 26). *Safety in metro Toronto housing communities.* Paper presented at Safer Communities: Working Together. Hosted by the Crime Prevention Council of Ottawa, Ottawa.

Wood, J. (2006). Research and innovation in the field of security: A nodal governance view. In J. Wood & B. Dupont (Eds.), *Democracy, society and the governance of security.* Cambridge: Cambridge University Press.

Wood, J., & Dupont, B. (Eds.). (2006). *Democracy, society and the governance of security.* Cambridge: Cambridge University Press.

Wood, J., Fleming, J., & Marks, M. (2008). Building the capacity of police change agents: The Nexus Policing Project. *Policing and Society, 18*(1), 78–94.

Wood, J., & Shearing, C. (2007). *Imagining security.* Cullompton, Devon: Willan Publishing.

Wood, J., Shearing, C., & Froestad, J. (2011). Restorative justice and nodal governance. *International Journal of Comparative and Applied Criminal Justice, 35*(1), 1–18.

Woods, N. (2000). The challenge of good governance for the IMF and the World Bank themselves. *World Development, 28*(5), 823–841.

World Bank. (1980). *World development report.* Washington, DC: The World Bank.

World Bank. (1981). *World development report.* Washington, DC: The World Bank.

World Bank. (1992). *Governance and development.* Washington, DC: The World Bank.

World Bank. (1994). *Governance: The World Bank's experience.* Washington, DC: The World Bank.

World Bank. (1997). *World development report.* Washington, DC: The World Bank.

World Bank. (2001). *World development report 2000/2001: Attacking poverty.* New York: Oxford University Press.

Yamin, A.E. (2005). The future in the mirror: Incorporating strategies for the defense and promotion of economic, social and cultural rights into the mainstream human rights agenda. *Human Rights Quarterly, 27,* 1200–1244.

Young, I. (2000). *Inclusion and democracy.* Oxford: Oxford University Press.

Zamora, M. (1979). Review of revolution from above: Military bureaucrats and development in Japan, Turkey, Egypt and Peru. *Annals of the American Academy of Political and Social Science, 441,* 201–202.

Zedner, L. (2009). *Security.* London: Routledge.

Zehr, H. (1990). *Changing lenses: A new focus for crime and justice.* Scottsdale, PA: Herald Press.

Zuern, E. (2002). Fighting for democracy: Popular organizations and post-apartheid government in South Africa. *African Studies Review, 45*(1), 77–102.

# Appendix

**Step 1—The Interview**   It is not necessary to go into great detail about the problem at this point, or to take notes. It is most important to listen, so as to avoid misunderstanding and to build trust with the disputants. The aim is to understand who is involved. In the movie *Scars*, the PC did not meet with Nandipha, which resulted in a lack of trust.

**Step 2—Organizing the Gathering**   **Inviting the right people** is one of the most important steps, and it comes before the gathering itself. In *Scars*, this step was not properly carried out in the beginning, which led to much wasted time later and to trouble with Nandipha, who objected that the PC had not spoken directly to her.

The PC can also invite people they think could be helpful.

If one or more disputants refuse to attend the proposed peacemaking gathering, peace committee members will go to speak to them to explain more fully what kind of meeting a peacemaking gathering is—for example, this is not a court, there will be no bullying and no punishment, and all those who attend will be treated with respect.

Peace committee members (at least two and no more than six) meet with all these people together in a peacemaking gathering. For the first few gatherings of a new peace committee, it is quite acceptable for all the peace committee members to be present in order to learn from the experience, but the number of those attending any particular gathering should be reduced as soon as possible, so that disputants and other community members do not feel intimidated.

**Step 3—Facilitating and Reporting**   It is important to know **who is responsible for facilitating and reporting** each peacemaking gathering, in case there are problems that need to be followed up.

The names of all PC members present at the gathering are needed in order to prepare accurate payment schedules.

This is an important administration tool and this data, when analyzed, will be important for peace committee planning.

**Step 4—Opening the Gathering**   **Reading the peace committee code** at every gathering reminds PC members of how they are to behave, and it also informs the community members what kind of meeting this is and what they can expect. Reading the peace committee code shows how the peace committee works and it builds trust with the community participants.

**Step 5—Taking Statements**   Other disputants have to go outside at this point so that they can feel **comfortable and not intimidated** when they tell their story, therefore they can express themselves freely. This also ensures that the disputants don't start arguing and blaming each other. It also helps to build the disputants' (and the other community members') trust that this will be a fair process.

The various people with the problem are referred to as "disputants," and not "victims" and "offenders." These labels may prevent finding a solution for the problem since it emphasizes blaming. To move to the future, we have to let go of the past.

**Step 6—Modification of Statements**   This step **avoids further argument later on**, so that they can now move on to the next stage of the discussion. The purpose is not to find out what actually happened, but to find out how the participants see what happened. Each participant may have a different perception or point of view. This is not yet the time for a general discussion.

**Step 7— Related Problems**   This is an opportunity for people to discuss some of the **consequences of what has happened**, and what **patterns** they can see.

If people at this stage start to make suggestions for a plan of action, the facilitator should ask them to hang on to that idea and bring it up again later at the proper time (as part of Step 9).

**Step 8—The Root Cause**   People quite often try to skip this step and go straight to a plan of action. But why is this a necessary and important step? Why shouldn't they go straight to a plan of action after hearing the statements and clarifications? Because the plan of action is not likely to work if the probable root cause has not been discussed. It also **ensures that the problem doesn't happen again**.

**Step 9—Plan of Action**   Steps 8 and 9 are the most important part of the gathering—if the plan of action does not **deal directly with the root cause of the particular problem**, the problem is likely to go on happening, and everyone's time will have been wasted.

**Step 10—Commitment**   Do peace committee members decide on the plan of action? Definitely not—there is no point in forcing disputants or other participants to agree to a plan of action, because then they can ignore the plan of action and blame the peace committee for forcing them. The whole point is for the disputants (and the other participants, where appropriate) **to take full responsibilities for their actions**.

**Step 11—Register**   This information is important for understanding what kind of people are making use of the peace committee's service, and also for getting in contact with people in order to do exit interviews. Remember, the **quality of the information provided determines the quality of the information analysis** that will be available to make decisions on peace-building interventions.

**Step 12—Outreach**   Keeping people updated about PC activities and inviting them to participate in future activities.

**Step 13—Closure**   To provide appropriate closure for the gathering.

## Community Peace Programme

**Peace Committee Code**

01.07.06 - Ver 2                              Page 1 of 1

### MEMBERS OF PEACE COMMITTEES USE THESE GUIDELINES IN THE COURSE OF THEIR WORK

*It is important to remember that all the disputants in a gathering have their own free will. If a disputant doesn't feel comfortable with the process at any stage, he / she is free to leave the gathering*

1.  We help to create a safe and secure environment in our Community

2.  We respect the South African Constitution

3.  We work with the law

4.  We do not use force or violence

5.  We do not take sides in disputes

6.  We work in the community as a co-operative team, not as individuals

7.  We follow procedures which are open for the community to see

8.  We do not gossip about our work or about other people

9.  We are committed in what we do

10. Our aim is to heal, not to hurt

Community Peace Programme

English – PeaceBuilding Steps
01.10.08 - Ver 1                              Page 1 of 1

## PEACEBUILDING STEPS

Step 1          Decide which root cause the PeaceBuilding will address

Step 2          Decide on the proportions of the PeaceBuilding Fund to be used
                for each root cause

Step 3          Decide on the local service providers to carry out the PeaceBuilding
                initiative in accordance with the PeaceBuilding criteria

Step 4          Complete the PeaceBuilding MOU

Step 5          Attach the completed Service Providers Details for each service
                provider involved

Step 6          Submit the PeaceBuilding MOU and Service Providers Details
                Forms for authorization and payment

Step 7          Invite all stakeholders and partner organisations to the
                PeaceBuilding Activity

Step 8          Issue public announcement of PeaceBuilding Activity to local press
                and radio

Step 9          Finalise the PeaceBuilding Activity

Step 10         Complete and submit the PeaceBuilding Activity Report for
                payment

Community Peace Programme

PeaceMaking Case Report™
20.01.09

### PEACEMAKING CASE REPORT™

Please note all steps need to be completed in the following order and documented in this report. This is an absolute requirement for recognition that the dispute has been addressed according to the Steps in PeaceMaking for members of Peace Committees and the Peace Committee Code. No other minutes of the gathering will be required.

Name of Peace Committee   :      _____

Date Reported                :      _____

Prepared By  :  _____     ID Number  :  _____

### STEP 1 : THE INTERVIEW

Meet separately with the people directly involved in the conflict in order to find out what happened or what the problem seems to be.  Provide the following details of the people you interview  :

| Date | Name | Surname | Address | Employed |
|------|------|---------|---------|----------|
|      |      |         |         |          |
|      |      |         |         |          |
|      |      |         |         |          |
|      |      |         |         |          |
|      |      |         |         |          |
|      |      |         |         |          |
|      |      |         |         |          |
|      |      |         |         |          |

**STEP 2 : ORGANISING THE GATHERING**

Encourage them to come together in a Peace Gathering. Discuss with them what other people could also come who might help to find a peaceful, practical solution and record these names below :

| Name | Surname | Address and Contact Number | Employed |
|------|---------|---------------------------|----------|
|      |         |                           |          |
|      |         |                           |          |
|      |         |                           |          |
|      |         |                           |          |

**STEP 3 : RESPONSIBILITIES AT THE GATHERING**

Supply the following details :

| Date of Gathering | Name/s of Facilitator | Name/s of Secretary |
|-------------------|----------------------|--------------------|
|                   |                      |                    |
|                   |                      |                    |
|                   |                      |                    |
|                   |                      |                    |

Total number of hours spent in gathering : _____    Case No : _____

Referred by : _____ *(disputant, organisation, neighbour, family member, other)*

Name of Referrer : _____    Gender of Referrer : _____ (male/female)

Number of Times Postponed : _____    Reason for Postponement : _____

_____

_____

List names of Peace Committee members present. Note that after the Peace Committee has been in operation for 3 months, the number of Peace Committee members present at a gathering should not exceed 6.

| Name | Surname | Gender : Female/Male |
|------|---------|----------------------|
| 1. | | |
| 2. | | |
| 3. | | |
| 4. | | |
| 5. | | |
| 6. | | |
| 7. | | |
| 8. | | |
| 9. | | |
| 10. | | |

Total Peace Committee members present    :    _____

| Breakdown by Age and Gender | Female | Male |
|-----------------------------|--------|------|
| Children (less than 15 yrs) | | |
| Youth (15-25 yrs) | | |
| Adults (25-65 yrs) | | |
| Seniors (65+) | | |
| TOTAL MEMBERS | | |

### STEP 4 : OPENING OF GATHERING

- The facilitator opens the meeting by explaining why they are all gathered together

- The facilitator reads the Peace Committee Code to the gathering

## MEMBERS OF PEACE COMMITTEES USE THESE GUIDELINES IN THE COURSE OF THEIR WORK

*It is important to remember that all the disputants in a gathering have their own free will. If a disputant doesn't feel comfortable with the process at any stage, he / she is free to leave the gathering*

1. We help to create a safe and secure environment in our Community

2. We respect the South African Constitution

3. We work with the law

4. We do not use force or violence

5. We do not take sides in disputes

6. We work in the community as a co-operative team, not as individuals

7. We follow procedures which are open for the community to see

8. We do not gossip about our work or about other people

9. We are committed in what we do

10. Our aim is to heal, not to hurt

## STEP 5 : REPORT OF PARTY 1

Mr / Mrs / Ms _____ describes what happened as he / she saw it while the other person/s wait outside. The secretary should make notes in the space provided.

_____

_____

_____

_____

_____

_____

Why / how does she / he think it happened ?

_____

_____

_____

_____

_____

_____

## STEP 5 : REPORT OF PARTY 2

Mr / Mrs / Ms _____ describes what happened as he / she saw it while the other person/s wait outside. The secretary should make notes in the space provided.

_____

_____

_____

_____

_____

_____

Why / how does she / he think it happened ?

_____

_____

_____

_____

**STEP 5 : REPORT OF PARTY 3**

Mr / Mrs / Ms _____ describes what happened as he / she saw it while the other person/s wait outside.  The secretary should make notes in the space provided.

_____

_____

_____

_____

_____

_____

Why / how does she / he think it happened ?

_____

_____

_____

_____

_____

_____

**STEP 5 : REPORT OF PARTY 4**

Mr / Mrs / Ms _____ describes what happened as he / she saw it while the other person/s wait outside.  The secretary should make notes in the space provided.

_____

_____

_____

_____

_____

_____

Why / how does she / he think it happened ?

_____

_____

_____

_____

_____

_____

**STEP 6 : MODIFICATION OF REPORTS**

The secretary will read out the reports given in the presence of everyone. Those directly involved may briefly add to or modify what they have said previously in Step 5.

**STEP 7 : RELATED PROBLEMS**

All the people affected by what happened will be given the opportunity to tell how it affected them and what they think are the related problems. The facilitator will make sure that everyone has the opportunity to speak freely. The secretary will note each person's response in the space provided below :

Mr / Mrs/ Ms _____ says :

_____

_____

_____


Mr / Mrs/ Ms _____ says :

_____

_____

_____


Mr / Mrs/ Ms _____ says :

_____

_____

_____


Mr / Mrs/ Ms _____ says :

_____

_____

_____


Mr / Mrs/ Ms _____ says :

_____

_____

_____

**STEP 8 : IDENTIFYING THE SOURCES OF THE PROBLEM**

The facilitator will encourage all present at the gathering to consider what can be done to reduce the likelihood of this happening again. The secretary will note the sources of the problem and the name of the person who identified it in the space below :

| Sources of the Problem | Name |
|---|---|
| 1. | |
| 2. | |
| 3. | |
| 4. | |
| 5. | |
| 6. | |
| 7. | |
| 8. | |

**STEP 9 : PLAN OF ACTION PROPOSAL**

The facilitator will encourage all the people at the gathering to propose a Plan of Action that addresses the root causes identified above to ensure that this problem does not happen again.

| Action | Responsible person/s | When | Name of Monitor | Signature |
|---|---|---|---|---|
| 1. | | | | |
| 2. | | | | |
| 3. | | | | |
| 4. | | | | |
| 5. | | | | |

**STEP 10 : COMMITMENT TO THE PLAN OF ACTION**

All parties bound by the Plan of Action need to state and sign that they are satisfied with and committed to carrying out the plan of action.

| Name | Surname | Address | Contact No |
|------|---------|---------|------------|
| 1. | | | |
| 2. | | | |
| 3. | | | |
| 4. | | | |
| 5. | | | |
| 6. | | | |
| 7. | | | |
| 8. | | | |
| 9. | | | |
| 10. | | | |
| 11. | | | |
| 12. | | | |
| 13. | | | |
| 14. | | | |
| 15. | | | |
| 16. | | | |
| 17. | | | |
| 18. | | | |
| 19. | | | |
| 20. | | | |
| 21. | | | |
| 22. | | | |
| 23. | | | |
| 24. | | | |
| 25. | | | |

## STEP 11 : REGISTER

All participants at the gathering (excluding PC members) must add their details to the register for monitoring purposes.

| Name | Surname | Address | Contact No | Signature |
|------|---------|---------|------------|-----------|
| 1. | | | | |
| 2. | | | | |
| 3. | | | | |
| 4. | | | | |
| 5. | | | | |
| 6. | | | | |
| 7. | | | | |
| 8. | | | | |
| 9. | | | | |
| 10. | | | | |
| 11. | | | | |
| 12. | | | | |
| 13. | | | | |
| 14. | | | | |
| 15. | | | | |
| 16. | | | | |
| 17. | | | | |
| 18. | | | | |
| 19. | | | | |
| 20. | | | | |

Breakdown by Age and Gender

| | Female | Male |
|---|--------|------|
| Children (less than 15 yrs) | | |
| Youth (15-25 yrs) | | |
| Adults (25-65 yrs) | | |
| Seniors (65+) | | |
| TOTAL PARTICIPANTS | | |

## STEP 12 : OUTREACH

The facilitator will provide the following information to those present at the gathering :

Upcoming meetings        :        _____

Pamphlets                :        _____

Matters arising          :        _____

The secretary will note the names of people interested in participating in Peace Committee activities in the future :

| Name | Surname | Address | Contact Number |
|------|---------|---------|----------------|
| 1. | | | |
| 2. | | | |
| 3. | | | |
| 4. | | | |
| 5. | | | |
| 6. | | | |
| 7. | | | |
| 8. | | | |
| 9. | | | |
| 10. | | | |

## STEP 13 : CLOSURE

Close the gathering in some way that will show that those involved have committed themselves to the plan of action that would bring a better tomorrow.

Eg everyone at the gathering might wish to hold hands while a prayer is said, shake hands, embrace, sing etc. What PeaceMaking gesture was used ?

Peace gestures between :

| | | | | | |
|------|------|------|------|------|------|
| Disputants | Shaking Hands | Prayer | Song | Other | None |

| | | | | | |
|------|------|------|------|------|------|
| All Participants | Shaking Hands | Prayer | Song | Other | None |

# PEACEMAKING SUMMARY

| Area PC : | PC Case No : | Name of Organiser : |
|---|---|---|
| Peace Committee Name : | Name of Coordinator : | ID Number : |
| Date of Gathering : | Date Dispute Reported : | Average Days Elapsed : |

Referred by :   Disputant ☐   Organisation ☐   Neighbour ☐   Family Member ☐   SAPS ☐

| Name of Referrer : | Gender of Referrer (circle) :   Male  /  Female |  |
|---|---|---|
| Name of Capturer : | Date of Capturing : |  |
| Times Postponed : | Reason for Postponement : | Total no of hours spent in Gathering : |

Names of Peace Committee members at Gathering

1. _____      6. _____
2. _____      7. _____
3. _____      8. _____
4. _____      9. _____
5. _____     10. _____

Peace Committee members at Gathering :

|  | Female | Male | Total |
|---|---|---|---|
| Children (less than 15 yrs) |  |  |  |
| Youth (15-25 yrs) |  |  |  |
| Adult (25-65 yrs) |  |  |  |
| Senior (65 yrs+) |  |  |  |
| Total |  |  |  |

Disputants at Gathering :

|  | Female | Male | Total |
|---|---|---|---|
| Children (less than 15 yrs) |  |  |  |
| Youth (15-25 yrs) |  |  |  |
| Adult (25-65 yrs) |  |  |  |
| Senior (65 yrs+) |  |  |  |
| Total |  |  |  |

| Tick all underlying and related problems | Money-Lending | Theft | Non-Payment | Loan of Goods | Assault without weapon | Assault with sharp object | Assault with blunt object | Fighting | Assault with gun | Robbery – with the use of / threat of violence | Nuisance – urinating, noise, dumping | Extra-marital affair | Sexual harassment | Spousal Abuse | Child Abuse | Insults / Threats | Family Dispute | Neighbourhood Disputes | Attempted Rape | Rape | Damage to Property | Substance Abuse | Maintenance | Breaching of Contract | Misappropriation of Funds | Other (Specify) |
|---|---|---|---|---|---|---|---|---|---|---|---|---|---|---|---|---|---|---|---|---|---|---|---|---|---|---|
|  |  |  |  |  |  |  |  |  |  |  |  |  |  |  |  |  |  |  |  |  |  |  |  |  |  |  |

Sources of the Problem ?

Overcrowding / Land Issues ☐
HIV / AIDS ☐
Alcohol & Substance Abuse ☐
Lack of Safe Recreational Spaces ☐
Lack of Childcare Facilities ☐
Nutritional Problems ☐
Lack of Opportunities for Income Generation ☐
Buying Stolen Goods ☐
Environmental Problems ☐
Root Cause Other (please specify) ☐
_____
_____

Solutions of Problem ?

Payment or Compensation ☐
PeaceBuilding ☐
Referred to Police ☐
Refusal to Comply ☐
Other (please specify) ☐
_____
_____

Was their commitment to the Plan of Action ?        Yes / No        If not, why ? _____

PC Case Monitor : _____

Peace Gestures between :

| | | | | | |
|---|---|---|---|---|---|
| Disputants | Shaking Hands | Prayer | Song | Other | None |
| All Participants | Shaking Hands | Prayer | Song | Other | None |

Other Organisations Involved : _____

Community Participants at Gathering :

| | Female | Male | Total |
|---|---|---|---|
| Children (less than 15 yrs) | | | |
| Youth (15-25 yrs) | | | |
| Adult (25-65 yrs) | | | |
| Senior (65 yrs+) | | | |
| Total | | | |

Comments : _____

# Index

# A Call for Authors
# *Advances in Police Theory and Practice*

## AIMS AND SCOPE:

This cutting-edge series is designed to promote publication of books on contemporary advances in police theory and practice. We are especially interested in volumes that focus on the nexus between research and practice, with the end goal of disseminating innovations in policing. We will consider collections of expert contributions as well as individually authored works. Books in this series will be marketed internationally to both academic and professional audiences. This series also seeks to —

- Bridge the gap in knowledge about advances in theory and practice regarding who the police are, what they do, and how they maintain order, administer laws, and serve their communities
- Improve cooperation between those who are active in the field and those who are involved in academic research so as to facilitate the application of innovative advances in theory and practice

Police Reform in China

Mission-Based Policing

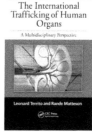

The International Trafficking of Human Organs

The series especially encourages the contribution of works coauthored by police practitioners and researchers. We are also interested in works comparing policing approaches and methods globally, examining such areas as the policing of transitional states, democratic policing, policing and minorities, preventive policing, investigation, patrolling and response, terrorism, organized crime and drug enforcement. In fact, every aspect of policing, public safety, and security, as well as public order is relevant for the series. Manuscripts should be between 300 and 600 printed pages. If you have a proposal for an original work or for a contributed volume, please be in touch.

**Series Editor**
Dilip Das, Ph.D., Ph: 802-598-3680
E-mail: dilipkd@aol.com

Dr. Das is a professor of criminal justice and Human Rights Consultant to the United Nations. He is a former chief of police and, founding president of the International Police Executive Symposium, IPES, www.ipes.info. He is also founding editor-in-chief of *Police Practice and Research: An International Journal* (PPR), (Routledge/Taylor & Francis), www.tandf.co.uk/journals. In addition to editing the *World Police Encyclopedia* (Taylor & Francis, 2006), Dr. Das has published numerous books and articles during his many years of involvement in police practice, research, writing, and education.

*Proposals for the series may be submitted to the series editor or directly to –*
**Carolyn Spence**
Senior Editor • CRC Press / Taylor & Francis Group
561-998-2515 • 561-997-7249 (fax)
carolyn.spence@taylorandfrancis.com • www.crcpress.com
6000 Broken Sound Parkway NW, Suite 300, Boca Raton, FL 33487

For Product Safety Concerns and Information please contact our EU
representative  GPSR@taylorandfrancis.com
Taylor & Francis Verlag GmbH, Kaufingerstraße 24, 80331 München, Germany

www.ingramcontent.com/pod-product-compliance
Ingram Content Group UK Ltd.
Pitfield, Milton Keynes, MK11 3LW, UK
UKHW021616240425
457818UK00018B/591